Praise for *The Nourishing As*

"Having watched Sophie's journey over the years, I'm not surprised at the professional detail and sheer culinary breadth of this marvelous book. Far more than a cookbook, *The Nourishing Asian Kitchen* brings the rich, authentic nourishing heritage of Asian foodcraft to all our tables. The theme is nutritional integrity; the result is health and delectable dining. Following this book's recommendations will turn you into a menu superstar for your family and friends."

—Joel Salatin, cofounder of Polyface Farm; author,
Everything I Want to Do Is Illegal

"Finally, an ethnic cookbook that truly celebrates the nourishing qualities of traditional diets! Through *The Nourishing Asian Kitchen*, Sophia Nguyen Eng empowers the home cook to rely upon ferments, broths, high-quality fats, and even offal to create authentically healthy dishes. This book is exactly what we need to help confront a global foodscape that has been cheapened by the industrial food system to the point that it is making us sick."

—Dr. Bill Schindler, author of *Eat Like a Human: Nourishing Foods
and Ancient Ways of Cooking to Revolutionize Your Health*

"I have been waiting a long time for an author who unapologetically celebrates traditional flavors enjoyed across Asia using the familiar fresh ingredients we can find in any grocery store. Traditional food is health food, and Sophia Nguyen Eng invites the novice and the expert into a culinary adventure that encapsulates generations of healing knowledge. It is sure to bring joy and health to you and your family for years to come."

—Cate Shanahan, MD, *New York Times* bestselling author
of *Deep Nutrition* and *The FATBURN Fix*

"Let's face it, we're not going to effect positive changes in nutrition without corresponding appeals to our taste buds and our hearts. In this exciting book, Sophia Nguyen Eng and her delightful family link wholesome, whole, and nutritious ingredients with pleasures for the palate and the warmth of tradition and community.

"A big 'thank you' to Sophie Eng and her lovely family for the consummation of this marriage between whole foods and the savory delights of traditional Asian cuisine. If you've sacrificed your favorite Eastern condiments on the altar of clean, additive-free food, take heart; these healthful and delicious recipes give them back to you, better than ever."

—Shawn and Beth Dougherty, authors of
The Independent Farmstead; owners of Sow's Ear Farm

"The best recipes are often those handed down from parents to their children—the dishes you learn to cook in your mother's and grandmother's kitchen. Sophia Nguyen Eng brings that culinary heritage to the forefront in her gorgeous cookbook. *The Nourishing Asian Kitchen* is a beautiful celebration of flavor, family, and nutrient-dense cooking. Her Bún Bò Huế has become a fast favorite in our home."

—Jennifer McGruther, NTP,
author of *The Nourished Kitchen*, *Vibrant Botanicals*,
and *Broth and Stock from the Nourished Kitchen*

"What an extraordinary book! I'd say cookbook but this truly is so much more. Eng doesn't just say 'Here's my food and gorgeous photographs,' she takes us into the most intimate of places, her home, and shows us how we too can feed our families in ours. Packed not just with delicious and practical recipes, it also has important, and oft-overlooked, advice on nutrition, sourcing, indigenous medicines, and closed-loop systems."

—Jeremy Umansky, coauthor of *Koji Alchemy*;
James Beard Award finalist; chef/owner
of Larder: A Curated Delicatessen & Bakery

The
Nourishing
Asian Kitchen

The
Nourishing
Asian Kitchen

Nutrient-Dense Recipes
for Health & Healing

Sophia Nguyen Eng

Foreword by Sally Fallon Morell
Food Photography by David K. Peng

Chelsea Green Publishing
White River Junction, Vermont
London, UK

Commissioning Editor: Brianne Goodspeed
Project Manager: Rebecca Springer
Copy Editor: Karen Wise
Proofreader: Hope Clarke
Indexer: Elizabeth Parson
Designer: Melissa Jacobson
Food Stylist: Christiane Hur

Printed in the United States of America.
First printing December 2023.
10 9 8 7 6 5 4 3 2 1   23 24 25 26 27

Our Commitment to Green Publishing
Chelsea Green sees publishing as a tool for cultural change and ecological stewardship. We strive to align our book manufacturing practices with our editorial mission and to reduce the impact of our business enterprise in the environment. We print our books using vegetable-based inks whenever possible. This book may cost slightly more because it was printed on paper from responsibly managed forests, and we hope you'll agree that it's worth it. *The Nourishing Asian Kitchen* was printed on paper supplied by Versa that is certified by the Forest Stewardship Council.®

Library of Congress Cataloging-in-Publication Data
Names: Eng, Sophia Nguyen, author.
Title: The nourishing Asian kitchen : nutrient-dense recipes for health & healing / Sophia Nguyen Eng ; foreword by Sally Fallon Morell ; food photography by David K. Peng.
Identifiers: LCCN 2023036774 | ISBN 9781645022169 (paperback) | ISBN 9781645022176 (ebook)
Subjects: LCSH: Cooking, Asian. | Nutrition. | BISAC: COOKING / Regional & Ethnic / Asian | COOKING / Farm to Table | LCGFT: Cookbooks.
Classification: LCC TX724.5.A1 N497 2023 | DDC 641.595—dc23/eng/20230831
LC record available at https://lccn.loc.gov/2023036774

Chelsea Green Publishing
White River Junction, Vermont, USA
London, UK

www.chelseagreen.com

To Mẹ, whose kitchen ignited my love for nourishing Asian cooking, and to Emily and Natalie, the bearers of our heritage and future traditions. May you savor the seasons and the flavors that connect us across time.

Contents

Foreword

These days, we're seeing a lot of interest in traditional diets—not only which foods healthy people ate in earlier times, but also how they prepared them. This shift in consciousness—from "what we eat doesn't matter" to "nutrient-dense traditional foods are the key to good health"—is occurring not just in the United States but worldwide.

Because the truth is, modern processed foods have invaded not just our own country but all areas of the world—from Africa to Beijing, processed foods based on rancid industrial seed oils, refined sugars, and fake flavorings like MSG fill the aisles of the supermarkets and hang from the rafters of rural markets and outdoor stalls. They have replaced the traditional offerings of street vendors and upstaged Mom's cooking at the family table.

Along with these modern ingredients come modern chronic diseases . . . and, little by little, citizens of the world are realizing that traditional foods did not cause such havoc, and that it's worth the effort to prepare the foods of our ancestors from scratch and to pay a little more for high-quality ingredients. Modern medicine produces many miracles, but true health is achieved only by providing our bodies with the nutrients they need.

Traditional diets embrace a number of important principles: the use of whole natural foods, including meat, eggs, raw whole-dairy foods, whole grains, fruits, and vegetables; the inclusion of nutrient-dense organ meats; the use of traditional natural fats, like butter, lard, poultry fat, and tallow; proper preparation of grains; and the inclusion of gelatinous bone broths, lacto-fermented foods, and unrefined salt.

Sophia Nguyen Eng's delightful cookbook shows us that these principles dominated traditional cooking in Asia as well as in other parts of the world.

The Nourishing Asian Kitchen focuses on traditional ingredients and preparation methods. Eng emphasizes the importance of using fresh, whole foods and teaches readers how to make their own seasonings and condiments. She includes sections on cooking techniques, such as stir-frying using traditional animal fats, fermentation to create delicious pickles, and preparing rich bone broths for satisfying soups and sauces. The chapter on organ meats is especially welcome.

The recipes in this cookbook draw on the rich culinary traditions of Vietnam, China, Japan, Korea, and other Asian countries and are designed to be nourishing as well as delicious. From comforting noodle soups and flavorful stir-fries to refreshing salads and sweet treats, there is something for everyone in this cookbook.

Whether you are a seasoned home cook or a novice in the kitchen, *The Nourishing Asian Kitchen* is perfect for anyone looking to explore traditional Asian cooking. The recipes are easy to follow, and the author provides helpful tips and tricks throughout the book to help readers achieve the best results possible. Best of all, your family will readily come to the table to enjoy these delicious offerings.

Sally Fallon Morell, President,
The Weston A. Price Foundation

Introduction

"Eat to live, do not live to eat!" was a lesson my grandfather taught me when I was a little girl following him around his backyard garden in San Jose, California. He was a man who didn't speak much and always had a serious demeanor, so I soaked in those moments when he did speak. And although I didn't know it at the time, his few simple words were setting a positive trajectory for our family's health for generations to come.

I am a first-generation Vietnamese American. My parents fled Vietnam by boat with my older sister, who was then two years old, the night before the fall of Saigon on April 29, 1975. My maternal grandparents followed four years later. Both generations—my parents and grandparents—settled in San Jose, first living together in the same house and later in the same neighborhood, a block apart.

Life wasn't easy for our immigrant family adjusting to a totally different life in California, but my parents always ensured that our family's basic needs were met. Our home was always filled with the aroma of delicious and nutritious food and, although both of my parents worked long hours to make

Family photo, 1983.

My first ducklings, 1984.

ends meet, my mother made it a priority to feed us well. Whenever she wasn't taking overtime shifts, I could find her in the kitchen.

My mother cooked nose-to-tail before it was a thing, using every part of an animal to cook delicious, nutrient-dense meals and leaving nothing to waste. She could stretch a whole broiler chicken into multiple meals: cooking down the head, neck, and bones for several hours to make porridge, the dark meat for cabbage and chicken salad, the breast meat for chicken phở—and even hot and spicy chicken feet and delectable chicken heart appetizers.

Growing up in Silicon Valley, I often felt like an outsider at the school lunch table. While other kids were munching on Lunchables and Fruit Roll-Ups, my mom had packed me pork floss, a finely shredded dry pork that other kids called "animal hair." For my fifth-grade field trip, my mother packed me bánh mì with chicken liver pâté (page 231) that made my backpack smell like a wet dog. But even while I was pining for Lean Cuisine, Coke, and strawberry-flavored gummy bears as an afterschool snack, I always jumped at the opportunity to go to the grocery store with my mother and help her prepare our family meals. I loved watching her pick out the freshest fruit, vegetables, fish, and poultry or negotiate for a better price. Alongside my grandfather's simple philosophy to eat to live, not live to eat, I absorbed these practical skills from my mother and carried them with me to college, my career, marriage, and motherhood.

In school, I was highly motivated by two goals: I wanted to attend a prestigious university and then get a high-paying job so I could one day repay my parents for the hard work and sacrifices they made for our family. I also wanted to study medicine so that I could help others attain

My grandfather, mother, and daughter, Emily, with opo squash from the backyard garden, 2013.

Sophia, speaking at Google Headquarters in San Francisco, CA, 2017.

health and healing; there was, I thought (and still do), no greater aspiration. After I graduated from high school, I enrolled in an accelerated seven-year dual BA/MD program at The George Washington University (GWU) in Washington, DC. I thought I was well on my way to achieving both goals.

But the best-laid plans are often disrupted by reality, and mine were no exception. After I launched into my studies at GWU, I began looking more carefully at the details of the program. There was only one class in nutrition! Doctors, I learned, receive minimal training in nutrition. When they counsel patients, if at all, most offer only outdated recommendations for a standard American diet (SAD)—the same dietary patterns that have coincided with a massive surge in diabetes, obesity, and chronic disease. I realized, somewhat painfully, that I'd received a better education in health and healing from my upbringing than I ever would in medical school. And so I decided to change course.

I completed my undergraduate degree in biology and a master's degree in clinical psychology, then moved back to the Bay Area to start a career in the tech industry. I led growth marketing campaigns at startup companies with few resources to achieve growth by as much as a factor of ten. Once again, I realized how valuable my upbringing had been: I applied my mother's humble art of stretching a budget for some of the most powerful and profitable companies in the world using my educational background in science and psychology.

Around this time, I crossed paths with Tim, a young man I'd attended high school with in San Jose who had just graduated from West Point and was beginning a career as a second lieutenant in the United States Army. We were both ambitious and organized and shared similar values and visions for our lives. But we also had big differences, specifically around food. While I

Tim and me on our wedding day, August 8, 2008.

grew up on nose-to-tail cooking, Tim grew up on Rice-a-Roni. During the early years of our marriage, most of our disagreements were related to comfort food—specifically Tim's nightly habit of munching on Nacho Cheese Doritos and Coke with two heaping scoops of Ben & Jerry's ice cream on the side.

Despite the unhealthy habits from his upbringing, Tim understood the importance of nutrition. He'd struggled with eczema for his entire life, ever since childhood. It was common for him to have white scratch marks all over his body from itching. Early in our marriage, sometimes I would wake up in the middle of the night thinking we were being hit with one of California's famous earthquakes, only to discover that it was Tim scratching in his sleep and shaking the bed! We intuitively knew there was a dietary or lifestyle component to his condition, so we began experimenting with eliminating various foods and changing certain household products. Lo and behold, when we switched from grain-fed supermarket beef to grass-fed and -finished beef, he immediately experienced relief from eczema. This was enough for Tim to get on board with a lifestyle change—which is not to say it was easy. Even as a West Point grad and army veteran, Tim says that his most challenging battles were not fought in the deserts of Baghdad but at home, around food, nutrition, and the struggle to change the eating habits he grew up with.

In 2010, self-described "lunatic farmer" Joel Salatin gave a talk at Google Headquarters in the Bay Area. Joel owns Polyface Farm in Virginia's Shenandoah Valley and became famous when Michael Pollan devoted a chapter to him in his bestselling 2006 book *The Omnivore's Dilemma*. Pollan described how Joel integrated animals into his farming operations in ways that have resulted in healthier food, happier animals, less waste, and an efficient, closed-loop farming ecosystem. Salatin calls himself a lunatic farmer because the evangelical Christian frequently finds himself at odds with regulatory recommendations and requirements, as well as modern agricultural practice. As Joel says, everything he wants to do is illegal—and yet his many loyal customers routinely travel great distances and pay a premium for his delicious, nutritious, and ethically produced food. Joel Salatin, Polyface Farm, and Michael Pollan shined a bright light on how broken the industrial agriculture system is, as well as the failures of regulatory bodies such as the USDA, FDA, and state health agencies.

At Google, Joel reminded us that, until relatively recently, there were no garbage trucks to cart waste away or landfills to dump trash in someone else's backyard. Chickens were the garbage disposal salvage operation on the homestead! When food spoils, you feed it to the chickens, and they give you eggs in return. What a gorgeously efficient circular system! Too many Americans "go green" by throwing their banana peels on a diesel-powered dump truck that travels to an off-site composting operation. Joel told those of us in the audience that if we really wanted to be "green," we should attach a chicken house to our corporate cafés so that the scraps go right out to the chicken house, the eggs come right back in, and we don't have to truck our garbage away or buy eggs from somewhere else.

Everything Joel Salatin said in that talk resonated with me—the systems-thinking efficiency, the commonsense frugality, and his respect for the land and the animals. It reminded me of the simple frugality of my mother and the common sense of my grandfather. Good food, good agriculture, and good health are inseparable, and traditional wisdom is often a much greater value than so-called modern improvements.

Since both Tim and I lacked farming experience, we enrolled in several workshops and conferences organized at Polyface Farm. We learned how to process meat chickens and rabbits and how to improve land for pasture. Our aim was to gain practical, hands-on experience and learn from the experts. And who better to learn from than Joel himself, the renowned farmer and practitioner of sustainable agriculture?

These hands-on workshops gave us the confidence to move out of Pleasant Hill, California, and purchase six acres in Lincoln, north of Sacramento,

With my parents and Joel Salatin, 2022.

Our family with Sally Fallon Morell, 2022.

along with our own chicken processing equipment and tractor. This homestead included chickens, goats, and sheep, which was a far cry from our urban backgrounds growing up in San Jose. In 2022, we moved our family and homestead to eastern Tennessee, where we built upon our successes and lessons learned in California. We even expanded our livestock and skill sets by adding dairy cows to the mix!

Joel's philosophy around food, farming, and nutrition quickly led me to the work of another renegade thinker: Sally Fallon Morell, author of *Nourishing Traditions*, founding president of the Weston A. Price Foundation, and founder of A Campaign for Real Milk. Sally is passionate about health and has made it her mission in life to advocate for a diet based on nutrient-dense foods and raw milk. *Nourishing Traditions*, based on the work of Weston A. Price, confirmed the teachings of my mother and grandfather about eating traditional foods.

Dr. Weston A. Price was a Canadian dentist who lived and practiced in Cleveland, Ohio, during the early part of the twentieth century. In his dental practice, Dr. Price noticed that the dental health of his patients, and children in particular, had been declining over time, and he suspected that it had something to do with the increasing availability of processed foods in the American diet.

Weston A. Price was a man on a mission. Driven to understand the surge in tooth decay, palate malformations, and other deteriorations in dental health, he embarked on a series of remarkable journeys to isolated regions around the world. From the villages of Switzerland to the Outer Hebrides, Africa, Australia, and Polynesia, he sought out communities where people still relied on their native diets of traditionally grown, raised, and prepared foods. These diets were a far cry from the processed industrial foods that were becoming increasingly popular in North America in the early twentieth century. Instead, they were rich in animal foods such as organ meats, shellfish, eggs, and butter, and packed with vital nutrients like fat-soluble vitamins A, D, E, and K, water-soluble vitamins like B complex and C, and a host of essential minerals.

With meticulous attention to detail, Price documented the foods people ate, how they were produced on the farm, and how they were prepared in the kitchen. And what he found was astonishing. In communities where people continued to rely on traditional foods, dental health was strong and overall health was robust. But in communities that had been introduced to processed industrial foods such as white flour, vegetable oils, and white sugar, the health of the people had deteriorated rapidly.

Price's research revealed a remarkable correlation between a diet rich in traditional nourishing foods, including high-quality meat, milk, grains, fruits, and vegetables, and optimal dental and overall physical health. This groundbreaking work inspired Sally Fallon Morell to co-found the Weston A. Price Foundation in 1999 with the goal of restoring "nutrient-dense foods to the human diet through education, research, and activism." Fallon's acclaimed cookbook *Nourishing Traditions* has sold millions of copies and presented a bold critique of the food pyramid, mainstream nutrition guidelines, the standard American diet, the low-fat fad, and the increasing reliance on processed foods. In line with Dr. Price's research, both Morell and Salatin advocate for humanely raised animals as an essential component of agriculture and human nutrition, emphasizing the importance of locally sourced meats, milks, cheeses, and fats from grass-fed/grass-finished and pasture-raised animals.

As an Asian American family striving to prioritize nourishing traditional foods, Tim and I encountered a challenge: the research of Dr. Price, upon which we based our approach, did not include studies on Asian countries. China and Japan in the 1930s, in particular, did not fit his criteria of isolated, nonindustrialized groups with diets based on indigenous foods and limited imports. Despite being considered "traditional" at the time, both nations had extensive histories of trade with other countries and already had established industries, including food production. This posed a dilemma for us as we sought to honor our cultural traditions while embracing a nourishing diet.

Take one example from our own family: Vietnam's rich culinary culture has been shaped by a variety of influences, including French colonialism in Indochina. The introduction of French flavors, ingredients, and cooking techniques transformed traditional Vietnamese dishes, creating a new and distinct flavor profile. The French introduced the baguette to Vietnam, which the Vietnamese adapted using rice flour to create bánh mì. (In fact, I am part French, which explains why I love Vietnamese and French food so much.)

Scaling Up

Tim and I were living in a small urban farmhouse on a corner lot with my parents and two daughters in the affluent city of Pleasant Hill, California, when we realized that if we were going to feed our family the most nutrient-dense food, we needed to learn how to grow it and produce it ourselves. In 2019, we started a quarter-acre homestead with a permaculture garden and five chickens in the middle of the San Francisco Bay Area.

A couple years later, we scaled up to six acres in Lincoln, California, just north of Sacramento, where we brought home our first sheep and goats. Tim began to focus on animal husbandry, while I specialized in growing vegetables using regenerative methods to improve soil health. We began rotational grazing with the animals, practiced no-till with the vegetable beds, incorporated cover crops and bio amendments to build soil organic matter, and planned and planted perennial polycultures with several different types of plants. This integrated approach fostered soil that was healthy and alive and enabled us not to use any pesticides on our land.

We continued to scale up: In addition to our sheep, goats, and laying hens, Tim tended to meat chickens, ducks, geese, and turkeys. Within one year, I produced more than 150 pounds of watermelon and hundreds of pounds of our own vegetables. With such abundance, we were

Our quarter-acre backyard urban homestead in Pleasant Hill, CA, in 2020.

Our Boer goats and East Friesian sheep on our six-acre homestead in Lincoln, CA, in 2021.

One hundred ducklings and two guard geese on our homestead in Lincoln, CA, in 2021.

determined not to let anything go to waste. This is when I really dug in to learning about fermentation, making krauts and kimchi. We also began eating our animals nose-to-tail to ensure that we (and our children) were receiving all of the available nutrients while minimizing waste. Everyone in our family could feel the difference in our physical and mental health as we became more and more nourished with foods such as nutrient-dense broths and fermented food from our own land.

Emily in the watermelon garden in Lincoln, CA, 2021.

Tim with a watermelon in Lincoln, CA, 2021.

A 34-pound watermelon from our garden in Lincoln, CA, 2021.

Many common vegetables, such as potatoes, artichokes, carrots, asparagus, and onions, were also introduced to Vietnamese cooking from the West. French influence extends beyond ingredients to cooking methods, with the use of butter, cheese, and wine all reflecting French culinary traditions. Even beef dishes like bò 7 món, a seven-course meal of beef, were created by French expats to celebrate the new availability of imported beef during the French colonial era. Vietnamese cuisine remains uniquely flavorful and diverse, a testament to the country's rich culinary history beyond French influences.

All of this meant that identifying the most nourishing traditions for our family was . . . complicated! Our family's cooking traditions included a lot of Vietnamese foods, of course, as well as a blend of Chinese and Taiwanese cooking from Tim's background. But over the years, our family's palate was shaped by where we lived in California and being exposed to some of the best Asian cuisine in the world, from Korean BBQ and Indian curry dishes to Thai noodles and fresh Japanese sashimi and more.

On top of all that, Tim and I had three (very different) generations under one roof. As my parents reached retirement age and began to have health issues, my mother and father left their home in San Jose and moved in with us. In 2011, we welcomed our first-born daughter, Emily, followed four years later by our daughter Natalie. Over the years, a lot of processed foodstuffs—especially condiments, marinades, and spices—had made their way into our pantry. We were a busy young family surrounded by four Whole Foods Markets and we loved our delivery of their Sperlonga bread.

One day, I decided to purge our pantry of these highly processed foods so we could start fresh with real, wholesome foods. My mother walked into the kitchen right as I opened the refrigerator and tossed a bunch of condiments and marinades into a big black garbage bag.

"If you throw away all of these condiments, what will we cook with?!" she exclaimed.

"I don't know yet, but we will figure it out!"

I knew that adopting Salatin's approach to agriculture and Fallon's approach to nutrition would serve our family well, but I wasn't entirely sure how to do it in the context of a modern first- and second-generation immigrant family. I was beginning to suspect that we were going to have to make it up as we went along.

When I explained to my mother why I was throwing out our processed soy sauce and hoisin sauce, however, she quickly got on board with the same kind of determination I'd witnessed when she bargained with the fishmonger for a better price on mackerel. Focusing on a few key staples was the first step in a years-long journey we took together to re-create the Asian dishes our family loved so they would be more nourishing and nutrient-dense.

Journey Toward Self-Sufficiency

On March 16, 2020, California went into a lockdown—complete with curfews—due to the Covid-19 pandemic. Although I already had an organic backyard garden in place at our home in Pleasant Hill, I knew our family needed a source of protein, especially if there was no guarantee we'd find what we needed on grocery store shelves. I had already been in contact with a "chicken lady" in Mill Valley, north of San Francisco, and could secure three egg-laying hens . . . for nearly $1,000! We bought them anyway because we didn't know how long the lockdown would last or what lay ahead, but from that point forward we seriously began our journey to truly understand the power of having a self-sufficient homestead.

As we saw with Tim's eczema, the proof of better health was all the evidence we needed to dedicate ourselves to this way of life. Over time, ailments that my parents suffered from improved. For my mother, that meant her hypertension diminished and congestive heart failure resolved. My father struggled with depression and obsessive-compulsive disorder (OCD), both of which also improved after we began eating real food as close to its natural state as possible.

I now believe that there is no one-size-fits-all approach to food, health, and nutrition. It's probably true that *every* family must grapple at some level with honoring their culinary traditions while rebuilding them for better nutrition, especially in the context of a convenience-driven modern society. I don't claim to have all the answers. This book is simply my offering of our family's beloved Asian recipes through the lens of nutrient-dense Wise Traditions principles. The Wise Tradition principles are not a diet, per se, but more a framework for making the best food choices for the human body, based on what has worked for humankind for millennia.

In other words, it is my attempt to fill a gap where Weston A. Price left off, as well as a passion project to spend as much time as I can in the kitchen with my mother in order to capture her recipes and preserve them for her grandchildren. This book and the homemade recipes in it were inspired by her and, while I enhanced them with everything I've learned from Joel Salatin, Sally Fallon Morell, and the Weston A. Price community, they all required her thumbs-up when she tasted each dish. And Mom did not go easy on me, I assure you! From our kitchen to yours, I hope you and your family enjoy these recipes as much as we do.

Different Dialects and Different Dishes

Growing up, I had wondered why my mother and father spoke different dialects of Vietnamese. My father's family came from Da Nang, a coastal city in Central Vietnam, whereas my mother's family was from Hanoi in the North. (During the early Vietnam War in the 1950s, members of both sides of my family fled south to Saigon, and my parents were the first of their families to ultimately leave Vietnam for the United States in 1975.)

In addition to speaking different dialects, my parents also craved different dishes—those they were accustomed to from their own childhoods. For example, my father favors spicy food from the city of Huế food; one of his favorite dishes is bún bò Huế, a spicy pork noodle soup. My mother loves anything "bánh," which refers to a wide variety of sweet or savory cakes, pastries, and other baked or steamed goods. In northern Vietnamese cuisine, bánh is particularly prominent and can be found in many forms, such as bánh mì (a type of sandwich made with a crusty baguette), bánh cuốn (steamed rice flour rolls stuffed with ground pork and mushrooms), bánh bao (steamed buns filled with pork and other ingredients), and bánh xèo (crispy rice flour crepes filled with pork, shrimp, and bean sprouts). These dishes can vary in preparation, ingredients, and shape depending on the region of Vietnam and the specific recipe.

CHAPTER 1

Getting Started

Our family's traditional foods have been passed down through generations of our Asian ancestors. I was fortunate to grow up with the vibrant flavors and textures of Vietnamese and French cuisine, while Tim's palate was shaped by the nuanced tastes of Chinese dishes. Despite our distinct cultural backgrounds, Tim and I have always shared a love for delicious food that continually draws us to explore the diverse culinary scene throughout California and wherever we travel to bring the flavors back to our home.

Since having children, we have come to appreciate the importance of preserving our family's traditional foods and culinary practices. Over the past twelve years, our family has rediscovered our Asian roots by incorporating traditional foods into our modern lifestyle. I believe that traditional foods are a cornerstone of our cultural heritage, and they offer numerous health benefits that we want to be able to share with others. By adopting a modern approach to our family's traditional foods, we can enjoy the best of both worlds—the flavors and nutrition of our ancestors' cuisine combined with the convenience and variety of today's food options. It's similar to what you may experience if you ever tried an Asian fusion restaurant, except our family ensures that each ingredient is cleanly sourced.

In many Asian societies, food is not just sustenance but also a fundamental part of cultural and social identity. As an Asian American, I sometimes worry about losing my ancestral heritage, so I love that I can help preserve it through making and eating these delicious dishes! Traditional foods are often associated with particular festivals, rituals, and ceremonies and are prepared with great care and attention to detail. There is no single correct definition for traditional food, much like there isn't one for sustainability.

However, since this cookbook is a compilation of recipes for what I consider to be traditional foods, I feel it's important to share my own definition of the term. My understanding of traditional foods is that they are the foods that have been consumed by certain cultural groups for many generations and have contributed to their good health and well-being. These foods are often simple and haven't been altered by modern agricultural or industrial processes. They are nutrient-dense and wholesome.

Traditional diets don't exclude meat and dairy and the saturated fat these foods provide. Instead, they emphasize the consumption of high-quality animal products from pasture-raised animals that are minimally fed with grains. Simple foods such as broth, eggs, fermented vegetables, and greens are essential parts of traditional diets.

My approach to nutrition is based on a holistic and sustainable perspective that values both taste and health. I don't believe in extreme diets that focus exclusively on animal-based or plant-based foods, as they don't align with how humans have traditionally eaten over the course of history. Instead, I advocate for a balanced approach that combines traditional practices with evidence-based research. By embracing this approach, we can cultivate a nourishing diet that promotes overall health and well-being.

Rediscovering Our Asian Roots: A Modern Approach to Our Family's Traditional Foods

Growing up in an Asian household in America, I was immersed in a rich tapestry of traditional foods that reflected my family's cultural heritage. From sourcing high-quality ingredients to preserving their freshness and nutritional value through fermentation, I learned the importance of culinary traditions passed down from generation to generation. The art of food preparation and cooking techniques taught by my mother emphasized efficiency without compromising on quality or presentation, a cherished legacy that has shaped my approach to food.

Incorporating traditional Asian foods into our daily meals has not only been a way to honor our heritage, but also a means to maintain our health and well-being. Many of these foods are nutrient-dense, packed with essential vitamins, minerals, and other antioxidants that support a robust immune system and reduce the risk of chronic diseases. This philosophy is in line with the groundbreaking research of renowned nutritionist Sally Fallon Morell, as detailed in her influential book *Nourishing Traditions*, and the pioneering work of Dr. Weston A. Price.

Drawing from our deep-rooted Asian heritage, this cookbook is a celebration of traditional foods and culinary wisdom. Through its pages, we not only share our family's treasured recipes, but also highlight the importance of incorporating Weston A. Price–inspired nutrient-dense foods into our diets for optimal health.

Guided by the principles of the Weston A. Price Foundation, this cookbook aims to rekindle your appreciation for the wisdom of our ancestors

and inspire you to embark on a culinary journey that blends cultural heritage with modern health-consciousness. Join us as we rediscover the nourishing traditions of Asian cuisine, one recipe at a time.

Guiding Principles

"Let food be thy medicine and thy medicine be thy food." —*Hippocrates*

In my pursuit of promoting healthier living for my family, I have spent years changing our eating habits and experimenting with various elimination diets. However, I found that many of these diets were not sustainable in the long run. In my quest for something that was simple to follow, sustainable for our family, and aligned with our culture and heritage, I discovered the Weston A. Price dietary guidelines as outlined in *Nourishing Traditions*. Through this process, I thought about my grandfather's perspective on food as being medicine and sustenance for the body. The

What Is Umami?

Umami is considered the fifth taste and is characterized by a savory, meaty, or broth-like flavor. It is found naturally in foods such as meat, fish, mushrooms, and fermented products. While umami is a taste that can be enjoyed by people of all cultures, it is often associated with Asian cuisine.

In many Asian cuisines there is a focus on balancing flavors, including sweet, sour, spicy, and umami, to create a harmonious and satisfying eating experience. This emphasis on balance is rooted in traditional beliefs about health and wellness. In traditional Chinese medicine, for example, foods are categorized by their energetic properties and flavors, and the goal is to achieve balance and harmony in the body by consuming a variety of different foods in moderation. This includes balancing yin (cooling) and yang (warming) foods, as well as the five basic flavors: sweet, sour, bitter, salty, and umami. It is believed that a balanced diet can help maintain physical health, prevent illness, and promote overall well-being.

Similarly, in Vietnamese cuisine, the balance of flavors is believed to promote good health and vitality. For example, sour flavors are thought to aid digestion and stimulate the appetite, while spicy flavors are believed to improve circulation and promote sweating, which can help cool the body in hot and humid climates. Umami-rich foods, such as fish sauce and fermented soy products, are also believed to be healthy, as they are high in protein and other nutrients.

Weston A. Price dietary guidelines provide a framework for healthier eating by focusing on how we source and prepare our ingredients so that they are more nutritious for our bodies. The purpose of this cookbook is to showcase how we can easily achieve this by cooking familiar Asian cuisines without compromising on the flavors we love.

The foundation of this book is based on the concept that throughout history, humans have cooked with taste as the primary focus rather than solely for health benefits. This approach has led to our natural taste preferences being aligned with what is most nourishing for our bodies. As a result, we tend to crave foods that are fatty and salty because, in their natural whole food forms, fat and salt are good for us. This book emphasizes the importance of consuming nutrient-rich foods with low toxicity levels, maintaining an appropriate macronutrient ratio, preparing historically appropriate dishes, incorporating natural umami flavors, including a variety of plant parts, and avoiding shortcuts. By adhering to these principles, we can create delicious and healthy meals that align with our natural cravings and support our overall well-being.

Weston A. Price Dietary Principles

The Weston A. Price Foundation is a nonprofit organization founded by Sally Fallon Morell that promotes a traditional, whole foods approach to nutrition based on the research of dentist and nutritionist Weston A. Price. The dietary principles of Dr. Price, often referred to as the "Principles of Traditional Diets," emphasize the consumption of nutrient-dense, unprocessed foods and avoidance of modern processed foods.[*]

First and foremost, minimize processed foods. Modern processed foods that are high in refined sugars, refined grains, artificial additives, and preservatives are the main factors that lead to poor dental and overall health, according to Dr. Price. Instead, replace these with whole, unprocessed foods, such as fresh fruits and vegetables, pasture-raised and grass-fed meats, wild-caught (not farmed) fish, eggs from pastured hens, raw and fermented full-fat dairy products, traditional fats, and properly prepared grains, nuts, and legumes. It is best to grow or raise these foods yourself or source them locally from reputable farmers and food producers who follow sustainable and organic practices.

---

* See Weston A. Price Foundation, "Timeless Principles of Healthy Traditional Diets," https://www.westonaprice.org/health-topics/abcs-of-nutrition/principles-of-healthy-diets-2.

Environmental Factors

I believe that the growing prevalence of food allergies and intolerances can be attributed to the changes in our modern environment. Due to our disconnection from nature and the ways of living that humans have had throughout history, we are more vulnerable to problematic foods, which can cause adverse reactions.

In the past, people consumed a variety of foods in their natural and unprocessed form. This allowed their bodies to adapt and develop tolerances to different types of foods. However, in our modern world, we are exposed to many new and processed foods that are not part of our evolutionary history. As a result, our bodies may not be able to recognize and tolerate these new foods, leading to allergic reactions or intolerances. Additionally, our modern lifestyle, including a lack of exposure to diverse natural environments and an over-reliance on antibiotics and other medications, may also contribute to the rise in food allergies and intolerances.

Throughout human history, people had plenty of exposure to nature, livestock, and a wide range of fresh, seasonal, and naturally fermented foods. However, in modern times, we have moved away from these traditional ways of living and eating. Additionally, industrial farming practices have led to soil depletion, resulting in less nutritious foods. Chronic lack of sleep and constant low-level stress are also contributing factors to a weakened immune system and an increase in food allergies and autoimmune-related health issues. The delicate balance of our gut microbiota, essential for optimal digestion and nutrient uptake, has been compromised by excessive use of antibiotics and antibacterial products. Neurologist Natasha Campbell-McBride has highlighted the correlation between learning disabilities and the foods we consume in her book, *Gut and Psychology Syndrome*. The quality of our diet and the health of our digestive system are pivotal factors that directly impact our overall well-being, and Dr. Campbell-McBride's research findings provide compelling evidence to support this stance.

Seek Out Organic, Locally Sourced Whole Foods

Choosing whole, unprocessed, unadulterated ingredients is the best way to make sure you are eating a nutrient-dense, nourishing diet. Organic standards do not allow the use of genetically modified organisms (GMOs) and prioritize biodiversity by promoting crop rotation and the use of cover crops. These practices can help protect the ecosystem and support the diversity of plant and animal species, which is essential for long-term sustainability. While quality food produced by quality farming practices might cost more, studies have shown that it requires less nutrient-dense food to make a person feel full in comparison to modern processed foods that contain refined sugars and trans fats.

Organic whole foods are considered to be more nutrient-dense than conventional foods due to several factors. One of the main reasons is that organic farming practices prioritize soil health through the use of organic matter, compost, and natural fertilizers instead of chemical alternatives. This results in nutrient-rich soil that supports the growth of plants with higher nutrient content.

Another factor is the avoidance of synthetic pesticides in organic farming. Instead, organic farmers rely on natural methods such as crop rotation, beneficial insects, and organic pest control measures. This results in fewer residues of synthetic chemicals in organic whole foods, potentially reducing the risk of exposure to these substances.

Organic foods are produced without the use of GMOs, which are plants or animals whose genetic material has been altered in a way that does not occur naturally. The topic of GMOs is complex, and they are controversial in terms of their safety and suitability for consumption. For our family's traditional cooking, we do not use GMOs and use only organic, whole food ingredients to be mindful of health, environmental, and ethical impacts.

Environmental impacts are a concern with GMOs. Some GMO crops are engineered to be resistant to certain pests or herbicides, which can lead to the development of pesticide-resistant pests or the contamination of non-GMO crops. One example is the insertion of genes from the soil bacterium *Bacillus thuringiensis* (*Bt*) into crop plants. This genetic modification produces a toxin that is lethal to specific pests, such as certain insects, thereby reducing the need for external pesticide application. Another example is the genetic modification of crops to be resistant to herbicides, such as glyphosate (Roundup). This allows farmers to use these herbicides to control weeds without harming the genetically modified crop. The goal of incorporating these traits into GMO crops is to enhance crop yield and reduce crop loss due to pests or weeds. However, there are considerations for environmental impacts, food safety, and broader socioeconomic implications to take into consideration with the harmful use of GMOs in our food. Additionally, there are concerns about the potential for genetically modified plants to crossbreed with wild relatives, leading to changes in natural ecosystems and other unintended consequences.

Ethical concerns related to GMOs include issues such as patenting of genetically modified seeds, corporate control of the food supply, and potential

Our family, at our east Tennessee homestead, August 2023.

negative impacts on small farmers and traditional farming practices. This concern is near and dear to our family's hearts because we believe that concentration of power and control over food production in the hands of a few large corporations will have negative social and economic consequences and that GMOs can contribute to the erosion of traditional farming practices and biodiversity.

In addition, conventional foods often undergo extensive processing, which typically involves the addition of preservatives, artificial flavors, and other additives that can reduce the nutrient content of the final product. On the other hand, organic whole foods are minimally processed, preserving their natural nutrient content.

Furthermore, organic farming practices often prioritize biodiversity, which can result in a greater variety of crops and livestock. Monocropping is commonly used in modern industrial agriculture to maximize yields and simplify management practices. It is often associated with large-scale commercial agriculture and the production of commodities such as corn, soybeans, wheat, and cotton. Monocrops are typically managed using mechanized equipment, synthetic fertilizers, and pesticides to optimize production and control pests and diseases. Concerns associated with monocropping include reduced biodiversity, increased risk of pest outbreaks and diseases, soil degradation, and dependence on synthetic inputs. Monocropping also has negative environmental impacts, such as soil erosion, nutrient depletion, and water pollution.

Like monocropping, industrialized animal farming has drawbacks, including issues related to animal welfare, environmental impact, and disease susceptibility. There is growing interest in more sustainable approaches to animal husbandry, such as mixed or diversified livestock farming, where multiple species of animals are raised together, often with a focus on regenerative practices that promote animal health, biodiversity, and sustainability. This diversity leads to a wider range of nutrients in the diet, as different plants and animals have different nutrient profiles.

It's extremely important to understand where your food comes from. This simple question—Where is our food coming from?—led me (and Tim) down a path where we now grow our own produce and raise our own meat. In this way, we not only have more control over the quality of our food, we also know that our animals have been raised and treated humanely and that our soil hasn't been tilled or sprayed.

Cooking Fats and Oils

As much as possible, avoid refined seed oils and man-made fats. Seed oils are typically highly processed and high in omega-6 fatty acids, which can lead to an imbalance in the omega-3 to omega-6 ratio in the body when consumed in excess. This imbalance has been linked to inflammation and other health issues. Some examples of refined seed oils to avoid include soybean oil, corn oil, cottonseed oil, canola oil, sunflower oil, safflower oil, and vegetable oil. These oils are commonly used in processed foods, fried foods, and many commercial cooking and baking applications.

Changing the oils in our diet was tough for my family, who used to love snacking on chips. Next time you go to the grocery store, try to find a snack that isn't made with seed oils. It may be difficult to find, but there are more and more alternatives being introduced that use healthier oils such as avocado or coconut.

Instead of seed oils, we now cook with the traditional fats and oils that have been used for centuries, using organic, unrefined coconut oil; organic, extra-virgin, and cold-pressed sesame oil and olive oil; and pasture-raised, grass-fed, organic sources of ghee (clarified butter), lard (from pastured pigs), and tallow (rendered beef or lamb fat). These traditional fats are more stable at high temperatures and have a healthier balance of saturated, monounsaturated, and polyunsaturated fats.

I know that advocating for the health benefits of traditional fats and oils may seem counterintuitive; to a degree, it is even for me. Growing up, I was taught that eating butter and animal fat leads to high cholesterol and heart disease. As it turns out, the margarine, vegetable oils, and other seed oils that were once advertised as healthier options are, in fact, extremely unhealthy. These products are highly processed, present numerous health hazards, and should be avoided. You are much better off with butter and animal fats. As with all food, it's important to source your fats well, such as from organic, pastured, or grass-fed animals. It's also good practice to vary the types of fats and oils you use.

Dairy

Milk and other dairy ingredients are not typically a big part of traditional Asian cuisines, so you may be wondering why they are included in my recipes. Dairy is a core component in the Weston A. Price dietary recommendations, and I've found that it makes good nutrition sense to include dairy—especially raw milk from our cow—as a part of our family's diet. While dairy is not entirely traditional, it is often incorporated into modern Asian fusion dishes and our favorite milk-based drinks and desserts such as Korean Strawberry Milk Tea with Honey Boba (page 260) and Condensed Milk Affogato (page 268). We've even found ways to make

The Crown Jewel of Every Homestead

The dairy cow is considered the crown jewel of the homestead for several reasons.

Milk production: Dairy cows are specifically bred for milk production, and they are highly efficient at converting their feed into milk. They can produce a large amount of milk on a daily basis, providing a steady supply of fresh milk for the homestead. Milk is a versatile and nutritious food that can be consumed as is or used to make a wide range of dairy products such as butter, cheese, yogurt, and more.

Self-sufficiency: Having a dairy cow on the homestead can provide a level of self-sufficiency. It reduces the reliance on external sources for milk and dairy products and allows homesteaders to have more control over their food supply. This can be particularly important in remote areas or during times of economic uncertainty, when access to store-bought dairy products may be limited.

Nutritional value: Milk is a good source of essential nutrients such as protein, calcium, vitamins, and minerals, making it a valuable addition to the homestead diet. Fresh, raw milk from a properly managed and healthy dairy cow is a highly nutritious food source for the entire family.

Sustainability: Keeping a dairy cow can be a sustainable practice as it allows for the utilization of available resources such as pastureland and feed. Additionally, cow manure can be used as a natural fertilizer for the homestead garden or crops, reducing the need for synthetic fertilizers.

Animal husbandry: Raising a dairy cow requires a certain level of animal husbandry skills, and many homesteaders find joy and fulfillment in caring for their cows. Building a relationship with the cow, learning about its behavior, and providing proper care and nutrition can be a rewarding experience and a way to connect with nature and the food production process.

these delicious treats more nutritious by using fresh raw milk from our family cow and natural sweeteners.

Raw milk is highly nutritious. It is packed with calcium and vitamins A, D, and K2, as well as healthy fat and beneficial bacteria that are excellent for gut health. These bacteria die during pasteurization—which the FDA would say is a good thing—but the pasteurized, homogenized reduced-fat milk that you find in the grocery store is of vastly inferior quality in terms of nutrition. Often, it is also pumped full of hormones like rBST to make cows produce more milk. If you don't have a local raw milk farmer, it can be difficult to source raw dairy, as it's not available in supermarkets in some

Tim with Ms. Brown.

states, but you can find a list of sources at RealMilk.com. If you decide to go the pasteurized route, I recommend dairy from grass-fed animals (such as Kalona SuperNatural products) for numerous reasons, including higher amounts of vitamin K2.

As with gluten allergies, there are many people who consider themselves to be lactose intolerant, Tim included. Although he loves ice cream, it never settled well in his stomach until we began making our own with raw cream milked from our Jerseys! People who consider themselves to be lactose intolerant might have an easier time digesting raw milk because lactase, the enzyme that helps you digest milk, is killed during pasteurization. Gut health also plays a role in lactose intolerance. Eating probiotic-rich foods (see chapter 4) may help improve your ability to digest dairy. Naturally, it's important to find what works best for your body and try challenging your tolerance occasionally. Keep in mind that improving gut health can take time, so trying dairy every few months can help you assess how your body is reacting to it. If your tummy is still tender, yogurt, kefir, sour cream, hard cheese, butter, and cream are often better tolerated than milk because they are fermented, and this process breaks down much of the lactose. However, tolerance can vary significantly from person to person.

A2/A2 milk comes from cows that naturally produce milk containing only the A2 beta-casein protein, without the A1 beta-casein protein. Some studies suggest that A2 beta-casein protein may be less likely to cause digestive discomfort in people with lactose intolerance compared to A1 beta-casein protein. However, evidence on the benefits of A2/A2 milk for lactose-intolerant individuals is still limited, and more research is needed to fully understand its effects. Some people may find relief from lactose intolerance symptoms by switching to A2/A2 milk or grass-fed dairy, while others may not experience any significant difference. Clarified butter or ghee, as well as cheese and yogurt made from goat's or sheep's milk, can also be alternatives for those who experience lactose intolerance from cow's milk products. Ultimately, it's important to listen to your body and find what works best for you when it comes to dairy.

The Farm-to-Consumer Legal Defense Fund

The Farm-to-Consumer Legal Defense Fund (FTCLDF; farmtoconsumer.org) was started by the Weston A. Price Foundation to protect the direct relationship between farmers and their customers, often (but not always) in the sale of raw milk and pasture-raised meats. It is designed to protect consumers' rights to buy food products directly from farmers without government interference. It also fills a need for farmers, homesteaders, and raw milk producers in receiving affordable legal representation to protect them.

Since its inception in 2007, FTCLDF has taken on several landmark cases, and while not every case in court has been victorious, homesteaders and farmers can now experience some reprieve and not feel isolated if they are targeted through legal action. Through the years, having this valuable resource has emboldened more people to grow their own food and no longer fear sharing their pasture-raised meats, organically grown crops, and fresh raw milk with others in their communities.

Essential Ingredients

This cookbook is a compilation of the recipes enjoyed by our multigenerational household on a daily basis, including those that bring us joy, those with roots in my parents' past, those that fuel us through long nights, and those that evoke memories of our travels. While there are many more I would have liked to include, my focus was on the most nourishing and nutrient-rich dishes using ingredients that are easily accessible in both urban and rural areas of North America. The following are some of these ingredients.

Fish Sauce

A number of Vietnamese dishes, particularly broths and soups, use fish sauce to add an extra layer of complex and savory umami flavor to the base. Similarly, Korean cuisine incorporates a bit of fried anchovy, while dried shrimp serves the same purpose in some Chinese dishes. Fish sauce is typically made by fermenting anchovies. Despite its initial fishy scent, adding it to a dish can result in a flavor that is full of umami and not at all fishy. It is best to choose varieties of fish sauce without added sugar or preservatives. Red Boat brand is my favorite.

Shrimp Paste

Southeast Asian cuisine often uses shrimp paste as a flavor enhancer. It is made from fermented shrimp and has a more potent flavor than fish sauce. You can find it without added preservatives in Asian grocery stores, or make your own using my recipe (page 84). For those who prefer a vegetarian or vegan option, you can use tamari instead (see below).

Coconut Aminos

Coconut aminos is a healthier alternative to soy sauce or tamari, as it is a gluten-free and soy-free condiment made from the sap of coconut blossoms. It also has a lighter taste than soy sauce or tamari. I use coconut aminos in marinades, sauces, dressings, stir-fries, and soups when I want to cut down on sodium while still adding a touch of sweet umami flavor.

Tamari

Tamari is a naturally wheat-free, fermented soy sauce that was introduced to Japan from China. Although it's best to avoid most forms of soy, I believe that fermented types such as tamari, miso, natto, and tempeh can be consumed in moderation. Tamari is the liquid byproduct of making miso paste, and it has a more pronounced and intense flavor compared to other soy sauces. To balance its sharp taste, I often use honey as a natural sweetener in my recipes. Tamari can be used as a condiment or an ingredient in stir-fries, marinades, dressings, and sauces. It is best to choose organic, traditionally fermented, and unpasteurized tamari made according to traditional methods to ensure that it is free from additives and preservatives. My favorite brand is Ohsawa.

Soy Sauce

Traditional soy sauce, also known as naturally brewed soy sauce, is made by fermenting soy beans with the help of specific molds and bacteria. The fermentation process can take months to develop the unique flavor profile and beneficial properties of the sauce. It is important to note that not all soy sauces available in the market meet these criteria. Many commercially available soy sauces are likely chemically processed, contain additives, or are made using shortcuts that do not involve traditional fermentation methods. I recommend looking for soy sauce brands that specify that they are using traditional brewing methods and that are free from additives or artificial ingredients. My favorites are imported straight from Japan from brands that continue to use the authentic Japanese methods of soy sauce fermentation.

Avocado Oil

Avocado oil has a high smoke point, which makes it a good option for cooking at high temperatures without breaking down and producing harmful compounds. Because most of the avocado oil out there is cut with other seed oils like canola oil, I recommend that you do your research to find a brand that is 100 percent avocado oil, such as Chosen Foods.

Flours and Starches

When it comes to baking, I prefer to use sprouted flour and fermented dough (sourdough) whenever possible. The fermentation process involved in sourdough creates a unique depth of flavor and improves the digestibility of gluten. I like to use a range of flours and starches in place of wheat flour and cornstarch. Choose high-quality, minimally processed, organic brands for maximum nutrient density.

- Rice flour is a staple in many Asian cuisines and is used for making rice noodles, rice cakes, and dumpling wrappers. Rice flour is my top choice for thickening.
- Sweet rice flour, mochiko in Japanese, is commonly used in Asian desserts. I like Koda Farms brand.
- Buckwheat flour is commonly used in Japanese cooking for making soba noodles.

- Sweet potato starch adds natural sweetness and unique texture to Korean dishes.
- Arrowroot starch serves as a gluten-free alternative to cornstarch for thickening sauces and stews.
- Tapioca starch, derived from the cassava root, is used as a thickening agent in soups, sauces, and desserts.
- Mung bean flour is used in various Asian desserts and snacks for its slightly sweet taste and smooth, silky texture when cooked.
- Coconut flour, made from dried and ground coconut meat, is used in some Asian cuisines for desserts and baked goods, providing a rich coconut flavor.

Sweeteners

I prefer to use pure raw honey and maple syrup as natural sweeteners, but their stronger flavors may not work in every recipe. In these cases, I often turn to granulated coconut sugar, which is made from the sap of coconut palm flower buds. Another favorite option is panela, a minimally processed whole cane sugar that retains many of the nutritional characteristics of the sugarcane grass. I most often source panela from Healthy Traditions.

Spices

Asian cuisines are renowned for their wide array of spices. Some of the spices I always keep stocked in my pantry include paprika, Saigon cinnamon, star anise pods, black cardamom seeds, fennel seeds, whole cloves,

ground turmeric, gochugaru (Korean red chili powder), and ground white pepper. In the Appalachian region where I live, we even forage for our own "Appalachian allspice," which we grind and use in everything from broths and rubs to marinades and ice cream.

When sourcing spices, it's important to look for non-GMO, nonirradiated, and non-EtO varieties. EtO (ethylene oxide) is a chemical compound commonly used to sterilize spices, herbs, and other food products to eliminate microbial contamination, insects, and pests. However, EtO is considered a potential carcinogen by the International Agency for Research on Cancer, and its use as a food sterilant has raised concerns about its potential health risks.

Asian spices available in US grocery stores are often shipped from overseas and have been found to contain high levels of lead. Out of a desire to source the highest quality spices and herbs, our family now prepackages herbal soup packs for our own relatives and friends to use. These are available online at JoyandJolie.com.

Asian Vegetables

Most of the greens I use in my dishes are what I can easily grow in my own backyard and what you may commonly find in North American grocery stores. These include bok choy, napa cabbage, kohlrabi, gai lan, mizuna, bitter melon, Thai basil, dill, lemongrass, daikons, and other radishes. Fresh cilantro and mint are commonly used to garnish Asian dishes. Although not an Asian green, watercress (one of the most nutrient-dense foods there is) grows wild here in the fresh spring mountain waters of the Appalachia, and I love using it in our Vietnamese Shaking Beef with Watercress Salad (page 182). The mild onion flavor of scallions (also called green onions) is featured in many Asian cuisines. They are a nutrient-rich addition to dishes such as stir-fries and soups and as a garnish.

Salt

Sea salt is typically less processed and undergoes minimal refining compared to table salt. As a result, it retains more of its natural mineral content, which can include magnesium, potassium, calcium, and other essential trace minerals. These minerals add flavor to the salt and provide additional nutritional value, making sea salt a more wholesome option compared to regular table salt, which is often heavily refined, stripped of its mineral content, and treated with anticaking agents and other additives to prevent clumping and improve shelf stability.

Many people find that sea salt has a more complex and nuanced taste compared to table salt, which can be relatively plain and one-dimensional in flavor. The unique taste of sea salt enhances the flavor of food and provides a more enjoyable culinary experience. Sea salt often has a coarser texture than table salt, which can provide a satisfying crunch, texture, or a burst of flavor when used as a finishing salt or added to the surface of foods.

Some people prefer sea salt due to environmental considerations. Sea salt is considered a renewable resource, often obtained through the evaporation of seawater. My favorite brand is Redmond Real Salt ancient fine sea salt, which is unrefined sea salt mined from an ancient sea bed in Utah and is marketed as being environmentally friendly and sustainably harvested. Frequently I also use other types of salt, such as Himalayan (pink) and Celtic (gray) sea salt. In contrast, regular table salt is often obtained through mining and may involve more extensive processing and environmental impacts.

Ginger

Ginger is a commonly used ingredient in many Asian culinary traditions. Its distinctive flavor and aroma add depth and complexity to a variety of nourishing dishes, such as soups, curries, and stir-fries. Ginger is also known for its potential healing properties, including anti-inflammatory, digestive, and immune-boosting effects.

In traditional Asian medicine, ginger is used to treat conditions associated with inflammation, such as arthritis. It is also believed to aid digestion by stimulating the production of digestive enzymes, improving gut motility, and reducing symptoms of indigestion, bloating, and nausea. Additionally, ginger is thought to have immune-boosting properties, thanks to its antioxidants and other bioactive compounds.

Furthermore, ginger is considered a warming spice in traditional Asian medicine and is often used in nourishing foods to help warm the body from the inside. This makes it a popular ingredient in soups, stews, and teas, especially during colder seasons or for individuals who are considered to have a "cold" constitution.

Garlic

In Asian cooking, garlic is a flavor superhero! It's used in so many different ways in Chinese, Japanese, Korean, Thai, Vietnamese, and other Asian cuisines. You'll find it minced or finely chopped and added to hot oil or butter to release its amazing flavor and aroma. It's used in stir-fries, soups, sauces, marinades, dressings, pickles, condiments, and spice pastes. It can be used with meat, poultry, seafood, veggies, and tofu, in either cooked or raw form. Some Asian cuisines even use it medicinally for potential health benefits, such as boosting the immune system and reducing inflammation.

Garlic is a culinary powerhouse that adds depth and complexity to Asian dishes, and it is a beloved ingredient in Asian kitchens.

Eggs

Eggs from pasture-raised, organically fed chickens are nutrient-dense, versatile, and commonly used in Asian cuisine. They are incorporated into a wide variety of dishes in various ways. In this cookbook, you will find my Aminos-Marinated Eggs recipe (page 145), a family favorite to which you can add your favorite protein. There are also several other ways to incorporate eggs into your Asian dishes. Stir-frying is a popular method, in which eggs are beaten and quickly cooked with fried rice, chow mein, or pad Thai, providing a luscious, silky texture and flavor. Asian-style omelets, such as Japanese tamagoyaki or Chinese-style egg foo young, are also common, with eggs being folded or rolled around fillings of vegetables, meat, or seafood. Eggs are also used to create delicate egg strands in dishes like egg drop soup or as binders in dumpling fillings or meatballs. Additionally, eggs are used in pancakes, batters, and coatings for deep-fried foods, such as tempura or Korean fried chicken, to create a crispy and golden crust. Steamed dishes, like Chinese steamed egg custard, use eggs to create a savory custard-like texture. Eggs are also used in making Chinese egg noodles, Vietnamese phở, and Japanese ramen, to enrich the dough and add flavor. Eggs are prized for their versatility and play a significant role in many traditional Asian dishes, adding richness, moisture, and flavor to the final dish. Many Asian cuisines also incorporate eggs from other fowl, like quail eggs (see page 167) and duck eggs.

The Great MSG Debate

Umami is one of the five basic tastes, along with sweet, sour, salty, and bitter. It is often described as a savory or meaty taste due to the presence of glutamate, an amino acid commonly found in foods such as meat, fish, mushrooms, and some vegetables. *Umami* is a Japanese word that translates to "pleasant savory taste," and it has been recognized as a distinct taste since the early twentieth century. It is known for enhancing the overall flavor of foods and adding depth to dishes. Umami can be found naturally in many foods, and it is also commonly used as a flavor enhancer in cooking and food production, sometimes in the form of monosodium glutamate (MSG).

MSG is a food additive commonly used to enhance flavor, and it is found in a variety of processed foods, such as canned soups, frozen dinners, and snack foods. Glutamate is considered an excitotoxin, essentially fooling the brain into thinking that the food tastes delicious, making us want to have more. The safety of MSG has been a topic of debate for many years. The US Food and Drug Administration (FDA) considers MSG to be "generally recognized as safe" (GRAS) for most people when consumed in typical amounts, and the junk food industry insists that MSG is a minor bother only for the rare sensitive individual and has no long-term consequences for the majority. But independent researchers are not so sure, citing neurological problems as the long-term impact of this excitatory substance, especially in children and the elderly.

In our family, we have made a conscious decision to avoid using additives in our cooking and instead opt for a traditional eating lifestyle. This means steering clear of ingredients such as MSG. We strive to consume whole, minimally processed foods in our meals. While the flavors of our dishes may not be exactly as we remember them from our childhood, our palates have adapted to appreciate the deliciousness of traditional, nourishing whole foods.

We do enjoy eating out on occasion, but when we visit restaurants we used to love, we often find that the food doesn't taste as good as we remember. For us, nothing beats the satisfaction of preparing and savoring wholesome, homemade meals in our own kitchen.

Seaweed

Nori, wakame, kombu, and other types of seaweed are popular ingredients in Asian cooking, used in a variety of ways. These nutrient-rich plants are prized in many Asian cuisines. In Japanese cuisine, nori is used to wrap sushi and rice balls, giving them a distinctive flavor and texture. Seaweed is also used in miso soup, on top of salads, and as a condiment to give any dish a natural salty flavor. In Chinese cuisine, seaweed is used in soups, stews, and stir-fries. It's often rehydrated and used as a main ingredient in salads and side dishes. In Korean cuisine, a seaweed known as gim is used to wrap rice and other fillings, similar to nori in Japanese cuisine. Seaweed is also used in Korean soups, stews, and side dishes.

Seaweed is known for its high nutritional value; it is a good source of minerals, vitamins and other antioxidants, and fiber. It is also believed to support thyroid function, aid digestion, and boost the immune system. Seaweed is considered a relatively sustainable ingredient because it requires minimal resources to grow and has a low environmental impact. Overall, seaweed is a versatile and nutritious ingredient that adds a unique umami flavor and texture to Asian dishes. Be sure to try the Korean Healing Soup recipe (page 119), which incorporates seaweed.

White Rice

White rice is a traditional staple in many Asian cuisines and is considered Weston A. Price–compliant when properly prepared through methods such as soaking, sprouting, or fermenting to improve its digestibility and nutrient availability. In Chinese cuisine, it is commonly used as a base for stir-fries, fried rice, and rice-based dishes such as rice bowls and rice cakes. It is also used in steamed dishes, where it absorbs the flavors of other ingredients. In Japanese cuisine, white rice is a central component of traditional meals, served alongside sushi, sashimi, tempura, and grilled meats. It is also used in rice balls and rice bowls. In Korean cuisine, white rice is a staple in dishes such as bibimbap, kimchi fried rice, and rice porridge. In this book, you will find recipes for these delicious rice dishes.

White rice is often considered a blank canvas that absorbs the flavors of other ingredients in the dish, making it a versatile base for a wide range of Asian dishes. It is cooked using different methods such as steaming, boiling, or stir-frying, depending on the dish and regional cuisine. Whether it's used as a side dish, a base for other ingredients, or in various rice-based dishes, white rice plays an integral role in Asian cuisine, providing texture, flavor, and nourishment.

Cooking Tools

I am a minimalist at heart and prefer to have no more kitchen equipment than necessary. To make the recipes in this book, there are several basic cooking tools that I recommend. These multifunctional tools allow you to save storage space in the kitchen as well.

Cast-iron skillets and woks are my favorite. Through the years, I've tossed out my nonstick pans and switched over to cast iron to avoid nonstick chemicals being cooked into my foods. While cast iron is heavier and requires regular maintenance of cleaning and seasoning, it is more versatile to use on different heat sources—including campfires! Cast iron is also what our ancestors cooked with.

A **cast-iron Dutch oven** is also another tool I love. For making broths and stocks, rendering fats, deep frying, and even baking my favorite sourdough boule, you cannot go wrong with a Dutch oven.

A **clay or cast-iron pot** is ideal for making nourishing Asian soups, stews, and broths because it is designed to distribute heat evenly and can help develop rich flavors in soups and stews.

In our family, we cook large batches of broths to feed six people for multiple days. I recommend an **8- to 12-quart stockpot** so that you can make enough nourishing bone broth to keep on hand to turn into a quick and hearty meal.

Preparing a whole foods diet requires more effort than a processed food diet, so having a **good, sharp chef's knife** is essential. While I prefer Japanese knives with handles that fit my hands well, brands like Wüsthof and J. A. Henckels are also great options. You do not have to spend a lot of money on cutlery. I shop at knife outlets near larger cities for the best overall quality and pricing. I recommend adding a **paring knife**, a **6-inch santoku knife**, and a **bread knife** to your collection. Also, it's important to learn how to sharpen your own knives or have them professionally sharpened at least twice a year. Sometimes you can find this service at your local farmers market.

A **rice cooker**, while not cheap, can make the process of cooking perfect rice much easier. Look for a rice cooker with different settings for different types of rice, as well as a "keep warm" function. I recommend purchasing one at an Asian grocery store.

Steaming is a common cooking method in Asian cuisine, used for vegetables, fish, dumplings, and more. A **steamer basket** can be used in a regular pot or wok to steam foods. Our family often uses this method as a way of reheating leftovers because we do not use a microwave. It allows for gentle and even heating, which helps retain the natural flavors, textures, and nutrients of the ingredients.

What Was a Traditional Vietnamese Diet?

The Vietnamese diet has varied depending on the region and the time period, but it has generally centered around vegetables, fruits, rice, and fish. Traditionally, many Vietnamese people haven't eaten a lot of meat due to high cost and low availability. When meat is used, pork is the most common, along with beef, goat, and chicken in certain regions.

The use of herbs and spices was also a significant aspect of the traditional Vietnamese diet, with many dishes featuring a blend of fresh herbs like mint, cilantro, and basil and spices like lemongrass, ginger, and star anise. Other common ingredients in traditional Vietnamese cuisine included soy sauce, fish sauce, and nước chấm, which are still widely used today. Many Vietnamese dishes were often served with a side of fresh vegetables and herbs, such as lettuce, cucumber, and bean sprouts, which added freshness and crunch to the meal.

French Influence

The French had a significant impact on Vietnamese cuisine during their colonial rule of Vietnam from the mid-nineteenth century to the mid-twentieth century. French cuisine was introduced to Vietnam during this period and gradually fused with existing Vietnamese culinary traditions to create a unique blend of flavors, ingredients, and cooking techniques.

One of the most notable French influences on Vietnamese cuisine is the use of baguettes and other wheat-based breads. These breads are now a staple in many Vietnamese dishes, such as bánh mì sandwiches. The French also introduced dairy products to Vietnam, leading to the incorporation of milk, butter, and cheese into Vietnamese cooking, resulting in dishes such as condensed milk coffee and buttery pâté chaud pastries. Overall, the French influence on Vietnamese cuisine brought new ingredients, cooking techniques, and flavors to Vietnam, resulting in a rich and diverse culinary tradition that continues to evolve and grow today.

I love using **wooden spatulas and chopsticks** for stirring, flipping, and serving. They are gentle on nonstick surfaces and can help prevent scratching or damaging your cookware. I also have several **spider skimmers** of various sizes for multiple uses like scooping up noodles and vegetables, deep-frying eggrolls, and skimming off scum from broths. I also highly recommend a **fish spatula**. It is my favorite tool to use for making foods where I need to flip delicately.

For our family, we bulk process our own meat. If you want to go this route, I recommend getting a **meat grinder or grinding attachment for your mixer** and a **deli-style meat slicer** for large quantities of meat as it saves on time and is well worth the investment.

Having these basic cooking tools in your kitchen can make it easier and more enjoyable to prepare nourishing Asian foods, while also allowing you to employ traditional cooking methods and techniques.

What Makes Asian Food Nourishing?

Asian cuisine emphasizes a balance of flavors and ingredients that results in well-rounded meals that provide a wide range of essential nutrients, such as vitamins, minerals, and other antioxidants. Many traditional Asian diets rely heavily on whole grains, fresh vegetables, and lean sources of protein such as fish and tofu. Asian cooking also frequently incorporates herbs and spices that are known for their health benefits. For example, ginger is known for its anti-inflammatory properties, while garlic is believed to have antibacterial and immune-boosting properties. Turmeric is another commonly used spice in Asian cuisine, known for its anti-inflammatory and antioxidant properties.

The cooking methods used in traditional Asian cuisines, such as stir-frying, steaming, and boiling, can help food retain its nutrients. Fermented and traditionally preserved foods, such as kimchi and miso, can introduce beneficial bacteria and enzymes to support gut health. Overall, the emphasis on fresh, whole, and minimally processed ingredients is the key to a balanced and nutrient-dense diet.

CHAPTER 2

Mastering the Basics

Of all world cuisines, Asian food stands out for its diversity and intricacy. Broth is one of its cornerstones, an indispensable ingredient in so many different dishes. Made from beef, chicken, fish, or pork, each type of broth relies on long simmering and enrichment with aromatics such as onion, garlic, and ginger. Incorporating broth as a base for a dish not only enhances flavors but also increases nutrient density thanks to an abundance of vitamins and minerals.

The specific types of cooking fats called for in Asian cuisines play a prominent role in shaping taste profiles. Whether using lard or tallow in Chinese and Vietnamese recipes or incorporating butter or ghee in Indian and Southeast Asian cooking, these rich ingredients define Asian cuisine. The harmonious fusion of different ingredients is the secret behind sophisticated flavors and numerous health advantages.

When it comes to culinary diversity within Asia, the abundance of unique and flavorful dishes is undeniable. From Japan's use of sticky rice in sushi rolls to China's unique forbidden black rice, with its high fiber content and umami flavor profile, there are plenty of options available. Other popular choices include sweet potato noodles and sprouted wild-rice recipes.

Vietnamese cuisine is well known for its unique balance of sweet, sour, salty, spicy, and umami flavors derived from fermented ingredients such as fish sauce and soy sauce. Amid the wondrous aroma of Mom's freshly cooked Vietnamese delicacies, her soups always took center stage. With her soups, she served side dishes loaded with a variety of delicious flavors and textures.

Bone Broths

Our family didn't have a lot of money when I was growing up, but one thing remained constant: healing soup on our table thanks to my resourceful mother. Now as a parent myself trying my best to balance work and home life, I have discovered how beneficial it is to keep bone broth ready so that preparing nutritious meals becomes easy even amid chaos. Mom knew all along what every good parent should do: ensure your loved ones are well fed no matter what circumstance they're in. The broths and stocks in this chapter are kept simple for greater versatility and serve as the base for most of our soup recipes.

Broths and stocks have similar nutritional benefits, but the specific nutrient content varies depending on the ingredients used and the method

of preparation. While broths are typically made by simmering meat and vegetables and tend to be richer in taste, stocks primarily rely on the use of bones. Importantly, homemade broths and stocks are generally free from added salt and preservatives typically found in store-bought varieties.

Broths are a staple across Korea, Vietnam, Japan, and many other countries. Each one offers its unique version. Japanese dashi is made by steeping kombu seaweed and bonito flakes, while Korean gomguk uses a blend of ingredients like beef or chicken bones plus ginger, garlic, and vegetables to create flavor-rich broths boasting anti-inflammatory properties known for their health benefits. And then there's phở; Vietnamese food lovers will recognize this well-seasoned soup made by boiling beef bones alongside aromatic charred onions and ginger, complemented by earthy spices like cinnamon and star anise.

The way to harness the benefits of bone broth is by slowly simmering animal bones over an extended period while incorporating a variety of top-notch vegetables, herbs, and spices. Across all Asian cultures, there exists a preference for utilizing only the highest quality bones from animals raised on pasture and fed only grass. This results in a flavorful, nutrient-dense broth with key components such as collagen and amino acids that work together to support overall vitality and kidney function.

> "Properly prepared, meat stocks are extremely nutritious, containing the minerals of bone, cartilage, marrow, and vegetables as electrolytes, a form that is easy to assimilate. Acidic wine or vinegar added during cooking helps to draw out these vital nutrients, as does cooking for a long time, sometimes upwards of forty-eight hours."
>
> —Sally Fallon Morell, *Nourishing Traditions*

Long, slow cooking facilitates maximum extraction of nutrients from both meat and connective tissues, resulting in a richness of collagen, gelatin, and vital minerals like calcium, magnesium, and potassium to support healthy bones, joints, skin, digestion, and the immune system. Adding acidic wine or vinegar and cooking for a long time are excellent ways to extract essential nutrients. Combining additional ingredients like goji berries, dried shiitake mushrooms, or astragalus root enhances those healing properties even more, according to many traditional Chinese medicine practices.

During my father's struggle with OCD and depression, I discovered the GAPS diet, which emphasizes homemade bone broth and fermented foods as part of the healing process. Through personal experience, I discovered the powerful effects that certain foods had on my father's mood and anxiety. Further research led me to uncover the intricate relationship between gut microbiota and mental health.

Soil microbiomes play an equally important role in health and nutrition. They are akin to Earth's digestive system, nurturing crops with vital nutrients necessary for human health. Regenerative agriculture is a holistic approach to farming that focuses on building soil health and increasing biodiversity on the farm. This can lead to better nutrition and health for both the land and the people who consume the food grown on it. We use regenerative practices in raising animals specifically for this purpose because their bones provide unmatched nutrients essential for a healthy gut. The meat and bones we consume come from the very animals that graze on our land, underscoring the special care we take in selecting each ingredient.

The legacy of our traditional Asian values motivates us to harvest every part of these pasture-raised animals with as little waste as possible. My grandfather's traditional approach to composting kitchen waste involved burying the scraps in his garden. But there is a more innovative and efficient way to use animal bones: they can be transformed into biochar—a form of charcoal made by heating organic matter without oxygen. When added to soil, biochar boosts fertility by elevating soil carbon and augmenting its water-holding capacity. It serves as a habitat for beneficial microorganisms while remaining in place for centuries or even millennia, effectively sequestering carbon and mitigating climate change. By utilizing bone-derived biochar, we establish a closed-loop system where waste is converted into an input stream for another process.

Incorporating nutrient-dense bone broths into our diet is just one step toward optimal health, but it has a ripple effect on other areas of our life, such as our food choices and how we source and prepare our meals. By understanding the interconnectedness of our gut health, our food, and the soil it grows in, we can make more informed choices about what we eat and how we live.

Tenderizing Lemongrass and Ginger

Gently pounding lemongrass and ginger helps break down the fibers and releases their flavors. For lemongrass, trim off the root end of the stalk and remove any tough outer layers. Then cut the stalk into pieces and use the back of a knife or a meat tenderizer to lightly crush each piece. For ginger, use a spoon to gently scrape off the skin. Then lightly pound the ginger with your tool of choice.

Pork Bone Broth

(SÚP HEO)

Pork is a hallmark of Vietnamese cuisine, and pork bone broth is a common ingredient in many Vietnamese dishes. Traditional Vietnamese cuisine has a strong emphasis on using every part of an animal and not wasting anything, so using pork bones to make broth is a practical and economical choice. Pork broth is mild in flavor, much like chicken broth, and its richness can add depth and complexity to many dishes. For nights we work late, Tim and I like to make a quick kimchi ramen noodle dish using this pork broth.

Yield: 2 gallons (7.5 L)

5 pounds (2.25 kg) pork bones
2 gallons (7.5 L) spring water
1 medium onion, cut in half
1 (5-ounce [140 g]) piece fresh ginger, tenderized (see page 44)
1 tablespoon black peppercorns

Fill a large stockpot with tap water and bring to a rolling boil over high heat. Carefully lower in the pork bones. Boil vigorously for 5 minutes to release any impurities, which will float to the top as scum. Dump the bones and water into a clean sink, then rinse the bones under running water to remove any clinging residue.

Clean the pot, then fill it with the spring water. Return the bones to the pot and add the onion, ginger, and peppercorns. Simmer the broth over low heat for 2 hours, skimming off any scum or fat that rises to the surface. Check every so often and add more water as needed to ensure that the bones remain covered.

Remove from the heat and allow the broth to cool, uncovered, for 1 hour. Strain the broth through a fine-mesh strainer, discarding the solids. For an even clearer broth, strain the liquid a second time through a coffee filter placed in a strainer.

If you don't plan on using the broth right away, allow it to cool to lukewarm. Pour it into a container with a spout to easily distribute it into quart or half-gallon (1 L or 2 L) jars. You can store the jars in the refrigerator for up to 2 weeks or in the freezer for up to 6 months. (If freezing, be sure to leave a little extra headspace in the jars before sealing.)

Fish Broth

(SÚP CÁ)

Fish broth, or fish fumet, is a faster, easier weeknight broth that doesn't require hours in the kitchen. This isn't the broth you want to boil violently and make in a rush. It's simmered for no longer than an hour and then allowed to steep. I prefer to use salmon, grouper, or bass, though any fish could work. It's a fantastic base that you can use to elevate soups, vegetables, and stir-fries. I also love using this simple and accessible broth for a quick, nourishing meal, adding shrimp or sliced fish, cabbage, scallions, cilantro, lime, and some spicy Vietnamese sa tế sauce with white rice.

Yield: 6 quarts (5.5 L)

1 pound (450 g) fish carcasses and heads
Shrimp shells (and heads, if available)
    from 1 pound (450 g) wild-caught
    shrimp (optional)
6 quarts (5.5 L) spring water,
    plus more as needed
1 tablespoon rice vinegar
3 shallots, peeled and quartered lengthwise
3 scallions, cut into 2-inch (5 cm) pieces
1 (5-ounce [140 g]) piece fresh ginger,
    halved and tenderized (see page 44)
1 lemongrass stalk, tenderized
    (see page 44)
1 head garlic, outer papery skin removed,
    cut in half crosswise
½ cup (8 g) cilantro sprigs
1 whole Thai chili (optional)
2 tablespoons (30 g) coarse sea salt
1 tablespoon rainbow peppercorns

Put the fish carcasses and heads and shrimp shells and heads, if using, in a large stockpot and cover with the spring water. Add the vinegar. Bring to a soft boil over medium heat and boil for 20 minutes. Skim off any scum or impurities that rise to the top of the broth.

Once the broth is clear, add the shallots, scallions, ginger, lemongrass, garlic, cilantro, Thai chili (if using), salt, and peppercorns. Reduce the heat to low and simmer for 45 minutes, skimming off any scum that rises to the surface and checking to ensure that the ingredients remain covered with water. Add more water if needed.

Remove from the heat and allow the broth to cool, uncovered, for 1 hour. Strain the broth through a fine-mesh strainer and discard any remaining solids. For an even clearer broth, strain the liquid a second time through a coffee filter placed in a strainer.

If you don't plan on using the broth right away, allow it to cool to lukewarm. Pour it into a container with a spout to easily distribute it into quart or half-gallon (1 L or 2 L) jars. You can store the jars in the refrigerator for up to 5 days or in the freezer for up to 6 months. (If freezing, be sure to leave a little extra headspace in the jars before sealing.)

Gelatinous Chicken Bone Broth
(SÚP GÀ)

Chicken bone broth is a staple in our household, and for good reason. Not only is it versatile and delicious, it's also incredibly nutritious! I like to throw in a few extra chicken feet for additional collagen, which has been shown to support gut health, improve skin elasticity, and promote healthy hair and nails.

Making chicken broth is an easy and delicious way to get the most out of your whole broiler chicken. When I was a child, my mother would always buy whole gà đi bộ, which means "walking chicken" in Vietnamese. She would have me cut the chicken to remove the innards, and sometimes we would find unlaid eggs inside the chicken! Now as we process our retired egg-laying hens, it brings me so much joy to see the excitement on my children's faces when they discover these hidden treasures.

If you make your chicken broth with good-quality chicken, preferably pasture-raised, it will be filled with free-range love and flavor that you won't ever find in store-bought bone broth. I like to use the remaining chicken meat to make Chicken Rice Porridge (page 136) or Vietnamese Chicken Salad (page 147) and use the feet for Chicken Feet Dim Sum Style (page 227).

Yield: 2 gallons (7.5 L)

1 (4-pound [1.8 kg]) pasture-raised
    chicken, rinsed
8 pasture-raised chicken feet, cleaned
2 gallons (7.5 L) spring water
2 tablespoons (30 mL) apple cider vinegar
1 red onion, cut in half
2 carrots, sliced lengthwise
2 celery ribs
3 scallions, cut into 2-inch (5 cm) pieces
1 lemongrass stalk, tenderized
    (see page 44)
½ cup (8 g) cilantro sprigs
2 thumb-size pieces fresh ginger,
    tenderized (see page 44)
5 garlic cloves, peeled
1 tablespoon white peppercorns, toasted
1 tablespoon black peppercorns, toasted

Remove the innards from the chicken cavity and reserve for another use (see page 225). Put the chicken and chicken feet in a large stockpot and cover with the spring water. Add the vinegar and let stand for 45 to 60 minutes. Bring to a soft boil over medium heat and boil for 20 minutes. Skim off any scum or impurities that rise to the top.

Once the broth is clear, add the onion, carrots, celery, scallions, lemongrass, cilantro, ginger, garlic, and white and black peppercorns. Reduce the heat to low and simmer for 2 hours, skimming off any scum or fat that rises to the surface.

Remove from the heat and allow the broth to cool, uncovered, for 1 hour. Strain the broth through a fine-mesh strainer, reserving the chicken meat and feet for other uses and discarding any remaining solids. For an even clearer broth, strain the liquid a second time through a coffee filter placed in a strainer.

Note: *In addition to feet, you can also use chicken heads, necks, and backs in your broth. Carcasses from whole roasted chickens, ducks, or turkeys can also be used to make broth.*

If you don't plan on using the broth right away, allow it to cool to lukewarm. Pour it into a container with a spout to easily distribute it into quart or half-gallon (1 L or 2 L) jars. You can store the jars in the refrigerator for up to 2 weeks or in the freezer for up to 6 months. (If freezing, be sure to leave a little extra headspace in the jars before sealing.)

Beef Bone and Marrow Broth
(SÚP BÒ)

I love bone marrow, and I love it even more when I can put it in a pot of beef broth to enhance its flavor and texture. After a long simmer, the marrow renders and the tendons soften. I remember, when I was a young child, using a straw to clean out the marrow inside whatever bones my mom had cooked. A nutritional powerhouse, bone marrow is a good source of healthy fats, vitamins, and minerals. Once it's done, I like to scrape the marrow out of the bones and spread it on toast, topped with pickled onions.

Yield: 2 gallons (7.5 L)

4 to 6 (2-inch [5 cm]) pieces grass-fed
    beef marrow bones and knucklebones
1 pound (450 g) boneless grass-fed
    beef chuck or other beef cut, cut into
    large pieces
2 tablespoons (30 mL) apple cider vinegar
1 onion, halved
1 (5-ounce [140 g]) piece fresh ginger,
    tenderized (see page 44)
2 gallons (7.5 L) spring water,
    plus more if needed
1 head garlic, outer papery skin removed,
    cut in half crosswise
3 scallions, cut into 2-inch (5 cm) pieces
1 tablespoon white peppercorns, toasted
1 tablespoon black peppercorns, toasted

In a large bowl, combine the beef marrow bones, knucklebones, and beef chuck. Add the vinegar and enough cold tap water to cover. Let stand for 45 to 60 minutes. Drain.

Meanwhile, preheat the broiler on low.

Put the onion, cut side up, and ginger on a rimmed baking sheet and broil for about 10 minutes, until slightly charred. Set aside.

Bring a large stockpot of tap water to a rolling boil. Carefully lower the marrow bones, knuckle-bones, and chuck into the boiling water. Wait for the water to return to a hard boil and boil vigorously for 3 minutes to release any impurities, which will float to the top as scum.

Dump the bones, beef, and water into a clean sink, then rinse the bones under running water to remove any clinging residue. Clean the pot, then fill it with the spring water. Return the bones and beef to the pot and add the charred onion and ginger, garlic, scallions, and peppercorns. Simmer the broth over low heat for 12 to 24 hours, skimming off any scum or fat that rises to the surface. Check every few hours and add more spring water as needed to ensure that the bones remain covered.

Remove the bones and meat with a slotted spoon and reserve for other uses. Strain the broth through a fine-mesh strainer and discard any remaining solids. For an even clearer broth, strain the liquid a second time through a coffee filter placed in a strainer.

If you don't plan on using the broth right away, allow it to cool to lukewarm. Pour it into a container with a spout to easily distribute it into quart or half-gallon (1 L or 2 L) jars. You can store the jars in the refrigerator for up to 2 weeks or in the freezer for up to 6 months. (If freezing, be sure to leave a little extra headspace in the jars before sealing.)

Cooking Fats

One of the toughest aspects of adopting a new, healthier lifestyle is changing our habits and using only healthy fats for cooking. Besides coconut, olive, and avocado oils, homemade butter and rendered fats from healthy animals are excellent sources of energy.

Animal fats like chicken fat (schmaltz), beef tallow, duck fat, and pork fat (lard) are extremely nutritious when eaten in moderation as a part of a balanced diet. These types of fats provide essential energy as well as vitamins A, D, E, and K. Beef tallow and duck fat, in particular, contain high amounts of vitamin K2, which has been associated with improved bone health, while chicken fat and pork fat are good sources of monounsaturated and polyunsaturated fats. These fats are also high in calories, so consume them in moderation.

The fat from pasture-raised animals has a distinct nutritional profile compared to those that are conventionally raised in concentrated animal feeding operations (CAFOs). For example, levels of omega-3 fatty acids are much higher in pastured animals. It is also worth noting that fat tends to concentrate toxins, which makes it even more crucial to ensure that the animals we eat have been raised organically. Prioritizing products that are organic and come from pastured animals helps ensure optimal nutritional value and reduce the risk of ingesting harmful toxins.

Lard and Tallow

Rendered pig fat, also known as lard, is a highly versatile animal-based cooking fat that is stable at high temperatures and a superior choice for frying. It can be made from back or leaf fat (from the area around the pig's kidneys), the latter of which has a more neutral taste.

Pork fat is primarily composed of monounsaturated fat, the same type of heart-healthy fat found in foods like avocados and olive oil. When pigs are raised on pasture with access to natural forage and ample sunlight, their meat and fat contain higher levels of important micronutrients like vitamin E, vitamin D, and selenium. As monogastric animals, pigs produce vitamin D in their skin and fat when exposed to sunlight, which makes pasture-raised pork an excellent source of this vital nutrient.

Tallow is rendered beef, lamb, or bison fat and has been used for cooking and many other purposes in cultures around the world for centuries. In fact, one of the most famous Chinese dishes, Peking duck, is traditionally roasted using tallow (see my recipe for Pan-Seared Honey-Miso-Orange Duck Breast, page 156).

As a general guideline, you can expect to get 1 to 2 cups (240–480 mL) of rendered fat for every pound (450 g) of pork fat or beef fat you start with.

▶ HOW TO RENDER LARD OR TALLOW

Start by cutting the fat into small pieces. You can use a sharp knife or a meat grinder to do this.

Put the fat in a heavy-bottomed pot or Dutch oven and add about 1 inch of water.

Set the pot over low to medium-low heat. As the fat heats up, it will start to melt, and the water will begin to boil. As the fat melts, it will release its liquid and begin to separate from the solid pieces. Continue to heat the mixture until the fat pieces have turned golden brown and the liquid is clear and no longer milky. Rendering lard or tallow will typically take 1 to 2 hours to complete. The cooking time will depend on the quantity of fat you are rendering and the temperature you are using. It's important to keep a close eye on the process to ensure the fat doesn't burn.

Carefully pour the rendered, liquid fat through a fine-mesh strainer to remove any solid bits. If you wish, you can strain it a second time through cheesecloth.

Allow the lard or tallow to cool slightly (but not until it hardens), then pour it into a clean, airtight container and store it in the fridge for up to 1 year or in the freezer for up to 3 years. An even more convenient option is to pour the rendered fat into a muffin tin or mini muffin tin and let it harden, then transfer the individual portions to a storage container to be refrigerated or frozen and used as needed.

Butter

Many Asian cuisines do not traditionally include butter, as dairy farming has been less common in Asian countries than in Europe and North America. However, with globalization and increased access to imported ingredients, butter has become more widely used in some Asian cuisines, particularly in fusion dishes and in countries with a history of colonialism.

Vietnamese cooking has incorporated butter dating back several generations, especially within communities in northern Vietnam, where my mother's family was originally from and where the French had significant influence during their colonial rule. The French brought with them their love for butter, and today you can see this influence in Vietnamese dishes such as bánh mì, which often features butter spread on the baguette.

I prefer to cook with unsalted butter and serve salted butter at the table. Butter is a whole food that contains essential nutrients such as vitamins A, D, E, and K2, as well as butyrate and other beneficial short-chain fatty acids. Butter is also a good source of conjugated linoleic acid (CLA), a type of fat that

Arachidonic Acid

Sally Fallon Morell recommends eating butter made from raw milk from grass-fed cows, which contains a compound called arachidonic acid, a type of omega-6 fatty acid. Arachidonic acid is an essential nutrient that plays a crucial role in many physiological processes, including brain function, growth and development, and the immune response. She argues that arachidonic acid is particularly important for pregnant and nursing women, infants, and children, as they have higher requirements for this nutrient.

The arachidonic acid content of butter is highest in butter made from raw milk from grass-fed animals. Pasteurization and confinement feeding practices can decrease the arachidonic acid content of butter, as well as other beneficial nutrients like vitamins A, D, and K.

has been linked to various health benefits, including reducing inflammation and improving insulin sensitivity. The fat in butter is more stable at high temperatures than many oils, making it a good choice for cooking and baking.

Raw-milk butter is often considered to be more nutrient-dense than other types of butter because it is made from unpasteurized milk, which is believed to contain more beneficial nutrients and enzymes than pasteurized milk.

Having a micro dairy farm on our homestead provides us with a source of fresh, nutritious dairy products that are free from the additives and processing that are often found in commercial dairy products. Making our own butter and ghee is a great way to connect with traditional foodways and build a deeper understanding and appreciation for the role that dairy products can play in a healthy, balanced diet.

▶ HOW TO MAKE BUTTER

Homemade butter has a fresher taste and is free from additives, making it a great addition to a healthy lifestyle. And it's so simple to make! The yield will depend on the amount of cream you start with; 1 quart of heavy cream will yield approximately 1 pound of butter.

If you have access to fresh, raw milk, start by skimming off the cream and letting the cream sit at room temperature for 1 hour. Once the cream is ready, pour it into a food processor or stand mixer (or butter churn, if you have one) and process until the solid butter separates out from the liquid buttermilk, which will take a minute or so.

Drain off the buttermilk and reserve it for another use, such as making pancakes or biscuits. Rinse the solid butter under cold water to remove any remaining buttermilk.

If you like, you can flavor the butter with salt, herbs, or spices.

Put the butter in a jar, cover, and store in the refrigerator for up to 6 months or in the freezer for up to 1 year.

Ghee

Ghee is a type of clarified butter that has been used in Indian cuisine for thousands of years. It is made by simmering butter, which causes the water and milk solids to separate from the fat. The milk solids are then removed, leaving behind a pure form of butterfat. Ghee has a rich, nutty flavor and a high smoke point, making it a popular choice for cooking and frying. It also has a long shelf life and is high in healthy fats like CLA and butyrate.

Depending on the water content of the butter you use to make ghee and how long you simmer it, you can expect a yield of 25 to 30 percent less ghee than the amount of butter you started with.

Start with high-quality unsalted butter. Grass-fed butter is often preferred for its richer flavor and higher nutrient content.

Cut the butter into cubes and put them in a heavy-bottomed saucepan. Heat over low heat, stirring occasionally, until the butter melts completely. Cook at a low simmer, allowing the water to evaporate and the butter start to foam. You will notice a layer of milk solids forming at the bottom of the pot. Keep simmering until the foam disappears and the milk solids turn golden brown. Remove the pan from the heat and let it cool for a few minutes.

Strain the liquid through a cheesecloth or fine-mesh sieve to remove the milk solids, leaving behind a clear, golden liquid—that is the ghee. Store the ghee in the pantry in a clean, sterile glass jar with the lid on tight. Freshest within the first 3 months, ghee is shelf stable for up to 12 months when stored properly.

Starches

Starches have been a staple in Asian diets for centuries, mainly because many Asian cultures relied heavily on agriculture, and starches like rice, noodles, and root vegetables were readily available and economical sources of sustenance. These starches could be stored for long periods and thus are the basis of many traditional dishes.

Rice is a staple in many Asian cuisines and is served alongside a variety of dishes. Some Asian cultures also incorporate starchy legumes such as soybeans, lentils, and mung beans, which may be used to make various types of tofu as well as traditional fermented foods like tempeh and natto.

Starchy foods provide energy and can help make meals more satisfying and filling. My parents still say that without enough cơm (rice), they aren't able to have a good night's sleep. When consumed in moderation as part of a balanced diet, starches are a nourishing component of a traditional diet.

How to Make Grains and Legumes More Nourishing
While grains and legumes are already nutritious, you can make them even more nourishing by using traditional cooking methods and adding some healthy ingredients. Here are some ideas:

Soaking: Soaking starches, such as rice, or legumes, such as beans, in water for several hours or overnight can help reduce antinutrients, such as phytic acid and gluten, and increase nutrient availability. For

example, soaking rice before cooking helps break down phytic acid, which can bind to minerals and inhibit their absorption. Soaking also softens grains, making them easier to digest.

Fermenting: Fermenting starches can increase their nutrient content and digestibility. For example, fermented rice or dosa batter (made from fermented rice and lentils) increases the availability of B vitamins and minerals, as well as breaks down antinutrients.

Sprouting: Sprouting grains and legumes can help reduce antinutrients and increase nutrient availability. Sprouting also increases the activity of enzymes, which can help break down complex carbohydrates and make them easier to digest. See "How to Sprout Wild Rice" (page 64) for a technique that can be used with other whole grains.

Cooking with bone broth: Using bone broth as a base for cooking starches adds minerals and gelatin, which can help improve gut and joint health.

Cooking with coconut milk: For a creamy and rich flavor, cook rice in coconut milk instead of water. This will add healthy fats and a tropical flavor.

Adding traditional fats: Adding traditional fats, such as butter, ghee, lard, schmaltz, or coconut oil, to cooked starches can increase nutrient absorption and provide healthy fats that are essential for hormone production and brain function.

Adding vegetables: Mix in some sautéed or roasted vegetables like broccoli, carrots, bell peppers, or mushrooms for added nutrition, fiber, and flavor.

Adding herbs and spices: Herbs and spices like turmeric, garlic, ginger, cumin, or coriander will enhance the flavor and nutritional value of your rice.

Topping with nuts or seeds: Sprinkle some chopped sprouted nuts or seeds like almonds, cashews, sesame seeds, or pumpkin seeds on top of your rice for a crunchy texture and extra nutrition. I also like to sprinkle some furikake on top of cooked rice, sushi, or udon noodles or as a topping for various Japanese dishes. It adds an extra layer of nourishment, flavor, texture, and visual appeal to meals.

Why Source Organic Rice?

Most rice found in Asian grocery stores that isn't specifically labeled organic is likely to be conventionally grown. This means that it may have been exposed to synthetic pesticides, herbicides, and fertilizers. These chemicals can leave residues, which can be harmful to human health when consumed in large quantities over time. Additionally, conventionally grown rice may be grown from genetically modified seed or irradiated to increase its shelf life.

Try to choose organic rice whenever possible; it is grown without synthetic pesticides and fertilizers and is not genetically modified or irradiated.

Organic rice is grown using sustainable agricultural practices that prioritize soil health, biodiversity, and water conservation. This can lead to a healthier and more resilient ecosystem, with fewer negative impacts on the surrounding environment, such as soil degradation and water pollution. Organic farming practices rely on natural methods of pest and disease control, such as crop rotation and the use of beneficial insects, which can result in fewer harmful residues in the final product. Some people also prefer to source organic rice because it is free from GMOs, which are often used in conventional agriculture to improve yields and resistance to pests and diseases.

Cooking Rice

Type of Rice	Description	Rice : Liquid Ratio by Volume	Cooking Time*	Recipe
Jasmine rice	Aromatic, slightly sweet flavor; fluffy and tender texture	1 : 1¾	18 to 20 minutes	**Kimchi Fried Rice:** Cook rice. Sauté onion, garlic, and kimchi; add cooked rice, fish sauce, and eggs.
Basmati rice	Fragrant, nutty flavor; long, slender grains	1 : 1¾	18 to 20 minutes	**Vegetable Biryani:** Cook rice with spices like ground cumin, coriander, turmeric, and garam masala. Sauté onion, garlic, and ginger; add mixed vegetables and cooked rice. Garnish with fresh cilantro; top with pumpkin seeds.
Glutinous rice	Sticky, chewy texture; often used in desserts	2 : 2¼	20 to 25 minutes	**Mango Sticky Rice:** Cook rice in coconut milk and sugar. Serve with fresh mango slices and a drizzle of sweetened coconut milk sauce; top with sesame seeds.
Arborio rice	Short, plump grains; high in starch	1 : 2½	45 to 60 minutes	**Rice Pudding:** Simmer rice in milk and maple syrup until creamy; add vanilla and ground cinnamon for flavor; top with cashews.
Forbidden black rice	Nutty, sweet flavor; high in antioxidants	1 : 2¼	30 to 35 minutes	**Forbidden Black Rice Sushi Rolls:** Cook rice, then stir in rice vinegar and salt. Lay sheet of nori shiny side down on sushi mat; spread thin layer of rice over nori, leaving 1-inch border at top, and fill with desired toppings. Roll sushi tightly using sushi mat and slice into rounds. Serve with tamari and pickled ginger.

* Cooking time is for the stovetop technique outlined in the recipes below. If using a rice cooker, use the same ratio of rice to water, but the timing may vary.

Jasmine Rice

Yield: 3 cups (600 g)

1 cup (190 g) jasmine rice

1¾ cups (415 mL) bone broth or spring water

> **Note:** The ratio of water to rice may vary depending on the brand of jasmine rice you use. Always refer to the package instructions for the best results.

Rinse the rice in a fine-mesh strainer under cold running water until the water runs clear. Put the rice in a bowl, cover with water, and soak for at least 30 minutes, or overnight. Drain.

In a medium saucepan, combine the rice and broth. Bring to a boil over high heat. Reduce the heat to low, cover, and simmer for 18 to 20 minutes, until all the water has been absorbed and the rice is tender.

Remove the pan from the heat and let it sit, covered, for 5 to 10 minutes to allow the steam to finish cooking the rice. Fluff the rice with a fork and serve.

Glutinous Rice (Sticky Rice)

Yield: 4 cups (700 g)

2 cups (415 g) glutinous rice

2¼ cups (530 mL) spring water

Rinse the rice in a fine-mesh strainer under cold running water until the water runs clear. Put the rice in a bowl, cover with water, and soak for at least 2 hours, or overnight. Drain.

Put the rice in a steamer basket lined with cheesecloth.

Pour the water into a pot or wok and bring it to a boil over high heat. Place the steamer basket in the pot and cover. Steam the rice for 20 to 25 minutes, until the rice is tender and sticky.

Remove the steamer basket from the pot or wok and let the rice sit for 10 to 15 minutes. Fluff the rice with a fork and serve.

Basmati Rice

Yield: 3 cups *(600 g)*

1 cup (180 g) basmati rice
1¾ cups (415 mL) bone broth or spring water
Pinch salt
1 tablespoon unsalted grass-fed butter
  (optional)

> *Note: The exact cooking time may vary depending on the brand of basmati rice, so be sure to check the package instructions and adjust the cooking time accordingly.*

Rinse the rice in a fine-mesh strainer under cold running water until the water runs clear. Put the rice in a bowl, cover with water, and soak for at least 30 minutes, or overnight. Drain.

In a medium saucepan, add the rice, broth, salt, and butter (if using). Bring to a boil over high heat. Reduce the heat to low, cover, and simmer for 18 to 20 minutes, until the water has been absorbed and the rice is tender.

Remove the pan from the heat and let it sit, covered, for 5 minutes to allow the steam to finish cooking the rice. Fluff the rice with a fork and serve.

Forbidden Black Rice

Black rice is very nutritious and gets its dark color from an antioxidant called anthocyanin. It's high in antioxidants, protein, and fiber and is a good source of iron.

Yield: 3 cups *(600 g)*

1 cup (180 g) black rice
2¼ cups (530 mL) bone broth or spring water
⅛ teaspoon fine sea salt

Rinse the rice in a fine-mesh strainer under cold running water until the water runs clear. Put the rice in a bowl, cover with water, and soak for at least 1 hour. Drain.

In a medium saucepan, combine the rice and broth. Bring to a boil over medium-high heat, then add the salt. Cover, reduce the heat to low, and simmer for 30 to 35 minutes, until all the water has been absorbed and the rice is tender.

Remove the pan from the heat and let it sit, covered, for 5 to 10 minutes. Fluff the rice with a fork and serve.

> *Note: If all the water has evaporated, but the rice is not fully cooked yet, add another 2 to 3 tablespoons water and cook for 5 more minutes. The perfect ratio of water to black rice and cooking time can vary depending on various factors such as the type of saucepan and lid you use, humidity in your area, altitude, and so on. It may be necessary to experiment to find the best ratio and timing for your specific cooking environment.*

▶ HOW TO SPROUT WILD RICE

Asian cultures have long valued consuming sprouted rice as a healthy dietary choice that allows optimal nourishment for the body. Wild rice is a great source of protein, fiber, and minerals like magnesium, zinc, and potassium, and sprouting wild rice increases its nutritional value, with higher concentrations of vitamins, minerals, and antioxidants than regular, nonsprouted grains. The process of sprouting rice also breaks down the phytic acid from the bran of the rice, which can inhibit the absorption of certain minerals in the body. Sprouted wild rice can be easier to digest than unsprouted rice, making it a good option for those with digestive issues or sensitivities. However, sprouting wild rice can be a bit challenging because the seed coat is very tough and needs to be softened before it will germinate.

Rinse the wild rice in a fine-mesh strainer or sprouting jar and remove any debris or broken grains. Put the wild rice in a bowl, cover with water, and soak for 24 hours. Drain the wild rice and rinse again.

Put the wild rice in a sprouting jar and cover with the sprouting lid, or use any glass container and cover with cheesecloth and a rubber band.

Keep the sprouting container at room temperature, out of direct sunlight. Rinse the wild rice with fresh water twice a day, making sure to drain off all the water. It's important to rinse and drain the rice frequently during the sprouting process to prevent mold growth.

After 3 to 5 days, the wild rice should start to sprout. Continue rinsing it twice a day until the sprouts are the desired length (usually about ¼ inch).

Once the wild rice has sprouted, rinse it well and cook it using your preferred method (see Korean Healing Soup, page 119). It will keep in the refrigerator for up to 3 days.

Note: Because of the toughness of wild rice's seed coat, it's normal for some of the grains to not sprout. Cooking times for sprouted wild rice may be shorter than for regular wild rice, so be sure to check it frequently as it cooks to avoid overcooking.

► HOW TO COOK SWEET POTATO STARCH NOODLES

Sweet potato starch noodles, also known as Korean glass noodles or dang-myeon, are a traditional Korean food made from sweet potato starch. While I was in graduate school in Los Angeles, I grew to love Korean food. No matter what I ordered as a main dish, sweet potato starch noodles were always on my plate.

Sweet potatoes are a rich source of complex carbohydrates, dietary fiber, and nutrients such as vitamin C, vitamin A, and potassium. These noodles are gluten-free, which makes them a great option for people with celiac disease or gluten sensitivities. They also have prebiotic properties, which means that they promote the growth of beneficial bacteria in the gut and can lead to better digestion, improved immune function, and other health benefits.

Sweet potato starch noodles are often served with kimchi, but they can also be used in a variety of dishes such as japchae (stir-fried noodles with vegetables and meat) and hot and spicy soup.

Here's how to prepare them: Bring a pot of water to a rolling boil over high heat. Add the sweet potato starch noodles to the boiling water, stirring gently to prevent sticking. Cook the noodles for 6 to 8 minutes, until they are tender but still slightly chewy.

Drain the noodles and rinse them under cold running water to cool them down and remove excess starch. Toss the noodles with a bit of sesame oil to prevent sticking, then add your choice of seasonings.

NƯỚC CHẤM

MẮM NEM

NƯỚC MẮM ME

NƯỚC MẮM GỪNG

GOCHUJANG

HOISIN SAUCE

MẮM RUOC

SAMBAL OELEK

SA TẾ

CHAPTER 3

Sauces and Seasonings

W hen I started to look more closely at the Asian sauces and condiments that I used to buy at the grocery store, I realized that many, if not all of them, contained unhealthy additives, seed oils, and preservatives to extend their shelf life. Because we were using them in almost every dish we cooked, I knew I would have to learn how to make these sauces and seasonings from scratch. Making your own sauces allows you to control the quality and freshness of the ingredients, as well as the amount of added sugar, salt, and other flavorings.

Our family appreciates the flavor and nutrition that homemade sauces and seasonings bring to all our meals. Making sauces from scratch allows us to use high-quality, fresh ingredients. Using herbs and spices that we forage from our food forest enhances the flavors even more. We have become so accustomed to the taste and health benefits of our food thanks to our homemade sauces that even eating out at our favorite restaurants in Napa and Los Angeles pales in comparison!

Vietnamese Dipping Sauce
(NƯỚC CHẤM)

We always have a mason jar of nước chấm (dipping sauce) or nước mắm pha (mixed fish sauce) in the refrigerator. Whenever my mother would ask me to grab the nước mắm (fish sauce), I would pick this one first. This is the Vietnamese dipping sauce that is often served with spring rolls, grilled meats, and many other dishes found in this book. Traditional nước chấm calls for sugar, but we have adapted this to use honey or maple syrup. Note that the flavor may differ slightly from traditional nước chấm due to the natural sweetener used.

Yield: 2 cups (480 mL)

¼ cup (60 mL) fish sauce or Fermented Anchovy Sauce (page 70)

¼ cup (60 mL) maple syrup or raw honey

2 tablespoons (30 mL) lime juice

1 tablespoon apple cider vinegar

1 garlic clove, minced

1 or 2 Thai chilies, sliced (optional)

⅔ cup (80 mL) spring water, warmed

In a small bowl, whisk together the fish sauce, maple syrup, lime juice, vinegar, garlic, and chilies (if using) until the sweetener is dissolved. Stir in enough warm water to thin the sauce to your desired consistency.

Taste and adjust the seasoning as needed. Serve nước chấm in small bowls for dipping spring rolls and egg rolls, or pour it over a rice or noodle dish as a sauce. Store in an airtight container in the refrigerator for up to 6 months.

Vietnamese Pineapple-Anchovy Dipping Sauce
(MẮM NEM)

This sweet and savory sauce is perfect for dipping spring rolls, grilled meats, or seafood. You can use canned pineapple for this recipe.

Yield: 1 cup (240 mL)

¼ cup (60 mL) fish sauce or Fermented Anchovy Sauce (page 70)
¼ cup (60 mL) pineapple juice
¼ cup (60 mL) spring water
2 tablespoons (30 mL) lime juice
1 tablespoon minced lemongrass
1 tablespoon maple syrup or raw honey
2 teaspoons finely chopped garlic
2 teaspoons finely chopped red chili (optional)
1 tablespoon finely chopped pineapple
1 tablespoon finely chopped fresh cilantro

In a bowl, whisk together the fish sauce, pineapple juice, spring water, lime juice, lemongrass, and maple syrup until well combined. Add the garlic and chili (if using) and stir to combine. Stir in the chopped pineapple and cilantro. Cover the bowl and let the sauce sit at room temperature for at least 1 hour to allow the flavors to meld together.

Before serving, stir the sauce and adjust the seasoning to taste. Store in an airtight container in the refrigerator for up to 1 week. If the sauce thickens, thin it out with a little bit of water.

Fermented Anchovy Sauce
(NƯỚC MẮM)

Fermented anchovy sauce, also known as fish sauce, is a condiment that is widely used in many Southeast Asian cuisines. Here's a simple recipe to make fish sauce at home. Although this is a year-long process, it is well worth the wait! I use fresh pineapple as it contains bromelain, which helps to break down proteins into their building blocks. This homemade sauce can be substituted in any recipe that calls for fish sauce.

Yield: about 1 quart (1 L)

5 pounds (2.25 kg) fresh anchovies or other small, oily fish
2 pounds (900 g) coarse sea salt
½ pineapple, trimmed and chopped

Rinse the anchovies under cold running water and drain well.

In a half-gallon (2 L) glass or ceramic container, layer the anchovies, salt, and pineapple, making sure to cover each layer of fish completely with salt. Continue layering until all the anchovies are covered in salt. Top with a 1-inch (2.5 cm) layer of salt.

Cover the container with a tight-fitting lid or plastic wrap and leave it at room temperature for 10 to 12 months to allow the fermentation process to take place. To determine when fish sauce is done fermenting, there are a few signs to look for. The color will gradually darken and develop a rich amber or reddish-brown hue. When the sauce reaches a deep, golden color, it is often an indication that fermentation is nearing completion. In the early stages, the sauce may have a pungent, fishy smell. As fermentation continues, the aroma will mellow and transform into a complex, savory scent. When the fish sauce has a pleasant, well-rounded aroma, without any off-putting odors, it is a sign that fermentation is likely complete or near completion. As for the taste, initially it may be quite salty and intense. Over time, the flavors will develop and become more balanced. This is the beauty of fish sauce, the harmonious balance of saltiness, umami, and complexity, and it is an indication that fermentation has progressed sufficiently.

When fermentation is complete, strain the sauce through a fine-mesh strainer and discard the solids. The dark brown liquid should be clear and free of any cloudiness and have a strong, salty aroma. You may notice a separation of sediment at the bottom, which is normal for traditionally fermented fish sauce. Store in an airtight container in a cool, dark place for up to 1 year.

Tamarind Dipping Sauce
(NƯỚC MẮM ME)

This tangy, spicy, and slightly sweet sauce is great to use as a dressing for refreshing salads and rice or noodle bowls. I also love this sauce with a simple baked fish wrapped in rice paper or as a dipping sauce for spring rolls. In Asian markets you can find tamarind pressed into blocks or as a paste. You can also buy dried whole tamarind pods in Latin markets. If using pods, peel off the skin and cut off the stringy parts, then cut the fruit into small pieces for this recipe. If using tamarind paste, the intensity may vary, so experimentation is needed to find the right ratio for this sauce.

Yield: 1 cup (*240 mL*)

¼ cup (60 mL) tamarind paste

¼ cup (60 mL) spring water, warmed

¼ cup (60 mL) fish sauce or Fermented Anchovy Sauce (page 70)

¼ cup (60 mL) maple syrup

¼ cup (30 g) chopped shallots

1 or 2 Thai chilies, chopped (optional)

In a bowl, mix together the tamarind paste and warm water until the paste has dissolved. Add the fish sauce, maple syrup, shallots, and Thai chilies (if using) and stir until well combined.

Taste and adjust the seasoning to your liking. Store in an airtight container in the refrigerator for up to 1 week.

Butter Fish Sauce

This sauce is like liquid gold! You will need to start with clarified butter, or ghee, making it a two-step process, but I promise you the results will be worth it. Making your own clarified butter is easy and also much more cost-effective than store-bought. Use this as a dipping sauce for lobster and other fish dishes.

Yield: about 1 cup (240 mL)

1 cup (240 g) ghee (page 57), melted
2 tablespoons (30 mL) maple syrup
1 tablespoon lime or lemon juice, or more as needed
2 tablespoons (30 mL) fish sauce or Fermented Anchovy Sauce (page 70), or more as needed
1 garlic clove, minced
1 Thai chili, finely sliced

In a bowl, combine the ghee, maple syrup, and lime juice to taste. Add the fish sauce in small increments to your liking. Sprinkle with the garlic and Thai chili before serving. Store in an airtight container in the refrigerator for up to 1 month.

Ginger Fish Sauce
(NƯỚC MẮM GỪNG)

This sweet and tangy sauce is a perfect accompaniment to poached chicken or duck. This is also my favorite sauce to use as a dressing or dipping sauce for a savory and slightly spicy Vietnamese chicken and cabbage salad.

Yield: about 1 cup (240 mL)

¼ cup (60 mL) fish sauce or Fermented Anchovy Sauce (page 70)
¼ cup (60 mL) spring water, warmed
2 tablespoons (30 mL) lime juice
2 tablespoons (30 mL) maple syrup or raw honey
1 (2-inch [5 cm]) piece fresh ginger (about 2 ounces [55 g]), peeled and finely chopped
2 garlic cloves, finely chopped
1 or 2 Thai chilies, sliced (optional)

In a small bowl, combine the fish sauce, water, lime juice, and maple syrup. Mix until the sweetener dissolves. Add the ginger, garlic, and the chilies and stir to combine.

Let the sauce sit for 10 minutes before serving. Store in an airtight container in the refrigerator for up to 2 weeks.

Tonkatsu Sauce

This sauce always takes me back to Fort Benning, Georgia, where my husband, Tim, was stationed before he was deployed to Iraq and where he introduced me to his special tonkatsu burgers. One busy night of packing before he left, he cooked up some beef patties and served them over rice, generously drizzling them with Kikkoman katsu sauce. Tim also loves using this sauce on his deep-fried pork cutlets. Inspired by Tim's love for this sauce, I created my own version that I sometimes call "Timkatsu" sauce. This sauce is perfect for dipping or drizzling over grilled meats and vegetables or as a topping for burgers.

Yield: about ½ cup (120 mL)

¼ cup (60 mL) tamari

2 tablespoons (30 mL) raw honey
    or maple syrup

2 tablespoons (30 mL) apple cider vinegar

2 tablespoons (30 mL) tomato paste

1 tablespoon fish sauce or Fermented
    Anchovy Sauce (page 70)

1 tablespoon lemon juice

1 garlic clove, minced

½ teaspoon grated fresh ginger

In a small bowl, whisk together all of the ingredients until well combined. Taste and adjust the seasoning. Store in an airtight container in the refrigerator for up to 1 week.

Fermented Black Bean Sauce

This savory, earthy, and aromatic black bean sauce recipe adds authenticity and depth of flavor to all your favorite Chinese recipes. It is a versatile sauce that can be used as a condiment, a marinade, or even a stir-fry sauce—I especially love it with seafood and vegetables! I prefer to make my own fermented black beans from scratch (recipe follows).

Yield: 1 cup (*240 mL*)

½ cup (70 g) fermented black soybeans
  (see below)
1 small shallot, chopped
3 tablespoons (27 g) minced garlic
1 tablespoon grated fresh ginger
5 tablespoons (75 mL) sesame oil
¼ cup (60 mL) Gelatinous Chicken
  Bone Broth (page 48)
2 tablespoons (30 mL) dry sherry
  or rice vinegar
2 tablespoons (30 mL) soy sauce or tamari
1½ teaspoons coconut sugar
1½ teaspoons red chili flakes (optional)
1 teaspoon arrowroot starch

Combine the fermented black beans, shallot, garlic, and ginger in a food processor and process until finely minced.

Heat the sesame oil in a small saucepan over medium heat. Add the black bean mixture from the food processor and cook for 2 to 4 minutes to allow the flavors to meld. Stir in the broth, sherry, soy sauce, coconut sugar, chili flakes (if using), and arrowroot. Cook over medium-low heat for 10 minutes, stirring occasionally to prevent sticking. Remove from the heat and let cool. Store in an airtight container in the refrigerator for up to 1 month.

Note: *This sauce is salty, so when using it in stir-fries or other dishes, I recommend starting with a small amount and adjusting according to taste.*

▶ HOW TO FERMENT BLACK SOYBEANS (DOUCHI)

Fermented black beans have a nice umami flavor. You can use them in sauces or eat them on their own as a snack. For this recipe you'll need dried black soybeans (I prefer using organic, non-GMO black soybeans) and a culture to help the beans ferment. The culture can be whey culture, brine from lacto-fermented vegetables, or even plain kombucha.

Here's how to make them: Put the soybeans in a bowl, cover with warm water, and soak for 24 hours in a warm place. Drain.

Transfer the beans to a saucepan and cover with plenty of fresh water. Bring to a boil and let the beans boil for 10 minutes, then reduce the heat to a low simmer for 50 to 60 minutes, until the beans have softened and some of the outer shells have opened.

Drain the beans, transfer to a bowl, and allow them to cool. Add about a tablespoon of culture per cup of beans. Mash the beans with a spoon to break the skins and lightly bruise the beans, which will allow the culture to get into the beans and convert the starch in the beans into probiotics.

Transfer the beans to a sterilized jar and seal tightly. Let sit for 3 days in a warm place to complete the fermentation process. Release the gas in the jar every day and reseal. Once the beans are done fermenting, store in the fridge for up to 6 months.

Vietnamese Mayonnaise

Vietnamese mayonnaise has a tangy, slightly sweet flavor that is perfect to mix with other sauces. It's great as a condiment for sandwiches and spring rolls or as a dipping sauce for fried foods. You can add gochujang or sriracha to the mayonnaise for an added kick! I love it in a deconstructed bánh mì sandwich—paired with pâté on toast and pickled onions.

Yield: about 1 cup (*240 mL*)

2 large pasture-raised egg yolks

2 tablespoons (30 mL) rice vinegar or white wine vinegar

¼ teaspoon Dijon mustard (optional)

¼ teaspoon fine sea salt

¼ teaspoon garlic powder

¼ teaspoon onion powder

1 cup (240 mL) avocado oil

1 tablespoon lime juice

1 tablespoon fish sauce or Fermented Anchovy Sauce (page 70)

1 teaspoon maple syrup (optional)

In a large bowl, whisk together the egg yolks, vinegar, mustard, salt, garlic powder, and onion powder until smooth and well combined.

While whisking continuously, gradually pour the avocado oil into the egg mixture in a thin, steady stream. Keep whisking until the mixture is fully emulsified and has the consistency of mayonnaise. Alternatively, you can use an immersion blender, countertop blender, or food processor on a low setting and slowly drizzle in the oil to get it to the right thickness.

Add the lime juice and fish sauce and whisk until well combined. Taste the mayonnaise and adjust the seasoning as needed, adding the maple syrup if desired. Store in an airtight container in the refrigerator for up to 1 week.

Gochujang

Gochujang is a fermented chili paste that is a staple ingredient in Korean cuisine. Its uniquely spicy, slightly sweet, and savory flavor adds depth and complexity to all sorts of dishes. When I was pregnant, all my cravings were for some good Korean barbecue, just so I could put gochujang on everything. This homemade gochujang can be used as a condiment, marinade ingredient, or seasoning in a variety of dishes to add a spicy and savory kick. Traditional gochujang recipes sometimes call for ingredients that are hard to find outside of Korea. This recipe is adapted with easier-to-find ingredients that are still nourishing; I kept it gluten-free by using red miso instead of the traditional barley malt powder.

Yield: about 2 cups (480 mL)

1 cup (240 g) organic red miso paste
½ cup (40 g) gochugaru
    (Korean red chili powder)
3 tablespoons (45 mL) raw honey
1 tablespoon fine sea salt
2 teaspoons garlic powder
2 teaspoons rice vinegar
1 teaspoon sake (rice wine)
½ cup (120 mL) spring water,
    or more as needed

In a medium bowl, whisk together the miso, gochugaru, honey, salt, garlic powder, rice vinegar, and sake until well combined. Gradually stir in the water, 1 tablespoon at a time, until the paste reaches the desired consistency—thick and concentrated or smooth and spreadable. Store in an airtight container in the refrigerator for up to 1 month.

Miso

At the heart of authentic Asian nourishment lies the appeal of traditionally made organic miso. Cultivated through the meticulous fermentation processes, organic miso respects the harmony of nature and nurtures our bodies. Miso is known for its rich umami flavor and is used as a base for many soups, marinades, sauces, and more. It is made through the fermentation of soybeans, rice, or other grains using koji (a type of fungus) and salt. The fermentation process and the use of koji gives miso its unique taste and contributes to its nutritional value. While miso is mostly associated with Japanese cuisine, fermented bean pastes similar to miso can also be found in other Asian cultures, particularly in China and Korea. However, miso has evolved into a distinct culinary tradition in Japan, and it remains a cherished and versatile ingredient in Japanese cooking.

There are three distinct varieties of miso: White, yellow, and red miso. Each type carries its unique characteristics and culinary applications, offering a diverse range of tastes to savor.

White Miso Delicate and sweet white miso, also known as shiro miso, is crafted through a shorter fermentation process. Its pale color and mild flavor make it a wonderful choice for those new to miso. White miso's gentle taste lends itself well to dressings, light soups, and marinades. Its subtle complexity can enhance dishes without overpowering the other flavors.

Yellow Miso Yellow miso, or shinshu miso, embodies a balance between white and red miso. With a medium fermentation period, yellow miso boasts a nuanced flavor profile. It's slightly earthy and savory, making it versatile for both soups and sauces. The depth it adds complements heartier dishes while maintaining a delightful subtlety.

Red Miso Bold and robust red miso, often referred to as "aka miso," undergoes the longest fermentation. Its deep flavor, coupled with a rich umami taste, makes it a standout in hearty stews, savory broths, and bold marinades. Red miso's potency is ideal for lending depth to strong-flavored ingredients and creating complex, soul-satisfying dishes.

Exploring the world of white, yellow, and red miso invites a journey through varied tastes, textures, and culinary possibilities. These miso varieties encapsulate the essence of Asian tradition while offering endless avenues for culinary creativity in both traditional and contemporary dishes.

Hoisin Sauce

Hoisin sauce is a staple condiment in many Asian cuisines, particularly Chinese cuisine, where it is often used as a dipping sauce or a glaze. For Vietnamese phở, a popular noodle soup dish, it is offered at the table to add a sweet, savory, and slightly tangy flavor. I also use it as a base for my Vietnamese Peanut Dipping Sauce (page 81). Traditional hoisin sauce is made from fermented soy bean paste to give the sauce a thick consistency and a deep and tangy flavor.

Yield: about 1½ cups (360 mL)

5 tablespoons (75 mL) Fermented
   Black Bean Sauce (page 74; see Note)
¼ cup (60 mL) tamari or soy sauce
1 tablespoon rice vinegar
1 tablespoon raw honey or maple syrup
1½ teaspoons sesame oil
1½ teaspoons garlic powder
¼ teaspoon Chinese five-spice powder
¼ teaspoon ground black pepper

Combine all of the ingredients in a food processor or blender and process until smooth, 20 to 30 seconds. Store in an airtight container in the refrigerator for up to 1 month.

> **Note:** You can substitute store-bought Chinese fermented black bean sauce, such as the one from One Culture Foods, or yellow miso, but the flavor will be different.

Sesame Oil

Both sesame oil and toasted sesame oil are used in various culinary applications, but they have different flavors and purposes. Sesame oil is made from raw sesame seeds and has a light color and a mild, nutty flavor. It is commonly used as a finishing oil or as a flavor enhancer in Asian cuisines. Sesame oil is suitable for both cooked and uncooked applications, adding a subtle sesame aroma and flavor to dishes. It can be used in marinades, stir-fries, dressings, and sauces.

Toasted sesame oil, also known as dark sesame oil, is made from roasted sesame seeds. It has a more intense and robust flavor compared to regular sesame oil. Toasted sesame oil is typically used as a condiment or flavoring oil rather than for cooking with heat. It adds a rich, smoky, and nutty taste to dishes and is one of my favorite flavors to add to a simple fried rice dish. Due to its strong flavor, it is usually used sparingly in dressings, dips, noodle dishes, and drizzled over cooked foods.

Vietnamese Peanut Dipping Sauce

Traditional Vietnamese peanut sauce is popular as a dipping sauce for spring rolls or a sauce for grilled chicken or vegetables. If you prefer not to eat peanuts or have peanut allergies, you can make a similar sauce using almond butter or cashew butter instead.

Yield: about ¾ cup (180 mL)

½ cup (120 mL) natural peanut butter, almond butter, or cashew butter

2 tablespoons (30 mL) soy sauce or coconut aminos

1 tablespoon raw honey

1 teaspoon sesame oil

1 teaspoon Hoisin Sauce (page 80; optional)

¼ teaspoon cayenne pepper

¼ cup (60 mL) spring water, warmed

In a small bowl, whisk together the nut butter, soy sauce, honey, sesame oil, hoisin sauce (if using), and cayenne until well combined. Slowly add the water, whisking continuously, until the sauce reaches your desired consistency. Taste and adjust the seasoning as needed. Store in an airtight container in the refrigerator for up to 3 days.

Note: You can add other spices or herbs, such as ginger or cilantro, for additional flavor.

Black Garlic Butter

My mother loves garlic in every form—raw, fermented, pickled, cooked, you name it. She was the one who introduced me to fermented black garlic, which I especially love because it tastes more like candy than it does the pungent flavor of raw garlic. When fermented, garlic undergoes a chemical reaction known as the Maillard reaction, causing it to turn black and develop a soft, chewy texture and a sweet, slightly smoky flavor. Some studies have suggested that black garlic has more antioxidant activity than regular garlic, which may help reduce inflammation and prevent oxidative damage to cells. Black garlic may have beneficial effects on heart health as well, such as reducing cholesterol levels and improving blood flow. Here, I combine black garlic with raw butter to make a compound butter you can use as you would regular butter—to top a steak, rub on a chicken, or serve with steamed vegetables. Spread on sourdough bread and sprinkle with some salt—the children will devour it!

Yield: 1 to 1½ cups (*240–360 mL*)

1 to 2 black garlic heads, peeled

8 ounces (225 g) unsalted grass-fed butter
(preferably raw), softened

Use a mortar and pestle to combine the black garlic and butter until thoroughly and evenly mixed. Alternatively, you can use a spatula or a hand mixer.

Transfer the mixture to a glass container, pushing the compound butter down and spreading it evenly. Cover and refrigerate for at least 2 hours before serving. Store in the refrigerator for up to 6 months or in the freezer for up to 1 year.

Fermented Shrimp Paste

(MẮM TÔM)

A common flavor enhancer in Southeast Asian countries, mắm tôm is a very pungent and flavorful Vietnamese fermented shrimp paste. It used to be my least favorite ingredient because of its strong smell whenever my mother opened it up in the house, but to my surprise I found that it is the foundation of some of my favorite soups. You can sometimes buy blocks of premade shrimp paste, but it is difficult to source. With some simple ingredients, you can make fermented shrimp paste at home and use it to add depth to your Asian dishes. After fermenting for 7 to 10 days, mắm tôm is ready to incorporate into other dishes or serve as a dipping sauce with vegetables, grilled meat, or seafood.

Yield: 2 to 3 cups (240–360 mL)

2¼ pounds (1 kg) raw shell-on wild-caught shrimp, thawed if frozen

1 cup (240 mL) sake (rice wine) or dry white wine

½ cup (100 g) fine sea salt

Note: *Wild-caught shrimp taste better than farm-raised shrimp because they have a diverse diet and can swim freely. In addition, they may contain a different nutritional composition compared to farm-raised shrimp, which are typically fed a formulated diet that is designed to promote rapid growth. Shrimp farms have negative ecological effects as well.*

Any size or type of shrimp can be used for this recipe. Look for shrimp that have been frozen without chemicals such as sodium bisulfite and tripolyphosphate.

Clean the shrimp by removing the heads, legs, and veins, but leave the shells intact. Rinse the shrimp in cold water. Put the shrimp in a large bowl and pour the sake over. Let the shrimp soak at room temperature for 30 minutes. Drain.

Put the shrimp in a blender and add the salt. Blend on high speed until the mixture is smooth. Scrape the mixture into a container and place it in the oven with only the oven light on for 24 hours, stirring every 2 hours, and alternating between 2 hours with the light on and 2 hours with the light off. Alternatively, if the temperature where you are is at least 80°F (25°C), place the container outside, covered, for 24 hours, and stir every 2 hours.

Blend the mixture again and repeat the process of drying and blending each day for 7 to 10 days. When the shrimp paste is done fermenting, it should have a complex and savory aroma without any unpleasant or off-putting odors. It should also have a strong umami flavor with a blend of salty, savory, and slightly fishy notes. The taste should be balanced and not overpowering. You can use the shrimp paste immediately or store in an airtight container in the refrigerator for up to 1 month.

Sambal Oelek

The Southeast Asian pepper paste known as sambal oelek is one of the most common ways we enhance many noodle-based dishes. This fermented hot sauce is easy to make with jalapeños, serranos, or other hot peppers. When our summer garden is abundant with peppers, this is the recipe we use to preserve them for use throughout the year. For their color and flavor profile, I prefer using red jalapeños for sambal oelek. Red jalapeños are simply green jalapeños that have matured. As jalapeños ripen and turn red, they develop a sweeter, fruitier flavor and can also be slightly hotter than the green jalapeños. The membrane of the pepper contains the highest concentration of capsaicin, which gives the pepper its heat. By removing the membrane, you can control the spiciness of the sambal oelek to your preference.

Yield: about 2 cups (480 mL)

1 pound (450 g) red jalapeños
5 or 6 garlic cloves, peeled
1 tablespoon coarse sea salt

Note: *Fermenting chili peppers can produce a strong, pungent odor. Be sure to ferment the mixture in a well-ventilated area.*

Rinse the jalapeños and remove the stems. Slice them in half lengthwise and remove the seeds and membranes, if desired, or leave them in for a spicier sauce.

Put the jalapeños and garlic in a food processor and pulse until finely chopped. Transfer the mixture to a sterilized 1-pint (0.5 L) jar. Add the salt and mix well.

Loosely cover the jar with a lid or cloth and let the mixture sit at room temperature for 2 to 3 days, stirring once or twice a day. After 2 to 3 days, the mixture should start to bubble and ferment. Let it sit and ferment for another 2 to 3 days, or until it reaches the desired level of sourness.

Store in an airtight container in the refrigerator. It will continue to ferment slowly in the fridge and will last for several months.

Crispy Fried Shallots
(HÀNH PHI)

Crispy fried shallots are a versatile accompaniment to many dishes in various international cuisines. While Tim grew up with fried shallots as a garnish on steaks, green bean casseroles, and burgers, I enjoyed them on top of Vietnamese Chicken Salad (page 147), Vietnamese Chicken Noodle Soup (page 123), and Chicken Rice Porridge (page 136). A popular condiment in many Southeast Asian cuisines, premade fried shallots are not hard to find, but they are most often fried in palm oil and coated with wheat flour. Why buy these when you can make them at home with just a few simple steps? When you make your own fried shallots, you know the two simple ingredients used, and you will be left with one of my favorite fragrant oils for other uses.

Yield: 2 to 2½ cups (*180 g*)

1 pound (450 g) shallots, peeled and
   very thinly sliced
2 cups (480 mL) sesame oil

Line a rimmed baking sheet with two layers of paper towels. Squeeze the shallots in a paper towel to remove excess moisture. Spread out the shallots on the lined baking sheet and leave out to dry in the sun for a few hours, or on a paper towel over a cooling rack inside the house, until the shallots are dry.

Heat the oil in a large saucepan over medium heat. Add the shallots and cook, stirring frequently, until they are light golden brown and crispy, 8 to 10 minutes. Do not leave the shallots unattended, as they can quickly go from ready to burnt in just a matter of seconds.

Using a spider or fine-mesh strainer, transfer the crispy shallots to a paper towel–lined plate to drain. The shallots will continue to brown after removing them from the oil, so be sure to get them out of the oil before they get too brown.

Allow the crispy shallots to cool completely, then store in an airtight container at room temperature for up to 2 months.

Once the shallot oil has cooled, pour it through a fine-mesh strainer and store in a separate airtight container in the refrigerator for up to 1 month.

Vietnamese Preserved Lemons

(CHANH MUỐI)

Chanh muối translates to "salted lemon" and is a traditional way of preserving lemons in salt for a long, long time. My mother often had these preserved lemons sitting on the counter, ready for us to take hot or cold to alleviate various ailments, from nausea to the common cold. Tim and the children love using them to make a refreshing salty lemonade to enjoy in the summertime (see page 261). Make sure that you source organic lemons since you will be fermenting the lemons with the peels on. We use so many lemons that wherever we move, we always make sure to grow at least one lemon tree. This is one way we preserve our lemon harvest.

Yield: 1 quart (**1 L**)

6 to 8 organic lemons
   (depending on the size)
Sea salt

Wash the lemons well, scrubbing thoroughly to remove any dirt. Cut the lemons lengthwise into quarters, but do not cut all the way through the bottom. Generously salt the inside of the lemons. Pour a layer of salt into the bottom of a sterilized 1-quart (1 L) jar and place a layer of lemons inside the jar. Sprinkle with more salt, then continue to layer the remaining lemons and salt. Press down on the lemons to squeeze out some juice.

Wipe off any salt residue from the rim of the jar and loosely seal the jar with a lid so gases can escape during fermentation. Store the jar in a cool, dark place for about a month. Once fermentation is complete, you can store in the refrigerator for up to 1 year.

When removing the lemons from the jar, be sure to use a clean utensil every time to prevent contamination or mold.

Lemongrass Chili Oil
(SA TẾ)

Sa tế is a spicy chili oil that can enhance any dish with its bold flavor. The sauce's distinctive taste comes from a generous amount of garlic and aromatic lemongrass. My father often uses sa tế as a dipping sauce, to top his noodle dishes, and even on sandwiches for a spicy and aromatic flavor. It also goes well over any protein or rice to spice it up!

Yield: 1 cup *(240 mL)*

½ cup (50 g) chopped lemongrass
¼ cup (15 g) whole dried chilies,
    such as Thai or bird's eye
2 shallots, roughly chopped
1 head garlic, peeled and roughly chopped
½ cup (120 mL) sesame oil
2 tablespoons (30 mL) Sambal Oelek
    (page 85)
1 tablespoon gochugaru
    (Korean red chili powder)
1 tablespoon fish sauce or Fermented
    Anchovy Sauce (page 70)
1 tablespoon panela
½ teaspoon fine sea salt

In a food processor, combine the lemongrass, chilies, shallots, and garlic. Process until combined but still chunky.

In a small saucepan, heat the sesame oil over medium heat until it begins to shimmer. Add the lemongrass mixture, turn the heat to medium-low, and cook, stirring continuously, for 5 to 7 minutes, until it starts to brown. Stir in the sambal oelek and cook for another 5 minutes, being careful not to let it burn. Add the gochugaru and stir in the fish sauce, panela, and salt. Remove from the heat and allow to cool slightly.

Transfer the mixture to a container, cover, and let sit at room temperature for a few hours to allow the flavors to meld. Pour a thin layer of oil on top to keep the sa tế fresh longer and store in the refrigerator for up to 3 months.

Note: *This recipe can be easily adjusted to taste. If you prefer a spicier oil, add more sambal oelek.*

CHAPTER 4

Vegetables and Sides

My maternal grandfather and my mother instilled in me a love for fresh, homegrown produce. I remember spending countless hours in my grandfather's backyard garden as a child, listening to his stories and learning his tricks for keeping pests away from plants using unconventional methods like hanging CDs from trees. He also made his own compost from kitchen scraps and always had an abundance of persimmons, apricots, pears, oranges, and various herbs that he would eagerly share with neighbors, family, friends, and the local community. Today, I carry on this legacy by growing my own vegetables and herbs and using them to create delicious and healthy dishes that nourish both our bodies and souls.

When Tim and I purchased our first home in the San Francisco Bay Area, I planted some fruit trees and berry bushes, accompanied by a seemingly foolproof succulent garden from the Ruth Bancroft Garden & Nursery. I built my very first raised garden bed for my mom right outside the back door of our house that leads to the garden, and I planted the "phở bed"—just cilantro and scallions. Mom always said, "Don't bother making phở without them!" I learned how to succession-plant these crops to make sure we always had a steady supply right at our fingertips.

This built my confidence enough that I jumped into building four raised beds to grow vegetables for our spring rolls in the spring and summer and Asian greens for hot pot in the fall and winter. Before we knew it, we had shortened our food supply chain, we were spending more time together outside as a family, and we were having so much fun learning together.

When you grow your own food, you have better control over what goes into the soil and into your plants—and thus into your body. Gardening can be a rewarding and satisfying experience, providing a source of exercise, fresh air, and sunshine. However, not everyone has the time, space, or resources to grow their own food. Buying organic produce from local farmers can be a good alternative. Even as we were starting our homestead, we continued to support local farmers who raised their animals humanely and took care of their soil.

As our garden harvests became abundant, we would invite our neighbors, friends, and family over to our "U-Pick" to pick their own fresh produce. I wanted the children to hand-pick the vegetables and fruit themselves so they could experience something they would never get from the grocery store: the feeling of knowing where your food comes from!

We had such an overwhelming abundance of vegetables that my mom and I began fermenting them. As a kid, I used to think that fermenting was old-fashioned—and it is! Fermentation has been used by humans for thousands of years to extend the shelf life of foods, improve taste and texture, and make nutrients more available. Its popularity declined with the advent

of modern food preservation techniques such as canning, pickling, refrigeration, and chemical preservatives, but in recent years it has experienced a revival, and there's now renewed interest in fermentation and other traditional food preservation methods.

Make sure to use clean, sterilized utensils and jars for any fermented foods to avoid contamination during the fermentation process.

Traditional Asian Vegetables and Alternatives

Asian cuisine is known for its use of fresh, flavorful ingredients. Vegetables play a significant role in many dishes, but not all Asian vegetables are readily accessible in all parts of the world. Below, you'll find my family's favorite vegetables traditionally used in Asian cuisine, along with some more readily available substitutes.

Bok choy is popular in Chinese cuisine and is used in stir-fries and soups. Substitutes: Swiss chard, spinach.

Daikon radish is a winter vegetable used in many Asian cuisines, particularly Japanese, Korean, and Chinese. It has a mild, slightly sweet flavor and a crunchy texture. Substitutes: turnips, parsnips.

Edamame is a young soybean that is commonly used in Japanese cuisine. Substitute: lima beans.

From Kimchi to Kombucha

Fermenting vegetables is an ancient method of food preservation that has been used in many cultures. In Asia the practice dates back thousands of years. One of the earliest and best-known examples of fermented vegetables in Asia is the Korean dish kimchi, which is made by fermenting napa cabbage and other vegetables. Kimchi is a staple food in Korea and was originally made in large batches during the fall harvest season to preserve the vegetables for the winter months.

Sandor Katz, an American author and fermentation historian, has helped bring attention to the benefits and techniques of fermentation. Katz has studied various forms of traditional fermentation, including those used in Asian cultures. In most of Asia, fermentation has long been used as a way to preserve vegetables without refrigeration. The process involves the use of microorganisms, such as bacteria and yeast, to break down sugars and carbohydrates in the vegetables into organic acids and alcohol, which creates an acidic and tangy flavor.

In addition to kimchi, other fermented vegetables popular in Asia include Japanese pickles such as umeboshi (pickled plums), tsukemono (pickled vegetables), and nukazuke (vegetables pickled in rice bran), which are commonly eaten as a side dish or snack. In China, pickled mustard greens and pickled cabbage are used in cooking and served as a side dish.

Fermented vegetables are not only delicious, they are extremely nutritious. Fermentation can increase the bioavailability of certain vitamins and minerals, and the presence of probiotics can promote healthy gut bacteria. As a result, fermented vegetables have gained popularity in recent years as a health food, and many people around the world incorporate fermented vegetables into their diets.

Enoki mushrooms have a long, thin stalk and a small cap. They have a mild flavor and are often used in soups, stir-fries, and hot pots. Substitutes: shiitake mushrooms, white button mushrooms.

Gai lan. Also known as Chinese broccoli, gai lan has a slightly bitter taste and is often stir-fried or steamed. Substitutes: broccoli, broccoli rabe.

Kabocha squash is a type of winter squash that is commonly used in Japanese cuisine. It has a sweet flavor and can be roasted, boiled, or steamed. Substitutes: acorn squash, butternut squash.

Lotus root. This mild, crunchy root vegetable is used in many Asian dishes such as stir-fries and soups. Substitutes: water chestnuts, jicama.

Napa cabbage is a variety of Chinese cabbage commonly used in stir-fries, soups, and kimchi. Substitute: savoy cabbage.

Okra is a common ingredient in many Southeast Asian dishes and is also widely used in American Southern cuisine. Substitute: chayote squash.

Thai eggplant. This small, round eggplant has a slightly bitter flavor. It is commonly used in Thai cuisine in curries and stir-fries. Substitutes: Japanese eggplant, zucchini.

Water spinach (kangkong) is used in Southeast Asian cuisine and has a slightly bitter taste. Substitutes: spinach, Swiss chard.

While these substitutes might be similar in appearance and texture, they differ in flavor. For example, turnip is a good substitute for daikon in terms of texture, but it has a milder flavor. Likewise, shiitake mushrooms are a good substitute for enoki mushrooms in texture, but they have a stronger flavor. Nutritional value can also differ; for example, lotus root is a better source of fiber and vitamin C than water chestnuts are.

When we lived in the San Francisco Bay Area, we enjoyed access to a wide variety and abundance of Asian vegetables. When we moved to the country, many of these vegetables became hard to find in local markets, but my mother still wanted their unrivaled flavors and textures. That was when I started to grow these vegetables from seed in our backyard. Many Asian vegetables are easy to grow and thrive in a variety of climates, making them ideal for home gardening. By growing these vegetables yourself, you can ensure that they are fresh and free from harmful chemicals or pesticides, and you can have access to them whenever you need them.

Some Asian vegetables that are easy to grow include bok choy, napa cabbage, daikon radish, and herbs such as Thai basil, lemongrass, and cilantro. These plants are not only delicious and nutritious, but they also add a unique flavor and texture to your meals that cannot be replicated with substitutes.

Vietnamese Pickled Carrots and Daikon
(ĐỒ CHUA)

This sweet, sour, and crunchy side dish can make any meal pop. But it's also the culprit behind one of the most embarrassing moments of my childhood. For lunch at my fifth grade science camp, my mother packed me a bánh mì sandwich with extra đồ chua and pâté (the only way to eat bánh mì, in my opinion). I had to throw it away because of the smelly aroma coming out of my lunch bag that warm day. But I still love đồ chua, and when I make it at home, I can't resist adding more daikon. So go ahead, give it a try, but maybe don't pack it in your backpack on a hot summer day!

Yield: 2 cups (*480 mL*)

2 cups (480 mL) spring water

6 tablespoons (80 g) panela

1½ tablespoons fine sea salt, plus more for sprinkling

8 ounces (225 g) carrots

8 ounces (225 g) daikon radish

5 tablespoons (74 mL) apple cider vinegar

In a small saucepan, bring the water to a boil, then add the panela and salt and stir until dissolved. Remove from the heat and let cool to room temperature while you prepare the vegetables.

Wash and peel the carrots and daikon. Use a knife or a mandoline slicer to slice them into small or medium matchsticks. The smaller the pieces, the faster they will pickle.

Put the carrots and daikon in a bowl, sprinkle with salt, and massage for about 1 minute, then let sit for 30 minutes. Rinse thoroughly and squeeze out the excess moisture. Pack the vegetables into a sterilized 1-pint (0.5 L) glass jar.

When the brine solution has cooled, add the vinegar. Pour the brine over the vegetables until the jar is full, with 1 inch (2.5 cm) headspace. Cover the jar and let it sit at room temperature, checking every 12 to 24 hours, until it's pickled to your liking. This can take 2 to 4 days, depending on the temperature. Store in the fridge for up to 1 month.

No-Sugar Quick-Pickled Vegetables

This version of pickled vegetables is a great way for all the random vegetables in the refrigerator to come together as a nice, crunchy side dish. You can use any vegetables you have on hand, as long as you end up with about 2 quarts. I love when our children fish for their favorite vegetables in the colorful mason jar!

Yield: 2 quarts (2 L)

2 cups (480 mL) spring water
2 cups (480 mL) apple cider vinegar
2 tablespoons (36 g) Pickling Spice Mix
 (opposite)
1 tablespoon fine sea salt
8 cups (1.9 L) bite-size pieces
 of vegetables, such as:

- 2 small carrots, peeled and
 cut into matchsticks or coins
- 1 small head cauliflower, trimmed
 and cut into small florets
- 1 celery rib, sliced
- 10 snow peas
- 1 red bell pepper, seeded and
 cut into matchsticks

In a saucepan, combine the water, vinegar, pickling spice, and salt. Bring to a boil, then turn the heat down and simmer for 10 minutes.

Sterilize one half-gallon, two 1-quart, or four 1-pint (2 L, 1 L, or 0.5 L) jars. Distribute the vegetable pieces evenly into your jar(s). Pour the brine over the vegetables, leaving about ½ inch (13 mm) headspace at the top. Allow to cool slightly, then cover and refrigerate for at least 1 hour. Store in the refrigerator for up to 2 weeks.

Pickling Spice Mix

I put together this pickling spice mix as a timesaver to have on hand when you want to clear out the fridge and make quick meals. There are other options you can use for pickling spices; feel free to swap out some from the list below for a different flavor profile.

Yield: about ½ cup (*145 g*)

2 tablespoons (36 g) yellow mustard seed
2 tablespoons (36 g) dill seed
2 tablespoons (36 g) coriander pods
1 tablespoon allspice berries
1 tablespoon red pepper flakes (optional)
1 teaspoon whole cloves
Optional add-ins: cinnamon sticks (cut into small pieces), fennel seed, dried ginger, star anise, black peppercorns

Combine all the ingredients in a small jar, cover, and store at room temperature for up to 1 year.

Fermented Bean Sprouts
(DƯA GIÁ)

This healthy side dish is incredibly easy and fast to make. Our family makes this for Tết (Vietnamese Lunar New Year). I use mung beans that I first sprout for seven days, but you can also start with fresh bean sprouts. Be sure to use long sprouts that are not wilted or broken. In the Appalachian Mountains, we forage for wild onions in our backyard to use instead of garlic chives. This is an excellent side dish for caramelized dishes like braised pork and eggs (thit kho trung).

Yield: 2 quarts (1.9 L)

9 cups (2.1 L) spring water
2 tablespoons (28 g) fine sea salt
1 pound (450 g) mung bean sprouts
8 ounces (225 g) carrots, peeled and julienned
4 or 5 wild onion stalks or garlic chives,
    cut into 2-inch (5 cm) pieces

In a small saucepan, bring the water to a boil, then add the salt and stir until dissolved. Remove from the heat and allow the brine to cool to room temperature.

Sterilize one half-gallon, two 1-quart, or four 1-pint (2 L, 1 L, or 0.5 L) jars. In a large bowl, gently mix the bean sprouts, carrots, and wild onions. Distribute the mixture into your jar(s). Pour the cooled brine into the jars to completely cover the vegetables.

Cover the jars and let sit at room temperature for 1 to 2 days. To slow down the fermentation, place the jars in the fridge. After fermentation is complete (usually after 1 to 3 days), while the bean sprouts are still crunchy (not soggy), drain the liquid from the jars. Store in the refrigerator for up to 1 week.

► HOW TO SPROUT MUNG BEANS

Rinse the mung beans thoroughly under cool running water to remove any dirt or debris. Put the rinsed mung beans in a bowl or container and cover with water. Let soak for 8 to 12 hours.

Drain the mung beans and rinse again. Spread the soaked mung beans evenly in the bottom of a clean glass jar or sprouting tray. Cover the jar or tray with a breathable lid such as cheesecloth or mesh screen to allow proper airflow while preventing dust or insects from entering. Place the jar or tray in a cool, dark place away from direct sunlight.

Once every morning and again every evening, fill the jar or tray with water, swish it around, and then drain completely. Repeat the rinsing process every day for 3 to 5 days, until the mung bean sprouts have reached the desired length (usually 2 to 4 inches [5–10 cm]).

Give the sprouts a final rinse and drain well. Store the mung bean sprouts in a covered container in the refrigerator for up to 5 days.

Remember to practice good hygiene during the sprouting process by keeping equipment clean and washing your hands thoroughly before handling. Enjoy your home-grown bean sprouts in soups, salads, stir-fries, or any other dishes you like.

Pickled Red Onions
(HÀNH DẤM)

These crunchy pickles are on the secret menu at most phở restaurants. My dad would always ask for hành dấm with his bowl of phở, and as a child growing up, I never understood what the appeal was all about. But now, this tangy and slightly sweet onion topping completes my bowl of phở. I also love it with bánh mì sandwiches. It is super easy to make and can be enjoyed in just 15 minutes.

Yield: 2 cups (480 mL)

½ cup (120 mL) rice vinegar
½ cup (120 mL) spring water
1 teaspoon fine sea salt
1 large red onion, thinly sliced

In a small saucepan, heat the vinegar, water, and salt over medium heat until it comes to a simmer. Stir until the salt is dissolved. Remove the brine from the heat and let it cool for a few minutes.

Pack the onion slices into a jar. Pour the brine over the onions, making sure they are completely covered. If necessary, add a little more vinegar and water in equal parts to completely cover the onions. Cover and refrigerate for at least 15 minutes or up to 1 month.

Daikon Kimchi
(CỦ CẢI KIMCHI)

It's hard to pick my favorite kimchi, but the children and I love the crunchy chunks in this daikon kimchi. In our garden, I plant rows upon rows of daikon as a cover crop to break up compacted soil with its deep taproots. Daikon helps scavenge and recycle nutrients, which can help reduce the need for fertilizer. It's a great way for us to establish new garden beds, and as a huge additional bonus, each fall we end up with enough daikon to make countless jars of daikon kimchi to enjoy with friends and family throughout the year. Enjoy your daikon kimchi as a flavorful and probiotic-rich side dish with your meals!

Yield: 1 quart (1 L)

2 pounds (900 g) daikon radish, peeled and sliced into ¼-inch (6 mm) rounds

¼ cup (25 g) gochugaru (Korean red chili powder)

3 garlic cloves, minced

1 (1-inch [2.5 cm]) piece fresh ginger, peeled and minced

2 scallions, sliced

2 tablespoons (28 g) fine sea salt

Put the daikon in a large bowl. Add the gochugaru, garlic, ginger, scallions, and salt and mix until the daikon is evenly coated with the seasonings.

Pack the mixture tightly into a sterilized 1-quart (1 L) jar. Leave about 1 inch (2.5 cm) headspace at the top of the jar. Cover the jar and let it sit at room temperature for 2 to 3 days, until it becomes slightly sour and tangy. "Burp" the jar every day to release any gas that builds up from the fermentation process.

When the kimchi has reached your desired level of tanginess, transfer the jar to the refrigerator to slow down the fermentation process. Store for up to 3 weeks.

Easy Napa Cabbage Kimchi

While many traditional kimchi recipes include vinegar, fish sauce, and sugar, I opted for a simpler approach to achieve a rich and delicious flavor in this cabbage-based kimchi. This easy recipe is similar to making sauerkraut, but with a few additional ingredients to give it a bolder and spicier taste. To support local agriculture and make use of what's readily accessible, we use locally grown napa cabbage as the base for this recipe.

Yield: 1 quart (1 L)

1 head napa cabbage or white cabbage
2 tablespoons (28 g) sea salt
3 scallions, sliced
1 (2-inch [5 cm]) piece fresh ginger, peeled and grated
2 tablespoons (13 g) gochugaru (Korean red chili powder)
3 garlic cloves, minced
Spring water (optional)

Reserve 1 to 3 intact outer leaves of the cabbage and set aside for later use.

Cut the remaining cabbage into bite-size pieces and put in a large bowl. Add the salt and mix thoroughly. Set aside for 30 minutes to draw moisture out of the cabbage.

Massage the cabbage and salt with your hands until the cabbage starts to release its liquid. Let it sit for 2 hours, tossing occasionally.

In a medium bowl, combine the scallions, ginger, gochugaru, and garlic, and mix with clean hands until it forms a paste. If it's too dry, add a teaspoon at a time of spring water.

Drain the liquid from the cabbage. Add the scallion mixture and toss gently until all the cabbage is covered with the paste.

Using a wooden spoon, transfer the kimchi to a sterilized 1-quart (1 L) jar. Press down the kimchi firmly as you add it to the jar to release any air pockets.

Fold the cabbage leaves that you had set aside to form a "lid" that will fit the top of your jar. This will prevent bits of cabbage from floating to the top. Push the kimchi down until it is submerged in the liquid. You can also put a fermenting weight on top of the kimchi to keep it submerged. Place fine cheesecloth over the top of the jar and secure it with a rubber band.

Leave the jar to ferment at room temperature for 24 to 48 hours, until it reaches your desired level of sourness. Taste it periodically to monitor the fermentation process. Once the kimchi has fermented to your liking, cover the jar with a lid and transfer to the refrigerator to slow down the fermentation process. Store for up to 3 weeks.

Variation: Turmeric-Ginger Kimchi

This is a flavorful and colorful variation on the traditional Korean kimchi. Not only does the seasoning add an earthy and spicy flavor, but turmeric is known for its anti-inflammatory and antioxidant properties and ginger is believed to aid digestion and boost the immune system. We enjoy drinking the brine straight as a probiotic-rich health tonic.

Add 1 tablespoon ground turmeric to the seasoning paste mixture. To prevent turmeric-stained hands, use gloves when tossing it with the cabbage.

Vegan Japchae

Japchae is one of our family's favorite dishes. It is quick and easy to make and is also the most flavorful way for me to sneak in vegetables—including bell peppers, mushrooms, kale, or zucchini—to increase the nutrient density of this dish. It is gluten-free and rich in dietary fiber and also contains important vitamins and minerals such as vitamin C, potassium, and magnesium. This version is vegan, and you can add protein-rich ingredients like thin slices of tempeh. Sweet potato noodles, also known as Korean glass noodles or dangmyeon, are made from sweet potato starch and are a popular ingredient in many Korean dishes.

Yield: 4 to 6 servings

1 cup (20 g) dried wood ear mushrooms, sliced

3 tablespoons (45 mL) tamari or coconut aminos

2 tablespoons (30 mL) sesame oil

2 tablespoons (30 mL) maple syrup

2 garlic cloves, minced

3 tablespoons (45 mL) toasted sesame oil, divided

1 large red onion, sliced

2 medium carrots, peeled and julienned

1 red bell pepper, sliced

2 cups (60 g) spinach, torn if large

8 ounces (225 g) sweet potato noodles, cooked (see page 65)

Thinly sliced tempeh (optional)

Put the dried mushrooms in a bowl, cover with warm water, and let soak for 1 hour. Drain.

In a small bowl, whisk together the tamari, sesame oil, maple syrup, garlic, and 1 tablespoon of the vegetable oil; set aside.

In a large skillet or wok, heat the remaining 2 tablespoons vegetable oil over medium-high heat. Add the onion and cook until translucent, 3 to 4 minutes. Add the mushrooms and cook for 2 to 3 minutes. Add the carrots and bell pepper and cook for 2 to 3 minutes, until slightly softened. Add the spinach and cook until wilted, 1 to 2 minutes.

Add the cooked sweet potato noodles and tempeh (if using). Pour the tamari mixture over the top. Toss everything together until well combined and the noodles and vegetables are evenly coated. Serve warm or at room temperature.

Gluten-Free Vegetable Tempura

Tempura—battered and fried vegetables or seafood—is popular in many Asian countries, where it is often served as a main dish in a traditional multicourse meal, usually accompanied by side dishes such as soup and rice. This gluten-free and healthier twist on the classic dish relies on arrowroot starch for a deliciously crunchy and satisfying texture.

Yield: 4 to 6 servings

1 cup (160 g) rice flour
½ cup (64 g) arrowroot starch
1 teaspoon baking powder
1 teaspoon fine sea salt
1 large pasture-raised egg
1 cup (240 mL) ice-cold spring water
Avocado oil, for frying
3 to 4 cups (200–400 g) assorted bite-size vegetables, such as cauliflower, mushrooms, zucchini, shiso, bok choy, sweet potato, broccoli
Simple Tempura Dipping Sauce (below) or Vietnamese Dipping Sauce (page 68), for serving

In a large bowl, whisk together the rice flour, arrowroot, baking powder, and salt.

In a small bowl, lightly beat the egg, then whisk in the ice-cold water.

Pour the egg mixture into the dry ingredients and whisk until just combined. Do not overmix; the batter should be lumpy.

Pour oil to a depth of 2 inches (5 cm) in a deep frying pan or wok. Heat to 350°F (175°C). Place a wire rack on a rimmed baking sheet or line with paper towels.

One at a time, dip the vegetable pieces into the batter, shaking off any excess, and carefully lower into the hot oil. Work in batches so as not to crowd the pan. Fry for 2 to 3 minutes, turning once, until the batter is golden brown and crispy. Remove the tempura from the oil using a spider or slotted spoon and drain on the rack or paper towels for 5 minutes before serving.

Serve the tempura hot, with the dipping sauce of your choice.

Simple Tempura Dipping Sauce

Yield: ½ cup, or 120 mL

¼ cup (60 mL) mirin or rice vinegar
¼ cup (60 mL) tamari or soy sauce
2 tablespoons (30 mL) maple syrup

Combine all the ingredients in a bowl and mix together thoroughly. Use right away or store in an airtight container in the refrigerator for up to 1 month.

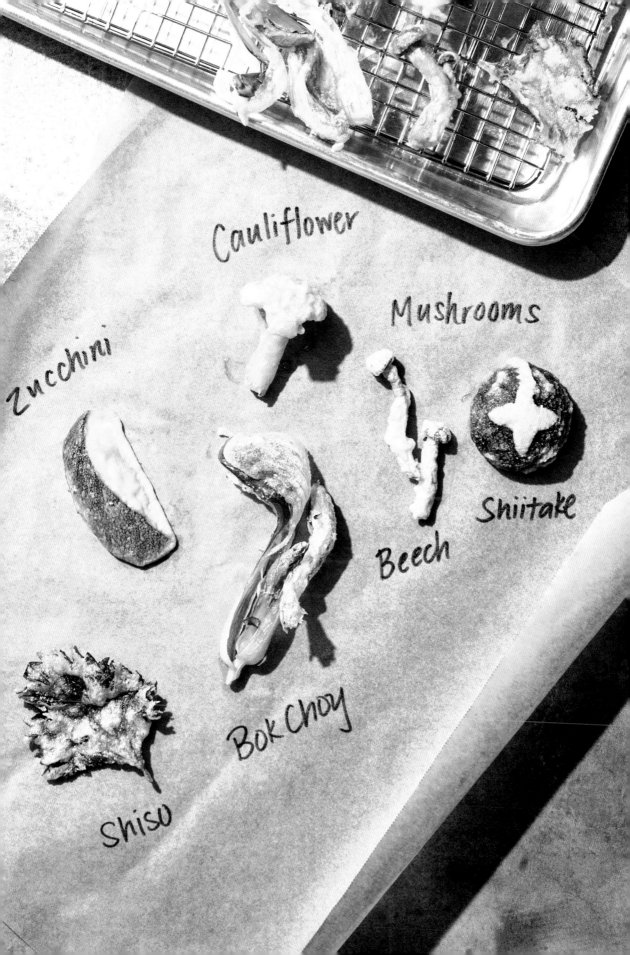

Cauliflower

Mushrooms

Zucchini

Beech

Shiitake

Bok Choy

Shiso

Wild Bibimbap

Bibimbap is a popular Korean dish that translates to "mixed rice" in English. It is a nutritious and colorful bowl of rice topped with various vegetables, protein, and often a fried egg. There are countless variations of bibimbap and many regional adaptations. What I love about this recipe is that most of these banchan (Korean side dishes) are adapted to make use of wild and foraged edibles we can find in the Appalachians and Northern California.

One version of this dish is known as dolsot bibimbap, which is served in a Korean stoneware bowl, making a delicious crispy rice. In our home, grandparents and grandkids both love crispy rice, so I have adapted the technique to a cast-iron skillet. I've used forbidden black rice here, but you can use white rice, brown rice, or even cauliflower rice. Most of the banchan can be prepared ahead of time and refrigerated until you are ready to eat.

Yield: 2 to 4 servings

Forbidden Black Rice, cooked and cooled
(page 63)
Sesame oil, for the pan
Fiddlehead Fern Banchan (page 112)
Stinging Nettle Banchan (page 114)
Mushroom Banchan (page 115)
Aminos-Marinated Eggs (page 145)

To assemble the bibimbap, put a base layer of cooked rice in the bottom of each bowl, dolsot, or cast-iron skillet. To achieve a crispy rice for bibimbap in a cast-iron skillet, preheat the skillet over medium-high heat and allow to preheat for a few minutes. It's important to use a well-seasoned cast-iron skillet for better non-stick properties and heat distribution. Add a generous amount of sesame oil to the preheated skillet. Carefully add the cooled rice and press down on it gently, compacting it slightly. Let the rice cook undisturbed for a few minutes to allow the bottom layer to crisp up.

Once the rice is crispy, transfer it to a serving dish and use it as a base for your bibimbap. Add the banchan in sections around the perimeter of the bowl, place an egg in the center, and serve.

Fiddlehead Fern Banchan

(GOSARI NAMUL)

Fiddlehead ferns grow wild in certain parts of the United States and Canada. We have foraged for fiddleheads in Northern California and the Appalachians. They're extremely tasty and quite nutritious, being high in antioxidants, iron, potassium, and even omega-3 fatty acids. You may be able to find them at the farmers market in season or dried.

Yield: 2 to 4 servings

1 ounce (28 g) dried Bracken Fernbrake Gosari fiddlehead ferns *or* 1 cup (120 g) fresh fiddlehead ferns

1 teaspoon tamari or coconut aminos

1 teaspoon minced garlic

1 tablespoon unsalted grass-fed butter

¼ cup (60 mL) Gelatinous Chicken Bone Broth (page 48) or Beef Bone and Marrow Broth (page 50)

1½ teaspoons toasted sesame oil

1½ teaspoons toasted sesame seeds

1 scallion, sliced

Put the fiddlehead ferns in a bowl, cover with water, and soak for at least 4 hours, or overnight, at room temperature.

Bring a medium saucepan of water to a boil. Drain the fiddleheads and add them to the boiling water, making sure they are completely submerged. Boil for 30 minutes, then turn off the heat and let cool in the pan of water. Drain and rinse well under cold running water.

Go through the fiddleheads and trim any hard woody bits from the stems. Cut into 3- to 4-inch (7.5–10 cm) lengths.

Put the fiddleheads in a bowl, add the tamari and garlic, and set aside to rest for 10 to 15 minutes.

Melt the butter in a large skillet over medium heat. Add the fiddleheads and sauté for 5 minutes. Pour in the broth and cook for another 5 minutes, stirring occasionally. Add the sesame oil, sesame seeds, and scallion and stir well. Serve immediately, or store in an airtight container in the refrigerator for up to 4 days.

▶ HOW TO FORAGE FOR FIDDLEHEAD FERNS

Foraging for fiddlehead ferns can be an enjoyable way to connect with nature and discover a delicious wild edible. Here are some guidelines to help you safely forage for and prepare fiddlehead ferns:

- Fiddlehead ferns emerge in the spring, usually around April or May, depending on your location. Look for the tightly coiled green shoots resembling the head of a fiddle or a violin.
- Learn to correctly identify fiddlehead ferns so you avoid consuming the wrong plant. Fiddleheads are typically found on ostrich ferns (*Matteuccia struthiopteris*). There are unique characteristics such as the brown papery scale on the young shoots and a distinctive U-shaped groove on the inside of the stem.
- Harvest only a small portion of the fiddleheads from each fern plant, leaving enough to allow for future plant growth and reproduction.
- Always source from clean areas, free from pollution such as runoff or contaminated soil. Stay away from fiddleheads that grow near highways or heavily sprayed agricultural fields.
- Use a sharp knife or scissors to cut the fiddleheads at the base, leaving a few inches of the stem attached.
- Once you've gathered your fiddleheads, rinse them thoroughly under cold running water to remove any dirt or debris. Trim off any brown or wilted parts.

Foraging Safety

Hundreds of years ago, our ancestors depended on foraging as a primary means of obtaining food before the industrialization of the food system. Foraging for wild edible foods is not only a way to feel more connected to the land but can also provide a sense of self-reliance. It is also an enjoyable pastime! However, it's important to proceed with caution and consume only those plants and fungi you can positively identify. Consult a regional foraging book or venture out with a trusted guide until you know what you're looking for.

Stinging Nettle Banchan
(SIGUMCHI NAMUL)

Traditionally, sautéed spinach is used in bibimbap, but once you've tried stinging nettle banchan, it's hard to go back! Stinging nettle is considered a medicinal plant thanks to its many health benefits. It is high in vitamins A, C, and K as well as minerals such as iron and calcium. It also contains antioxidants and anti-inflammatory compounds. Stinging nettles grow wild in Northern California, and we could forage for these all over our land. Always harvest before the plants flower.

When foraging and preparing stinging nettles, be sure to wear gloves or use tongs to avoid getting stung. The stinging sensation is a sharp, burning pain accompanied by itching and irritation. This lasts for a few minutes or a few hours, depending on the individual's sensitivity, and generally subsides on its own. By cooking the stinging nettles, you neutralize the sting and make them perfectly safe to eat. If stinging nettles don't grow wild near you or you don't have access to them where you are, simply substitute spinach.

Yield: 2 to 4 servings

8 ounces (225 g) stinging nettles
1 garlic clove, minced
1 scallion, sliced
1 teaspoon tamari or coconut aminos
½ teaspoon toasted sesame oil
1 teaspoon toasted sesame seeds

Bring a large pot of water to a boil. Wearing gloves, rinse the stinging nettles under cold running water. Add the nettles to the boiling water and blanch for 30 seconds to 1 minute. Drain the nettles and rinse under cold running water. Squeeze out the excess water and cut the nettles into bite-size pieces.

Put the nettles in a bowl, add the garlic, scallion, tamari, sesame oil, and sesame seeds, and stir well. Serve immediately, or store in an airtight container in the refrigerator for up to 4 days.

Note: Stinging nettles have diuretic properties and should be avoided by individuals who have low blood pressure or kidney disease or who are pregnant. If you have any of these conditions, consult with a doctor before consuming stinging nettles.

Mushroom Banchan
(BEUSEUS NAMUL)

You can use any variety of mushrooms for this dish, such as button, shiitake, beech, or oyster mushrooms, whether foraged or store-bought. Dried mushrooms will also work; just soak them in water overnight and drain before slicing. This banchan is delicious when we make it with lion's mane and oyster mushrooms that we forage on our land!

Yield: 2 to 4 servings

1 tablespoon unsalted grass-fed butter
8 ounces (225 g) mushrooms, thinly sliced
1 garlic clove, minced
2 teaspoons tamari or coconut aminos
1 teaspoon toasted sesame oil
1 teaspoon toasted sesame seeds

Melt the butter in a large skillet over medium-high heat. Add the mushrooms and stir-fry until they begin to brown, 5 to 8 minutes. Add the garlic and sauté for 2 minutes.

Remove from the heat and stir in the tamari, sesame oil, and sesame seeds and stir well. Serve immediately, or store in an airtight container in the refrigerator for up to 4 days.

Zesty Vegetable "Lo Mein" Zucchini Noodles

This healthier and gluten-free twist on classic lo mein noodles is a great addition to a family meal or gathering, as a main dish on its own or over rice. The colorful and nutritious vegetables combined with the flavorful sauce make this a satisfying and nourishing meal that the whole family will love. A spiralizer makes quick work of preparing the zucchini noodles, but if you don't have one, you can purchase store-made "zoodles" or use a julienne peeler.

Yield: 4 servings

3 tablespoons (45 mL) coconut oil or ghee

3 garlic cloves, minced

1 tablespoon grated fresh ginger

3 to 4 cups (200–400 g) bite-size vegetables, such as sliced bell peppers, sliced mushrooms, shredded carrots, small broccoli florets, and/or snow peas

2 to 3 medium zucchinis, spiralized

¼ cup (60 mL) Gelatinous Chicken Bone Broth (page 48)

2 tablespoons (30 mL) tamari or soy sauce

2 tablespoons (30 mL) toasted sesame oil

1 tablespoon arrowroot starch

¼ cup (10 g) chopped fresh cilantro (optional)

Fine sea salt and ground black pepper

In a large skillet or wok, heat the coconut oil over medium-high heat. Add the garlic and ginger to the wok, and cook, stirring, for 2 minutes. Add the vegetables and cook until they start to soften, 3 to 4 minutes. Add the zucchini noodles and continue to stir-fry until tender, 2 to 3 minutes.

In a small bowl, whisk together the broth, tamari, sesame oil, and arrowroot. Pour the sauce over the vegetables and stir until the sauce has thickened and evenly coats the noodles and vegetables.

Top with the cilantro, if using, and season with salt and pepper to taste. Serve hot.

CHAPTER 5

Soups

For thousands of years, many Asian cultures have believed that the secret to health and healing lies in balancing the body's internal systems. This belief is reflected in traditional Chinese medicine (TCM), which views the body as a holistic entity and makes no clear distinction between food and medicine. In fact, "yi chi tong yuan" is a Chinese saying that states that food and medicine are from the same source. This perspective has led to a deep respect for the healing properties of food, which is woven into the fabric of everyday Asian cuisine.

While some medicinal herbs and ingredients are particularly potent and used only for severe illnesses, many are as common in Asian cooking as ketchup and mustard are in America. Most traditional Asian recipes use a wide array of herbs, spices, and other seasonings, such as ginger, garlic, scallions, star anise, and cinnamon, that have been shown to have a variety of health benefits. For example, ginger is used to aid digestion and relieve nausea, while garlic has antimicrobial and immune-boosting properties.

After I gave birth to my first child, my mother began to return to some of the traditions she had grown up with. She would recount stories of the dire circumstances surrounding childbirth in underdeveloped Asian countries and emphasized the importance of taking care of the health of both the mother and baby.

My mother would tell of her mother-in-law, who had taken great care of her while she recovered from childbirth, unable to even leave the bed for forty days. I remember many meals of her gà ác (evil chicken) stew, made with black chicken, which is believed in Vietnamese culture to have healing properties. Other Asian healing soups after childbirth include pork trotters or pork feet, believed to help with lactation. My Korean friend brought over a seaweed soup as part of my postpartum recovery, as this healing soup is believed to provide nourishment and support during this crucial time.

In the West, there has been a recent resurgence of interest in reviving traditional foods and preparation techniques. This has led to a blending of East and West, with many Western recipes incorporating traditional Asian ingredients and cooking techniques, with a shared emphasis on seasonal and locally sourced foods. The body's needs change throughout the year, and consuming foods that are in season and grown locally can provide the nutrients and energy needed to support optimal health.

Korean Healing Soup

(MIYEOK-GUK)

Korean seaweed soup, known as miyeok-guk, is traditionally eaten on birthdays and by new mothers, as it is believed to have healing properties. This soup was a godsend when my Korean friend dropped it off for me when I had just given birth to my second child at home. This is so easy to prepare and digest that, for the first year after giving birth, I would eat this soup every day! This soup can be served with rice on the side for a more filling meal. I like it with sprouted wild rice (see page 64) and Turmeric-Ginger Kimchi (page 105). Adding an egg is optional, but it contributes a rich texture and also adds nutrient density and an extra boost of protein.

Yield: 2 to 4 servings

4 ounces (115 g) dried miyeok
   (Korean seaweed)
½ pound (225 g) grass-fed beef flank
   steak or brisket, sliced thinly
6 cups (1.5 L) spring water
2 tablespoons (30 mL) toasted sesame oil
2 tablespoons (60 mL) tamari
2 tablespoons (18 g) minced garlic
Fine sea salt and ground black pepper
1 large pasture-raised egg, beaten (optional)
1 scallion, thinly sliced (optional)

Put the miyeok in a bowl, cover with cold water, and let soak for at least 30 minutes, until it has expanded and become soft.

Meanwhile, in a large pot, combine the beef, spring water, sesame oil, tamari, and garlic. Season with salt and pepper to taste. Bring to a boil and skim off any foam. Reduce the heat to low and simmer for 1 hour, or until the beef is tender.

Drain the miyeok, rinse it thoroughly, and squeeze out the water. Add the miyeok to the pot and simmer for an additional 20 minutes, until the miyeok is tender.

If using the egg, pour it into the soup and stir until it is cooked.

Garnish with scallions, if you like, and serve hot.

Oxtail Beef Phở
(PHỞ ĐUÔI BÒ)

When I would come home from track meets in high school, I always craved a bowl of this perfect oxtail beef phở, with wide noodles, brisket, and rare beef. A beautiful bowl of phở is a sensory delight. The steam rising from the bowl carries the rich aroma of slow-cooked bone broth, warming spices, and fresh herbs. The broth itself is a deep, golden-brown color, clear and shimmering, with a rich depth of flavor that is both savory and comforting. Thin slices of tender, rare beef float in the broth, along with silky rice noodles that are soft and chewy. The bowl is garnished with a vibrant mix of fresh herbs, chili peppers for a touch of heat, and a squeeze of lime juice. The finished bowl of phở is a masterpiece of balance and complexity, a harmony of textures and flavors that is both nourishing and deeply satisfying.

My father likes to crack a raw egg into his bowl of phở. This variation is most commonly found in Hanoi, where my mother's family is from. The egg cooks slightly in the hot broth, creating a creamy texture and adding richness to the soup. Make sure you use fresh, high-quality eggs from a trusted source if you choose to include them in your phở. If you have many eggs from your backyard chickens, as we do, this is a delicious and nourishing way to use them in your family meals.

You can substitute zucchini noodles or tagliatelle for the rice noodles. The bone marrow in the oxtail adds extra flavor and is a good source of protein, iron, collagen, and gelatin.

Yield: 8 to 10 servings

4 pounds (1.8 kg) grass-fed oxtail, cut into 2- to 3-inch (5–7.5 cm) chunks

1 to 2 pounds (450–900 kg) grass-fed beef marrow bones

2 pounds (900 kg) grass-fed beef brisket

1 pound (450 g) grass-fed eye of round, thinly sliced

2 gallons (7.5 L) spring water

5 star anise pods

3 whole cloves

1 cinnamon stick

2 tablespoons (36 g) black cardamom seeds

Rinse the oxtail, marrow bones, and brisket under cold water and place in a large pot. Fill with cold water and bring to a boil. Skim off the impurities, then drain. Rinse out the pot and return the parboiled oxtail, marrow bones, and brisket to the pot. Add the spring water and bring to a boil.

Meanwhile, in a small skillet, combine the star anise, cloves, cinnamon, black cardamom seeds, coriander seeds, and fennel seeds and toast over high heat for 3 to 4 minutes. Transfer the toasted spices to a spice bag or tea strainer. (Alternatively, you can put the spices directly in the pot of broth and strain them out before serving.)

1 tablespoon coriander seeds

1 tablespoon fennel seeds

1 large onion, halved

1 (4-inch [10 cm]) piece fresh ginger, halved

1 tablespoon sea salt

5 tablespoons (74 mL) fish sauce or
   Fermented Anchovy Sauce (page 70)

3 tablespoons (45 mL) maple sugar or
   coconut sugar (optional)

FOR SERVING

1 (16-ounce [454 g]) package fresh wide
   noodles or dried flat rice noodles
   (pad thai)

Bean sprouts

3 scallions, sliced lengthwise

½ small yellow or red onion, very thinly
   sliced, or Pickled Red Onions (page 102)

½ cup (20 g) fresh cilantro leaves

4 to 6 Thai basil sprigs

4 to 6 mint sprigs

Fresh Vietnamese culantro or sawtooth
   (optional)

Lime wedges

Bird's eye chilies, sliced (optional)

Hoisin Sauce (page 80)

Sriracha or Sambal Oelek (page 85)

To char the onion and ginger, turn a gas stove burner to high heat or a grill to medium-high. Using tongs, carefully place the onion and ginger directly on the burner or grill grates. Allow them to cook undisturbed for a few minutes, until the bottoms are charred and blackened. Use the tongs to flip the onion and ginger to char the other side. Once charred, remove the onion and ginger from the heat and allow to cool slightly. Using your fingers or a knife, peel off the blackened outer layers of the onion and ginger and discard. (Alternatively, you can place the onion and ginger on a rimmed baking sheet and broil them in the oven. Keep an eye on them so they don't burn!)

Add the spice bag, onion, and ginger to the broth. Simmer for 1 hour, occasionally skimming off the scum that rises to the top.

Add the salt, cover, bring to a low simmer, and cook for 4 hours. Skim off any foam that rises to the surface.

Remove the oxtail and brisket from the pot and set aside to cool. Once the meat is cool enough to handle, thinly slice the brisket, cover, and set aside.

Simmer the broth with the marrow bones, uncovered, for another hour.

Strain the broth through a fine-mesh strainer, discarding any solids. Return the broth to the pot and add the fish sauce and sugar (if using). Season with additional salt or fish sauce to taste.

Cook the rice noodles according to the package instructions until chewy. Rinse under cold water and drain.

To serve, divide the noodles into serving bowls. Pour the broth over the noodles and top with the oxtail meat, sliced brisket, eye of round slices, bean sprouts, scallions, onion, and herbs. Offer lime wedges, chilies, hoisin sauce, and sriracha or sambal oelek sauce on the side.

Store leftovers in an airtight container in the refrigerator for up to 3 days or in the freezer for up to 6 months; if freezing, make sure to leave at least 1 inch (2.5 cm) headspace in your jars.

Oxtail Beef Phở

Vietnamese Chicken Noodle Soup
(PHỞ GÀ)

This soup is so simple to put together and is enjoyed by all ages in any kind of weather! The children tell me that they could eat this every day, so it's something we have at least weekly, even in the heat of the summer. This is a much lighter variation of beef phở, and my mother's secret is to always have some black cardamom on hand. If you were out of all your spices, this is truly the only one you would need for a good bowl of phở gà. I also use dried jujubes and daikon for a natural and medicinal sweetener. You can substitute zucchini noodles or homemade tagliatelle for the rice noodles. For increased nutrient density and an extra crunch without affecting the flavor profile of the soup, I quickly blanch some bok choy and cut it up for the family to enjoy.

Yield: 4 to 6 servings

10 cups (2.4 L) spring water,
   or more as needed
½ daikon, peeled and quartered (optional)
10 dried jujube apples *or* 1 (4-ounce [115 g])
   Fuji apple
1 (4- to 5-pound [1.8–2.3 kg])
   pasture-raised chicken
5 star anise pods
3 whole cloves
1 cinnamon stick
2 tablespoons (36 g) black cardamom seeds
1 tablespoon coriander seeds
1 tablespoon fennel seeds
1 large onion, halved
1 (4-inch [10 cm]) piece fresh ginger, halved
1 tablespoon sea salt
5 tablespoons (74 mL) fish sauce or
   Fermented Anchovy Sauce (page 70)
3 tablespoons maple sugar or coconut
   sugar (optional)

In a large pot, combine the water, daikon (if using), and jujube apples and bring to a boil. Add the chicken, plus more water if needed to cover the chicken, and return to a boil.

Meanwhile, in a small skillet, combine the star anise, cloves, cinnamon, black cardamom seeds, coriander seeds, and fennel seeds and toast over high heat for 3 to 4 minutes. Transfer the toasted spices to a spice bag or tea strainer. (Alternatively, you can put the spices directly in the pot of broth and strain them out before serving.)

To char the onion and ginger, turn a gas stove burner to high heat or a grill to medium-high. Using tongs, carefully place the onion and ginger directly on the burner or grill grates. Allow them to cook undisturbed for a few minutes, until the bottom is charred and blackened. Use the tongs to flip the onion and ginger to char the other side. Once charred, remove the onion and ginger from the heat and allow to cool slightly. Using your fingers or a knife, peel off the blackened outer layers of the onion and ginger and discard. (Alternatively, you can place the onion and ginger on a rimmed baking sheet and broil them in the oven. Keep an eye on them so they don't burn!)

continued on page 124

FOR SERVING

8 baby bok choy

1 (16-ounce [454 g]) package dried flat rice noodles (pad Thai)

Garnishes:

- ½ cup (20 g) fresh cilantro leaves
- 3 scallions, sliced lengthwise
- ½ small yellow or red onion, very thinly sliced, or Pickled Red Onions (page 102)
- 4 to 6 Thai basil sprigs
- 4 to 6 mint sprigs
- Bean sprouts
- Lime wedges
- Fresh Vietnamese culantro or sawtooth (optional)
- Bird's eye chilies, sliced (optional)
- Hoisin Sauce (page 80)
- Sriracha or Sambal Oelek (page 85)

Add the spice bag, onion, and ginger to the broth. Simmer for 1 hour, occasionally skimming off the scum that rises to the top.

Remove the chicken from the pot and pierce through the thigh with a chopstick or fork to check if the juices run clear. If not, return it to the pot to simmer for a while more, until fully cooked. Set aside to cool.

Remove the daikon, apples, spice bag (or whole spices), onion, and ginger from the broth. Season the broth with the salt, fish sauce, and sugar, if using.

Remove the chicken meat from the bones and cut it into ½-inch (13 mm) pieces for easy handling with chopsticks. Alternatively, you can hand tear the chicken pieces and add them directly to the bowls.

Bring a large pot of water to a boil. Add the bok choy and blanch for 1 to 2 minutes. Drain the bok choy and cut into bite-size pieces.

Cook the rice noodles according to the package instructions until chewy. Rinse under cold running water and drain.

To serve, divide the noodles into each serving bowl and top with chicken meat and bok choy. Ladle in the hot broth and top with your choice of garnishes. Offer hoisin sauce and sriracha or sambal oelek at the table.

Store leftovers in an airtight container in the refrigerator for up to 4 days or in the freezer for up to 6 months; if freezing, make sure to leave at least 1 inch (2.5 cm) headspace in your jars.

Time hacks: You can start with Gelatinous Chicken Bone Broth (page 48) and simmer for 1 hour with the spices, onion, and ginger and serve with chicken meat. Alternatively, use the carcass from a rotisserie chicken to make the broth, then serve the meat with the soup.

Vietnamese Sweet-and-Sour Tamarind Soup
(CANH CHUA CÁ)

Canh chua cá has been enjoyed for centuries. The soup has its roots in the Mekong Delta region of Vietnam, where freshwater fish are abundant and tamarind trees grow plentifully. It was originally created as a way to use up fish that had been caught in the river, and the sour flavor of tamarind was added to balance the fishy taste. Over time, the recipe evolved to include other tart ingredients such as pineapple or vinegar, as well as a variety of fresh vegetables and herbs.

Today, canh chua cá is a popular dish throughout Vietnam and a staple of many Vietnamese households, enjoyed both at home and in restaurants. It is typically served with steamed rice. This soup is the perfect umami complement to Vietnamese Caramelized Fish (page 220).

Yield: 4 to 6 servings

1 tablespoon sesame oil
1 small onion, thinly sliced
2 garlic cloves, minced
1 to 2 tablespoons (15–30 mL) tamarind paste
1 quart (1 L) Fish Broth (page 47) or spring water
1 small pineapple, peeled, cored, and cut into bite-size pieces
1 medium tomato, chopped
½ cup (75 g) chopped okra
1 or 2 bird's eye chilies, thinly sliced (optional)
1 pound (450 g) firm white fish fillets (such as cod or tilapia), cut into bite-size pieces
1 cup (90 g) bean sprouts
¼ cup (10 g) chopped fresh cilantro
1 tablespoon fish sauce or Fermented Anchovy Sauce (page 70)
1 tablespoon panela or coconut sugar
Fine sea salt and ground black pepper
Steamed rice (pages 62–63), for serving

Heat the oil in a large pot over medium-high heat. Add the onion and garlic and sauté for 2 to 3 minutes, until fragrant. Stir in the tamarind paste, fish broth, pineapple, tomato, okra, and chilies (if using). Bring to a boil, then reduce the heat and let simmer for 10 to 15 minutes, until the pineapple is tender.

Add the fish and simmer for 5 to 7 minutes, until the fish is cooked through.

Add the bean sprouts and cilantro and simmer for 1 to 2 minutes, until the bean sprouts are slightly softened.

Season the soup with the fish sauce, panela, and salt and pepper to taste. Serve hot, with steamed rice. This dish is best eaten the day it is made.

Vietnamese Pork and Shrimp Tapioca Noodle Soup

(BÁNH CANH GIÒ HEO)

Nothing compares to this comforting and flavorsome broth with thick, chewy noodles. It's a less well-known soup compared to phở and bún bò Huế, perhaps because not many restaurants serve it, but it's a versatile, comforting dish that appeals to all ages. It's especially easy to whip up on busy days when you don't want to spend so much time in the kitchen. Cleaning pork with vinegar before making soup is a common practice in some culinary traditions; the process removes impurities and odors from the meat and improves the texture as well.

Yield: 4 to 6 servings

½ cup (120 mL) apple cider vinegar
1½ cups (360 mL) spring water
1 pound (450 g) pasture-raised pork hock
1 pound (450 g) pork belly (optional)
1 onion, peeled
1 large daikon, peeled and quartered
1 large carrot, peeled and quartered
1 pound (450 g) large wild-caught shrimp, peeled and deveined
3 tablespoons (45 mL) fish sauce or Fermented Anchovy Sauce (page 70)
1 tablespoon coconut sugar (optional)
Fine sea salt and ground black pepper

FOR SERVING

4 to 6 pasture-raised quail eggs (optional)
Tapioca Udon Noodles (opposite) or store-bought udon noodles, cooked
2 cups (80 g) chopped fresh cilantro
Crispy Fried Shallots (page 86)
3 scallions, sliced

> **Note:** I recommend sourcing pasture-raised quail eggs from a local farmer, or you can also use chicken eggs as an alternative.

To clean the pork, combine the vinegar and water in a large pot. Submerge the pork hock and belly (if using) in the mixture and let it soak for 15 to 20 minutes. Drain, then rinse the pork under cold running water to wash away any remaining vinegar and debris. Pat the pork dry.

Rinse out the pot, fill it with fresh water, and bring to a boil. Add the pork and bring to a boil again, then boil for 10 minutes, skimming off any scum that rises to the surface. Drain.

Rinse the pot again, put the pork in, and cover with fresh water. Add the onion, daikon, and carrot. Bring to a boil and simmer for 45 minutes to 1 hour, skimming off any scum from the top, until the pork is cooked through. Strain the broth, discarding the spent vegetables. Remove the pork hock and pork belly and set aside until cool, then slice the pork belly.

Add the shrimp to the broth and cook for 5 to 8 minutes, until cooked through. Using a skimmer, scoop the shrimp out of the broth and set aside. Season the broth with the fish sauce, coconut sugar (if using), and salt and pepper to taste.

Meanwhile, if using the quail eggs, bring a small pot of water to a boil. Reduce the heat to medium-low and carefully add the quail eggs. Simmer for 3 to 4 minutes. Fill a large bowl with ice and cold water. Using a slotted spoon, transfer the eggs to the ice bath for at least 5 minutes to cool, then peel and halve the eggs.

To serve, divide the noodles into serving bowls. Add some pork, shrimp, and 2 quail egg halves to each bowl. Sprinkle with the cilantro, fried shallots, and scallions. Ladle the hot broth over the noodles and serve immediately.

Tapioca Udon Noodles

2 cups (256 g) tapioca starch
2 cups (320 g) rice flour
½ teaspoon fine sea salt
2½ cups (600 mL) spring water, heated
1½ teaspoons sesame oil

Note: *If you don't want to make udon noodles from scratch, look for preservative-free fresh or frozen udon noodles in Asian markets.*

Bring a large pot of water to a boil. Fill a large bowl with ice and cold water.

In a large bowl, whisk together the tapioca starch, rice flour, and salt. Add the hot spring water and the oil and mix with a spatula or wooden spoon until a shaggy dough forms. Use your hands to knead the dough for 3 to 5 minutes, until it becomes smooth and elastic.

Press portions of the dough through a potato ricer into the boiling water. Do not stir until the noodles begin to rise to the top of the water, then gently stir the noodles, being careful not to break them.

Use a spider or slotted spoon to transfer the noodles to the ice bath. This will stop the noodles from cooking further and keep them chewy. Drain and serve right away.

Vietnamese Crab Noodle Soup
(BÚN RIÊU)

Bún riêu is a flavorful Vietnamese rice noodle soup that boasts a unique blend of sweet and tangy tomato flavors. This soup is traditionally prepared with a variety of seafood ingredients, including crab and shrimp, which add depth and richness to the dish. The combination of savory broth, tender noodles, and fragrant herbs make bún riêu a satisfying and popular meal. This is a simplified and budget-friendly version of the traditional recipe, which is known for being complex and challenging to prepare.

Yield: 4 to 6 servings

FOR THE CRAB MEATBALLS

3 large pasture-raised eggs

6 to 8 ounces (170–225 g) crabmeat
  (preferably fresh)

8 ounces (225 g) ground pasture-raised pork

1 bunch scallions, sliced

1 tablespoon fish sauce or Fermented
  Anchovy Sauce (page 70)

FOR THE SOUP

½ cup (120 mL) apple cider vinegar

1 pound (450 g) pasture-raised pork bones

½ cup (120 mL) sesame oil

1 head garlic, minced

1 bunch scallions, cut into 2-inch (5 cm) pieces

3 tomatoes, cut into wedges

3 quarts (3 L) spring water

1 large onion, sliced

2 teaspoons fine sea salt

½ cup (85 g) pineapple chunks, fresh or
  canned (drained)

3 tablespoons (45 mL) fish sauce or
  Fermented Anchovy Sauce (page 70)

1 tablespoon Fermented Shrimp Paste
  (page 84; optional)

FOR SERVING

1 (16-ounce [454 g]) package rice vermicelli,
  cooked

Crispy Fried Shallots (page 86; optional)

½ large onion, thinly sliced

1 bunch scallions, thinly sliced

Fresh mint leaves (optional)

To prepare the crab meatballs, beat the eggs in a large bowl. Add the crabmeat, ground pork, and scallions and mix well. Season with the fish sauce. Set aside in the refrigerator until needed.

To clean the pork bones, add the vinegar to a large pot of water. Submerge the pork bones and let soak for 15 to 20 minutes. Drain, then rinse the bones under cold running water to wash away any remaining vinegar and debris. Pat the bones dry.

Rinse out the pot, fill it with fresh water, and bring to a boil. Add the pork bones and bring to a boil again, then boil for 10 minutes, skimming off any scum that rises to the surface. Drain.

Rinse the pot again, put the bones in, and cover with the spring water. Bring to a boil and simmer for 1 hour.

In a separate pot, heat the oil over medium heat. Add the garlic and scallions and sauté until fragrant, about 2 minutes. Add the tomatoes and stir well, then cover and cook for 3 minutes. Add the onion, salt, pineapple, fish sauce, and shrimp paste (if using), and pour into the pork broth. Scoop walnut-size portions of the crab mixture, roll into balls, and add to the broth. Cook until the meatballs float to the surface, about 3 minutes.

To serve, divide the noodles into the serving bowls, then ladle the soup with meatballs over the noodles. Top with fried shallots, sliced onion, scallions, and mint, if desired.

Vietnamese Spicy Beef Noodle Soup
(BÚN BÒ HUẾ)

Bún bò Huế originated in central Vietnam in the city of Huế, where my father's family is from. After my parents were married, my mom learned to make this dish by visiting multiple street food vendors to try different variations and perfect her recipe. When my parents emigrated to Seattle in 1975, my mom began making it for friends and family. She became well known for this delectable, full-bodied Vietnamese soup with beef and noodles, loaded with an array of exciting and flavorful ingredients. Rice noodles are traditional, but we have been using regular spaghetti since my mother came to America when there were few if any Asian grocery stores! If you don't want to use spaghetti, you can use rice noodles, zucchini noodles, or ramen noodles (gluten-free, if desired).

Yield: 4 to 6 servings

FOR THE BROTH

3 tablespoons (45 g) fine sea salt, divided

½ cup (120 mL) apple cider vinegar, divided

2 pounds (900 g) grass-fed beef bones

2 pounds (900 g) pasture-raised pork hock, sliced 1-inch (2.5 cm) thick

5 quarts (4.75 L) spring water

2 pounds (450 g) grass-fed beef shank

1 large onion, peeled

4 lemongrass stalks, tough outer layer removed, tenderized (see page 44), and chopped

1 large daikon, peeled and quartered (optional)

10 dried jujube apples or 1 (4-ounce [115 g]) Fuji apple

2 tablespoons (30 g) coconut sugar or panela

2 tablespoons (30 mL) Fermented Shrimp Paste (page 84), divided

¼ cup (60 mL) fish sauce or Fermented Anchovy Sauce (page 70)

To make the broth, fill two large pots with water and add 1½ teaspoons of the sea salt and ¼ cup (60 mL) of the vinegar to each. Add the beef bones to one pot and the pork hock to the other and bring to a boil. Boil each for 3 to 5 minutes, until the impurities rise to the top. Drain and rinse the beef bones and pork hock well under cold running water.

Rinse out one of the pots and put the beef bones and pork hock in it. Add the spring water, beef shank, onion, lemongrass, daikon (if using), jujube apples, coconut sugar, and remaining 2 tablespoons sea salt and bring to a boil. Lower the heat to medium-low and simmer, skimming occasionally, until the pork hock is tender, about 45 minutes. Fill a bowl with ice and cold water. Transfer the pork hock to the ice bath. The beef shank should be cooked through but not yet tender; transfer it to a cutting board. Return the broth to a simmer.

In a small bowl, combine 1 tablespoon of the shrimp paste with ½ cup (120 mL) room-temperature water and stir well till dissolved. Let sit for 30 minutes to settle the dregs. Pour off the top part of the mixture and stir it into the soup.

¼ cup (60 mL) sesame oil

1 tablespoon annatto seeds

¼ cup (25 g) minced lemongrass

2 tablespoons (35 g) minced shallot

1 tablespoon minced garlic

FOR THE SOUP

1 pound (450 g) spaghetti or cassava noodles

8 ounces (225 g) grass-fed beef brisket,
    thinly sliced

8 ounces (225 g) Pork Loaf (page 135), sliced

FOR SERVING

½ cup (60 g) thinly sliced yellow onion

½ cup (20 g) chopped fresh cilantro leaves

½ cup (30 g) thinly sliced scallions

2 limes, cut into wedges

2 cups (180 g) bean sprouts

2 jalapeños, stemmed, seeded,
    and thinly sliced

To make the sa té oil, heat the oil in a small sauce-pan over medium heat, then add the annatto seeds. Wait 30 seconds for them to release their color. Strain, discard the seeds, and return the oil to the pan. Add the lemongrass, shallot, and garlic and sauté until fragrant, about 5 minutes. Lower the heat to medium-low, and cook, stirring, for 2 minutes, or until thickened. Remove from the heat and let the oil cool, then add it to the simmering broth with the fish sauce.

Let the broth cook at a rolling simmer for a total of 3 hours. About 50 minutes before it will be done, add the brisket and return to a simmer until the meat is cooked through and tender. Discard the onion, lemongrass, daikon (if used), apples, and beef bones. Season to taste with additional salt and fish sauce if needed.

Cook the spaghetti according to the package instructions until al dente.

Slice the beef shank.

Divide the spaghetti into serving bowls. Top with the beef shank, pork hock, and pork loaf, then ladle that fragrant and delicious broth over the top. Sprinkle with sliced onion and cilantro and serve with lime wedges, bean sprouts, and jalapeños.

Vietnamese Spicy Beef Noodle Soup

Pork Loaf

(CHẢ LỤA)

Vietnamese pork loaf, also known as Chả Lụa or giò lụa, is a popular component in many Vietnamese dishes. You can use it in bánh mì sandwiches or as a topping for rice noodles.

Yield: 4 servings

1 pound (450 g) ground pork
¼ cup (32 g) tapioca starch
¼ cup (60 mL) fish sauce or Fermented
  Anchovy Sauce (page 70)
¼ cup (60 g) panela
3 garlic cloves, minced
½ teaspoon fine sea salt
½ teaspoon ground black pepper
½ cup (120 g) crushed ice
Sesame oil or banana leaves, for the pan

In a large bowl, combine the pork, tapioca starch, fish sauce, panela, garlic, salt, and pepper. Mix well, until all the ingredients are evenly incorporated.

Add the crushed ice and use your hands to mix everything together. Transfer the pork mixture to a food processor and blend into a smooth paste.

Oil a loaf pan or round baking pan that will fit in a large stockpot. (Alternatively, you can line it with banana leaves or parchment paper for easy removal.) Scrape the pork mixture into the pan, pressing down gently to remove any air pockets.

Place the pan in the stockpot and add enough water to come about three-quarters of the way up the sides of the pan. Bring the water to a boil over high heat, then reduce the heat to low and cover the pot with a lid.

Allow the pork loaf to steam for about 1 hour, or until it is firm and fully cooked. To test if it's done, insert a toothpick or knife into the center of the loaf— if it comes out clean, the loaf is cooked. Remove the pan from the stockpot and let it cool to room temperature, then slice and serve.

Chicken Rice Porridge
(CHÁO GÀ)

After making Gelatinous Chicken Bone Broth (page 48), I often divide the remaining cooked chicken meat in half and make two complementary dishes from one whole pasture-raised chicken—this porridge and Vietnamese Chicken Salad (page 147). These are great, budget-friendly dishes to share with friends and family.

Yield: 2 to 4 servings

1 cup (190 g) jasmine rice or glutinous rice

8 to 10 cups (2–2.4 L) Gelatinous Chicken Bone Broth (page 48) or spring water

1 pound (450 g) bone-in, skin-on pasture-raised chicken breasts or thighs

2 or 3 garlic cloves, minced

1 teaspoon grated fresh ginger

Fine sea salt and ground black pepper

Optional toppings: sliced scallions, chopped fresh cilantro, Crispy Fried Shallots (page 86), sliced fresh ginger, fish sauce or Fermented Anchovy Sauce (page 70), tamari, Lemongrass Chili Oil (page 90)

Put the rice in a bowl, cover with water, and soak overnight. Drain, rinse the rice under cold running water, and drain again. Repeat until the water runs clear. For a smooth porridge, put the rice in a strainer, set it over a bowl, and put it in the freezer for 2 hours.

In a large pot, bring the broth to a boil over high heat. Add the chicken, garlic, and ginger, reduce the heat to medium-low, cover, and simmer for 30 to 45 minutes, until the chicken is fully cooked and falls off the bone. Using tongs, transfer the chicken to a cutting board and, when cool enough to handle, slice the meat, discarding the bones.

While the chicken is cooling, increase the heat to medium-high and add the rice to the pot. Cook, stirring occasionally, until the rice is fully cooked and has the desired consistency, 30 minutes to 1 hour. Add more liquid for a more soup-like consistency or continue to simmer to thicken up to the consistency of porridge.

Return the sliced chicken to the pot. Season with salt and pepper to taste. Serve hot, with your desired toppings.

Variations

By adding additional grains to your porridge, you can increase the nutrient density and make a more satisfying and nourishing dish. I recommend substituting one of the following grains for half of the rice:

Brown rice adds a nutty flavor and extra fiber to your porridge.
Quinoa is high in protein and provides a slightly crunchy texture.
Steel-cut oats are less processed than rolled oats and add a pleasantly chewy texture.
Millet is a gluten-free grain that is high in protein and has a slightly sweet flavor.
Buckwheat is another gluten-free grain that adds a nutty flavor to porridge.
Amaranth is a tiny grain that is high in protein and has a slightly sweet and nutty flavor.

Nourishing Hot Pot Family Dinner

In the fall and winter, when harvests of kohlrabi, peas, bok choy, napa cabbage, chrysanthemum greens (my favorite!), and squash are abundant, you will find me setting up a hot pot station on many chilly nights, even busy weekdays. Hot pot is a social and interactive meal where friends and family gather around the pot, share food, and engage in conversation while enjoying a comforting and flavorful meal together. All the prep can be done quickly, and cooking is enjoyed together over a pot of nourishing broth. It's one of my favorite ways to host dinner with our friends at home. Your guests will do their own cooking at the table, so no cooking is needed prior to the party!

Hot pot is a simple cooking method that crosses over nearly every Asian cuisine—Chinese, Japanese, Korean, Vietnamese, Thai, Mongolian, and more. In recent years, it has taken off in mainstream restaurants that serve buffet-style meats and vegetables. It involves a communal pot filled with simmering broth placed at the center of the dining table. The pot is heated using a portable stove (either electrical or butane stove). I appreciate this soup not only for its flavorful broth but for its nourishment as well, and we love bringing the restaurant home by making our own!

The broth can be plain or flavored with herbs, spices, and other seasonings to create a rich and aromatic base. We have a "yin yang" style hot pot and like to offer our two favorite soup bases at the same time. One side is spicy for the adults, and the other is a non-spicy option loved by the children! When sourcing the herbs and aromatics, avoid the prepackaged soup bases with preservatives sometimes found in Asian grocery stores.

The ingredients are flexible: mix and match, or offer it all! We like to make this fun and ask the children to come up with new ingredients to add to the pot.

Broth of your choice, such as Miso Soup
Base (recipe below) and/or Thai Tom Yum
Hot Pot Soup Base (page 142)
Thinly sliced boneless meat such as beef
rib eye, lamb shoulder, pork belly or
shoulder, or chicken
Seafood such as shrimp, squid, fish fillets,
or scallops, cleaned and sliced
Vegetables such as Asian greens, okra,
kohlrabi, peas, squash, daikon, taro,
sweet potatoes, and/or mushrooms,
cut into bite-size pieces
Ramen, udon, or mung bean noodles,
parcooked
Equipment: a portable heat source
such as an electric hot pot burner or
tabletop gas burner

Place the portable burner in the middle of the table with a wide pot or a two-sectioned hot pot. Pour the broth(s) into the pot and bring to a boil. Place separate dishes of the ingredients on the table. Add the ingredients of your choice to the pot and simmer until they are cooked through. Using chopsticks, tongs, a skimmer, or a slotted spoon, remove cooked ingredients to individual bowls and eat right away.

Miso Soup Base

This is a very simple, nonspicy soup that is delicious and nourishing and perfect for children. We have so much joy watching them throw in veggies and meat on their own to cook!

Yield: 4 to 6 servings

1 tablespoon sesame oil
1 onion, sliced
4 garlic cloves, minced
2 quarts (2 L) Gelatinous Chicken Bone
Broth (page 48) or Beef Bone and
Marrow Broth (page 50)
2 tablespoons (30 mL) organic white
miso paste
Fine sea salt and ground black pepper

Heat the oil in a large pot over medium heat. Add the onion and garlic and brown lightly to release the aromatic flavors, about 5 minutes.

Add the bone broth and bring to a simmer. Add the miso to the simmering pot of broth, 1 tablespoon at a time, and stir to dissolve. Season to taste with salt, pepper, and more miso if desired.

Thai Tom Yum Hot Pot Soup Base

This soup base creates a delightful balance of sourness, spiciness, and herbal flavors. It is known for its distinct tangy, spicy, and savory taste, characteristic of Thai cuisine. I love to add cilantro, shallots, and garlic to further enhance the taste.

Yield: 4 to 6 servings

6 dried red chilies

1 tablespoon tamarind paste

2 lemongrass stalks, tough outer layer
   removed, each cut into 3 pieces

1 onion, sliced

1 shallot, chopped

4 garlic cloves, minced

5 thin slices fresh ginger

2 tomatoes, cut into wedges

1 cup (40 g) fresh cilantro leaves

3 tablespoons (45 mL) fish sauce or
   Fermented Anchovy Sauce (page 70)

1½ teaspoons paprika

2 quarts (2 L) Gelatinous Chicken Bone
   Broth (page 48) or Beef Bone and
   Marrow Broth (page 50)

Put the chilies in a bowl and add warm water to cover. Put the tamarind paste in another bowl and add ¼ cup (60 mL) warm water. Allow the chilies and tamarind to soak for 15 minutes.

Drain the chilies, remove the seeds, and cut them into 1-inch pieces.

Add the tamarind mixture and chilies to a food processor, along with the lemongrass, onion, shallot, garlic, ginger, tomatoes, cilantro, fish sauce, and paprika. Blend the ingredients into a paste.

Transfer the paste to a large pot. Pour in the broth and mix well, and bring to a boil. Bring to the table when ready to cook hot pot.

> **Note:** If you can't find tamarind paste, substitute 1½ teaspoons lime juice plus 1½ teaspoons brown sugar.

CHAPTER 6

Poultry and Eggs

When I was a kid, my mother loved to cook with gà đi bộ, or "walking chickens." These were chickens that were allowed to roam freely and eat a varied diet, resulting in meat that was richer and more flavorful than conventionally raised chicken.

When our family started to raise our own meat and egg-laying chickens, we saw and tasted the difference in quality that comes from pasture-raised birds. By fermenting their feed and supplementing with clabbered milk (naturally fermented raw or unpasteurized milk), we ensure that our chickens are getting a diverse and nutrient-dense diet, which translates into more nutritious and flavorful meat and eggs.

Not only do pasture-raised chickens taste better, they tend to be healthier and have a lower risk of disease. This is because we give them access to fresh air, sunlight, and open space, which allows them to live in a less stressful environment and exhibit natural behaviors. They are not subjected to the cramped and unsanitary living conditions of conventionally raised chickens, which can lead to the spread of disease.

Even if you cannot raise your own chickens, you can encourage more ethical farming practices by choosing to purchase pasture-raised poultry. Pasture-raised poultry help promote biodiversity and soil health by

grazing on pastureland, which can help to reduce soil erosion and nutrient depletion.

When we decided to venture beyond chicken and add ducks to the farm, we didn't start small: Tim ordered 100 ducks! He called them his "little soldiers" because they followed him around everywhere. When it came time to process them, they were much more challenging to defeather than chicken or turkeys, but we were delighted with the taste of the meat—plus the useful duck fat, which is high in vitamin K2, and the duck eggs, which have higher choline and vitamin B12 than chicken eggs.

As we continue to raise a variety of poultry, we have enjoyed numerous dishes that incorporate the unique flavors and textures of different types of poultry and eggs. From succulent Vietnamese "Rotisserie" Chicken Thighs (page 158) to Vietnamese Chicken Liver Pâté (page 231), there are endless possibilities when it comes to cooking with poultry.

Aminos-Marinated Eggs

(AJITSUKE TAMAGO)

These Japanese-style marinated eggs are a delicious addition on top of salads, ramen, or rice bowls like Wild Bibimbap (page 111). We love these eggs perfectly soft-boiled and slightly runny.

Yield: 4 servings

4 large pasture-raised eggs
¼ cup (60 mL) mirin
¼ cup (60 mL) coconut aminos, soy sauce, or tamari
1 tablespoon ume plum vinegar
¼ teaspoon ground black pepper
½ cup (120 mL) spring water
1 whole garlic clove

Bring a medium pot of water to a boil. Use a slotted spoon to gently lower the eggs into the pot. Set a timer for 6½ minutes and cook the eggs at a gentle boil. (If you prefer firmer or runnier yolks, adjust the cooking time by 30 seconds to 1 minute.)

While the eggs are cooking, fill a bowl with ice and cold water.

As soon as the timer goes off, use the slotted spoon to transfer the eggs to the ice bath to stop cooking. Let the eggs sit in the ice water bath for at least 5 minutes to cool down, then gently peel them and rinse under cold running water. Transfer the eggs to a narrow bowl or container—we use a quart (1 L) jar.

In a small bowl, whisk together the mirin, coconut aminos, vinegar, pepper, and water until well combined.

Pour the marinade over the eggs, making sure they are completely submerged (if not, find a smaller container). Add the garlic. Cover and refrigerate for at least 2 hours, or up to overnight.

When ready to serve, remove the eggs from the marinade and cut them in half lengthwise. Serve right away, or store in the refrigerator for up to 3 days.

Vietnamese Chicken Salad

(GỎI GÀ BẮP CẢI)

This chicken salad is second to none in my opinion! It is a popular dish in Vietnam and also in our home, because it allows me to stretch a poached or grilled chicken with a variety of fresh and pickled vegetables, herbs, and a sweet and tangy dressing. I often serve it with Chicken Rice Porridge (page 136), as the crispy and tangy salad is the perfect complement to the soft and creamy texture of the cháo. I like to take a spoonful of cháo and top it with a scoop of the chicken salad, drizzled with the dressing. I make it with three types of cabbage because they add a delectable crunch and texture to the salad, but you can use just green cabbage.

Yield: 4 to 6 servings

FOR THE DRESSING

6 tablespoons (90 mL) lemon juice

¼ cup (60 mL) fish sauce or Fermented Anchovy Sauce (page 70)

2 tablespoons (30 mL) rice vinegar

2 tablespoons (30 mL) maple syrup

1 teaspoon ground black pepper

FOR THE CHICKEN SALAD

3 cups (300 g) shredded cooked pasture-raised chicken

2 cups (200 g) finely shredded green cabbage

2 cups (200 g) thinly sliced napa cabbage

2 cups (200 g) thinly sliced savoy cabbage

1 carrot, peeled and shredded

3 radishes, thinly sliced

½ cup (45 g) bean sprouts

¼ red onion, thinly sliced

¼ cup (10 g) chopped fresh cilantro

¼ cup (10 g) chopped fresh mint

½ cup (60 g) chopped peanuts

3 scallions, sliced

1 Fresno chili, thinly sliced (optional)

¼ cup (20 g) Crispy Fried Shallots (page 86; optional)

Ginger Fish Sauce (page 72)

To make the dressing, in a small bowl, whisk together the lemon juice, fish sauce, vinegar, maple syrup, and pepper. Set aside.

In a large bowl, combine the chicken, cabbage, carrot, radishes, bean sprouts, and red onion. Pour some of the dressing over the chicken and vegetables and toss to combine. Add the cilantro and mint and toss again. Sprinkle the chopped peanuts, scallions, Fresno chili, and fried shallots (if using) on top of the salad.

Serve immediately, with the remaining dressing on the side for drizzling on each bite and the ginger fish sauce for dipping. Alternatively, you can cover and refrigerate the salad for up to 3 days and serve it chilled.

Ginger-Sesame Chicken Rice Bowl
with Broccoli

When my mother first came to America, she discovered that she could purchase the "leftover" pieces of the chicken—backs, necks, heads, and feet—at very affordable prices. She explained to me the importance of using every part of the chicken and how this dish reflected her resourcefulness and upbringing in Vietnam, where chicken can be very expensive. Years later, I continued to make this dish for myself on a shoestring budget in college. Now, when I make it for my family, it brings me back to those cherished memories of cooking with my mother.

Yield: 4 to 6 servings

1 cup (190 g) white jasmine rice
3 tablespoons (45 g) schmaltz or ghee
1 large onion, chopped
3 garlic cloves, minced
1 tablespoon grated fresh ginger
1¾ cups (415 mL) Gelatinous Chicken Bone Broth (page 48)
1 tablespoon fish sauce or Fermented Anchovy Sauce (page 70)
Fine sea salt and ground black pepper
1 cup (70 g) chopped broccoli
2 cups (250 g) shredded cooked pasture-raised chicken
Optional toppings: sliced scallions, toasted sesame seeds, sliced almonds

Rinse the rice under cold running water until the water runs clear. Drain.

In a large pot, heat the schmaltz over medium heat. Add the onion and cook until softened, about 5 minutes. Add the garlic and ginger and cook for another minute.

Add the rice and stir to coat with the onion mixture. Cook for 2 to 3 minutes, stirring occasionally, until the rice starts to turn translucent.

Add the broth, fish sauce, and salt and pepper to taste. Bring to a boil, then reduce the heat to low, cover, and simmer for 18 to 20 minutes, until the liquid has been absorbed and the rice is tender.

While the rice is cooking, steam the broccoli in a steamer for 3 to 4 minutes, until it is tender but still slightly crisp. Set aside.

When the rice is done, stir in the chicken and steamed broccoli. Let the mixture sit for a few minutes to allow the flavors to meld. Serve hot, topped with scallions, toasted sesame seeds, or sliced almonds, if desired.

Citrus-Glazed Chicken

Tim's grandfather was a Chinese immigrant who served in World War II and later became a chef at Chinese restaurants in Oklahoma and Illinois. Growing up, Tim heard many stories about his grandfather's cooking and how he brought the flavors of China to the Midwest. Today, Tim honors his grandfather's legacy by creating healthier and more nutrient-dense versions of Chinese dishes. This mandarin orange chicken is a perfect combination of savory and sweet, making it a delicious twist on the heavily processed and MSG-laden versions found in many takeout restaurants. Instead of deep-frying the chicken in vegetable oil, we pan-fry the chicken in traditional fats that are rich in nutrients. The orange zest infuses the dish with a bright, fresh citrus flavor, and the fresh broccoli adds a nice crunch. The cilantro is optional, but it adds a nice pop of color and fresh herbal flavor.

Yield: 4 to 6 servings

1 tablespoon arrowroot starch

½ teaspoon fine sea salt

¼ teaspoon ground black pepper

¼ teaspoon ground ginger

¼ teaspoon garlic powder

¼ teaspoon onion powder

¼ cup (60 mL) mandarin orange or clementine juice

1 tablespoon maple syrup

1 tablespoon tamari or soy sauce

1 tablespoon coconut oil or ghee

1 pound (450 g) boneless, skinless pasture-raised chicken thighs, cut into bite-size pieces

1 teaspoon grated mandarin orange or clementine zest

1 broccoli crown, cut into 1- to 2-inch (2.5–5 cm) pieces

Steamed rice (pages 62–63), for serving

Chopped fresh cilantro, for garnish (optional)

In a small bowl, whisk together the arrowroot, salt, pepper, ginger, garlic powder, and onion powder; set aside. In another small bowl, whisk together the orange juice, maple syrup, and tamari; set aside.

Heat the oil in a large skillet or wok over medium-high heat. Add the chicken and cook for 5 to 7 minutes, stirring occasionally, until it is lightly browned on all sides and cooked through.

Sprinkle the arrowroot mixture over the chicken and stir to coat the chicken evenly. Add the orange juice mixture and bring to a boil, then reduce the heat and simmer for 2 to 3 minutes, until the sauce has thickened.

Stir in the orange zest and broccoli and cook for 2 to 3 minutes, until the broccoli is crisp-tender.

Serve over rice, sprinkled with cilantro, if desired.

Vietnamese Egg Rolls with Turkey
(CHẢ GIÒ)

Unlike Chinese and Filipino egg rolls, which are typically filled with pork and wrapped with wheat-based wrappers, Vietnamese egg rolls are traditionally wrapped with rice paper and are deep-fried until crispy. This recipe is kosher and gluten-free, which means we can share it with more of our family and friends. My mother and I gather around the table to wrap, and the children love making their own shapes and sizes. These egg rolls are great to have in the freezer, ready to cook for a quick appetizer when guests come!

Yield: about 20 egg rolls

½ cup (10 g) dried wood ear mushrooms

4 ounces (115 g) mung bean noodles or glass noodles

½ cup (65 g) minced onion

1 cup (140 g) shredded carrot

6 garlic cloves, minced

1 large pasture-raised egg, beaten

¼ cup (60 mL) fish sauce or Fermented Anchovy Sauce (page 70)

1 teaspoon maple syrup

1 teaspoon fine sea salt

1 teaspoon ground black pepper

1 pound (450 g) ground turkey

20 to 25 (8-inch [20 cm]) rice paper wrappers

Duck fat or avocado oil, for frying

Vietnamese Dipping Sauce (page 68)

Note: *To make the egg rolls ahead of time, do a partial deep-fry so there is just a light browning on both sides of the egg rolls before taking them out of the oil. Allow them to cool, then store in an airtight container in the freezer for up to 6 months. Do not thaw before cooking.*

Put the dried mushrooms in a bowl, cover with warm water, and let soak for 1 hour. Drain and cut into small pieces. Rinse the mung bean noodles in hot water, then cut into shorter pieces.

In a large bowl, combine the mushrooms and noodles. Squeeze out the excess moisture from the onion by hand and add it to the bowl, along with the carrot, garlic, egg, fish sauce, maple syrup, salt, and pepper and mix thoroughly. Add the ground turkey and mix well.

Fill a large, shallow dish with warm water. Dip a rice paper wrapper into the water and let it soak for 5 to 10 seconds, until it is soft and pliable.

Place the wrapper on a clean, flat surface. Spoon 1 to 2 tablespoons (15–30 g) of the turkey mixture down the center of the wrapper. Fold the wrapper over the filling, tuck in the sides, then roll it up tightly, like a burrito. Repeat with the remaining wrappers and filling. Refrigerate for at least 30 minutes, or up to 4 hours.

In a large, deep skillet, add enough duck fat or oil to cover the egg rolls and heat over medium-low heat. Line a plate with paper towels. To check if the oil is ready, we do the "chopstick test." Touch a chopstick to the bottom of the skillet, and you should see some bubbles forming. Do not allow the oil to get too hot or you will burn the egg rolls. Working in batches so as not to crowd the pan, carefully add the egg rolls to the hot oil and cook until golden brown and crispy, 3 to 5 minutes. Using a spider or slotted spoon, transfer the egg rolls to the paper towels to drain.

Serve the egg rolls hot, with the dipping sauce.

Teriyaki Turkey-Stuffed Bell Peppers

Stuffed peppers are a common dish in many cuisines. This recipe provides a healthy twist on traditional by incorporating nutrient-dense ingredients such as coconut oil and shiitake mushrooms and using ground turkey instead of beef (although beef will work just as well). The combination of these ingredients, with the classic Asian flavors of fish sauce, ginger, and scallions, makes for a delicious and satisfying meal that the whole family will love.

Yield: *4 servings*

¼ cup (60 mL) tamari or soy sauce
2 tablespoons (30 mL) maple syrup
2 tablespoons (30 mL) apple cider vinegar
1 tablespoon grated fresh ginger
1 tablespoon arrowroot starch
1 tablespoon cold spring water
2 tablespoons (30 mL) coconut oil
1 pound (450 g) ground turkey
1 onion, chopped
3 garlic cloves, minced
1 cup (70 g) finely chopped broccoli
1 cup (60 g) sliced shiitake mushrooms
4 bell peppers (any color)
¼ cup (15 g) sliced scallions
Sesame seeds, for garnish

Preheat the oven to 375°F (190°C).

In a small bowl, whisk together the tamari, maple syrup, vinegar, and ginger. In another small bowl, whisk together the arrowroot and water to make a slurry. Pour the slurry into the tamari mixture and stir to make the teriyaki sauce; set aside.

In a large skillet, heat the oil over medium-high heat. Add the turkey and cook, stirring, until browned and fully cooked through, 8 to 10 minutes. Transfer the turkey to a bowl.

Add the onion and garlic to the skillet and sauté over medium heat until fragrant and softened, about 5 minutes. Add the broccoli and mushrooms and cook until tender and slightly browned, about 5 minutes.

Return the turkey to the skillet. Rewhisk the teriyaki sauce if necessary, pour it over the turkey mixture, and stir until everything is well coated and the sauce has thickened. Remove from the heat.

Cut the bell peppers in half lengthwise and remove the stems, membranes, and seeds. Place the pepper halves cut-side up on a rimmed baking sheet. Spoon the turkey mixture into the bell pepper halves and cover with aluminum foil. Bake for 20 to 25 minutes, until cooked through. Remove from the oven, sprinkle with the scallions and sesame seeds, and serve.

Five-Spice Quail

As a child, I would eagerly await weddings just to savor the rich flavors of this delectable dish, which was often served at special occasions. Even now, my children share my love for this savory quail recipe. To make it even more special, we now raise quail on our farm at my parents' request, providing both the eggs and the meat for the grandchildren to enjoy. If you don't raise your own quail, look for it at local farms or in the freezer section of Asian grocery stores. You can also use chicken legs and wings for this recipe. It's truly a dish that's close to our hearts.

Yield: 6 servings

6 quail
½ onion, minced
¼ cup (60 mL) tamari or soy sauce
2 tablespoons (30 mL) fish sauce or
   Fermented Anchovy Sauce (page 70)
2 garlic cloves, minced
1 tablespoon grated fresh ginger
1 tablespoon Chinese five-spice powder
2 teaspoons ground black pepper
Duck fat, lard, or avocado oil, for frying
2 scallions, sliced

Pat the quail dry with paper towels. In a large bowl, whisk together the onion, tamari, fish sauce, garlic, ginger, five-spice powder, and pepper. Add the quail to the bowl, turning them in the mixture to coat well. Cover the bowl and put it in the fridge to marinate for at least 2 hours, or preferably overnight.

When you're ready to cook, bring a large pot of water to a boil. Remove the quail from the marinade, letting the excess drip off. Add the quail to the pot and boil for 8 to 10 minutes, until they are fully cooked. Remove the quail from the pot and set them aside to dry.

Rinse and dry the pot (or use a deep fryer), and add enough oil to come halfway up the sides of the quail. Heat the fat or oil to 350 to 375°F (175–190°C). Line a plate with paper towels. Carefully add 3 quail to the hot oil and fry for 2 to 3 minutes on one side. Use tongs to carefully flip the quail over and fry for another 2 to 3 minutes, until crispy and golden brown. Using the tongs, transfer the quail to the paper towels to drain. Repeat with the remaining 3 quail. Sprinkle with the scallions and serve hot.

Vietnamese Garlic-Butter Chicken Wings

When Tim and I were dating, he would take me to fast food restaurants to share with me the food he loved eating. One of these times, we tried every flavor of chicken wings under the sun—including Tim's favorite, the garlic-butter variety. Every time I see the shape of a chicken wing now, I always think of Tim. When we process the chickens we raise on our farm, I separate the chicken wings and package them separately just to make this recipe. They are so easy to make, and we always have these ingredients on hand for a quick meal. For an extra touch of flavor and presentation, you can garnish the wings with scallions, cilantro, or sesame seeds.

Yield: 4 to 6 servings

FOR THE WINGS

¼ cup (32 g) tapioca starch

1 teaspoon garlic powder

1 teaspoon fine sea salt

¼ teaspoon ground black pepper

2 pounds (900 g) pasture-raised chicken wings, tips removed, drumettes and flats separated

Duck fat, lard, or avocado oil, for frying

FOR THE GARLIC-BUTTER SAUCE

4 tablespoons (60 g) unsalted grass-fed butter

2 garlic cloves, minced

¼ teaspoon fine sea salt

¼ teaspoon ground black pepper

1 tablespoon raw honey or maple syrup

1 tablespoon fish sauce or Fermented Anchovy Sauce (page 70)

Optional garnishes: sliced scallions, chopped fresh cilantro, toasted sesame seeds

To make the wings, in a large bowl, whisk together the tapioca starch, garlic powder, salt, and pepper. Add the chicken wings and toss until the wings are evenly coated with the mixture.

Add enough fat or oil to a large pot or deep fryer to cover the chicken wings and heat it to 375°F (190°C). Line a rimmed baking sheet with paper towels and set a wire rack over it. Working in batches if necessary, carefully add the wings to the fat and fry until golden brown and crispy, 10 to 12 minutes. Using tongs or a slotted spoon, transfer the wings to the wire rack to drain.

To make the sauce, in a small saucepan, melt the butter over medium heat. Add the garlic, salt, and pepper and cook, stirring occasionally, for 1 to 2 minutes, until the sauce thickens slightly. Add the honey and fish sauce and cook, stirring constantly, for an additional minute.

Put the fried chicken wings in a large bowl, add the garlic-butter sauce, and toss until they are coated evenly. Serve hot, with any remaining sauce drizzled over the top. Sprinkle with scallions, cilantro, or sesame seeds, if desired.

Pan-Seared Honey-Miso-Orange Duck Breast

This dish is one of the reasons we raise our own ducks! With just a few simple ingredients, the flavor of the duck shines through. Timing the perfect sear is essential to achieving a crispy skin and tender meat. The key is to cook low and slow to transfer the heat to the flesh through the buffer of the thick skin layer and give the fat time to render. With the honey-miso-orange sauce drizzled over the top, this dish is enjoyed by everyone in our family and is sure to impress your dinner guests with its flavor and presentation. Be sure to save the duck fat for future use.

Yield: 2 to 4 servings

2 (8- to 12-ounce [225–340 g]) boneless,
   skin-on duck breasts
Fine sea salt
½ cup (120 mL) Gelatinous Chicken
   Bone Broth (page 48)
3 tablespoons (45 g) unsalted
   grass-fed butter
Juice of ½ orange
¼ cup (60 mL) organic white miso paste
2 tablespoons (30 mL) raw honey
Steamed mustard greens,
   for serving (optional)

Pat the duck dry with paper towels. Use a sharp knife to score the skin in a tight crosshatch pattern about ⅛ inch (3 mm) apart, being careful not to cut into the flesh. Season with a sprinkle of salt.

Place the duck breasts skin side down in a cold stainless-steel pan. Turn the heat to low. Cook, removing any rendered fat with a spoon, until the skin is golden, 12 to 15 minutes. Turn the duck over, increase the heat to medium, and cook for 1 to 2 minutes, until cooked through. Transfer the duck to a plate.

Drain off all but 2 tablespoons (30 mL) of the rendered fat left in the pan (keep the brown bits). Add the broth and butter and bring to a simmer, scraping the bottom of the pan to deglaze. Once the butter is melted and the broth is slightly reduced, stir in the orange juice, miso, and honey. If you want a thicker sauce, simmer gently for a minute or two.

Serve the duck breasts on top of steamed mustard greens, if desired, and drizzle the delicious sauce over the top.

Vietnamese "Rotisserie" Chicken Thighs
(GÀ RÔTI)

This traditional Vietnamese dish is a real treat for your taste buds. Gà rôti is all about tasty chicken marinated with spices and then roasted to perfection. It's crispy on the outside and tender on the inside. I made this simple yet delicious dish throughout college, and my family still loves it as much today, served with sticky rice.

Yield: 4 to 6 servings

6 bone-in, skin-on pasture-raised
    chicken thighs

4 teaspoons (20 mL) fish sauce or
    Fermented Anchovy Sauce (page 70)

2 teaspoons tamari

1½ teaspoons raw honey

½ teaspoon Chinese five-spice powder

¼ teaspoon fine sea salt

3 shallots, minced

2 large garlic cloves, minced

2 tablespoons (30 mL) coconut oil or lard

1¼ cups (300 mL) fresh coconut water
    (from 1 coconut)

Steamed Glutinous Rice (page 62),
    for serving

Note: If you don't have coconut water, use chicken broth.

Put the chicken in a large bowl. In a small bowl, whisk together the fish sauce, tamari, honey, five-spice powder, and salt. Pour the mixture over the chicken, then stir in the shallots and garlic. Cover and marinate for several hours in the refrigerator or, if you're short on time, 20 to 30 minutes at room temperature.

Heat the oil in a large, deep skillet over medium heat. Remove the chicken from the marinade, shaking off the aromatics; reserve both the aromatics and the marinade. Add the chicken to the pan in a single layer and fry, turning frequently, for 10 to 15 minutes, until all sides are golden. Watch closely to avoid burning the chicken skin. (Alternatively, you can broil the chicken until all sides are golden.) Set the chicken aside on a plate.

Wipe the pan clean, discarding any remaining oil. Pour the reserved marinade and aromatics into the pan and return the chicken to the pan. Add enough coconut water so that the liquid comes halfway up the meat.

Bring to a boil, then lower the heat to medium to maintain a rolling simmer. Simmer for about 20 minutes, skimming off any foam and flipping the chicken once or twice, until the sauce is thickened to lightly coat the chicken. You may need to lower the heat slightly toward the end to prevent overcooking. Taste the meat and the sauce and season with more salt, fish sauce, tamari, or honey to taste. Serve hot, with sticky rice.

CHAPTER 7

Pork

Asian cultures have a rich tradition of using pork in their cuisines. In countries like China, Japan, Korea, and Vietnam, pork is considered a staple protein source and is featured in a variety of dishes, including soups, stir-fries, braises, and stews. From the more tender cuts like pork belly and pork loin to extra flavorful cuts like spare ribs and shoulder, different parts of the pig are used to cook a wide range of savory and delicious meals. Pork fat, often referred to as lard, is valued in Asian cooking as it provides a rich flavor and distinct texture. It is commonly used for frying and sautéing.

In Chinese cuisine, pork is considered a symbol of wealth and prosperity, and roast pork is often served for special occasions such as weddings and festivals. It is also commonly used in various preparations, including the famous char siu (barbecued pork), dumplings, and hot pot. In Japan, pork is used in dishes such as tonkatsu, breaded and deep-fried pork cutlets, and shabu-shabu, a delightful hot pot meal. In Korea, pork takes center stage in dishes such as bulgogi (marinated and grilled pork). In Southeast Asian cuisine, pork shines in traditional recipes such as Vietnamese caramelized pork spare ribs; Filipino adobo, a flavorful meat stew; and Thai pad kra pao, a pork stir-fry. Indonesia and Malaysia also feature pork prominently in their traditional cooking.

While certain parts of Asia have cultural or religious restrictions on pork consumption, it continues to be a widely versatile ingredient throughout much of the continent. When sourcing pork, it is important to find ethical and reputable producers who raise pigs on pasture, where they have access to fresh air, open fields, and a natural diet. Pasture-raising methods for pigs can result in pork that is more nutrient-rich compared to conventionally raised pork—not to mention more flavorful meat with fewer contaminants.

If you have personal, cultural, or religious reasons for not consuming pork, you can easily modify many of these recipes by substituting another lean protein, such as chicken or turkey. By making this simple substitution, you can still enjoy the flavors and textures of these delicious dishes while honoring your dietary preferences or restrictions. Whether making stir-fries, soups, or grilled favorites, you can adapt the recipes to suit your needs and continue to explore a wide variety of flavors and culinary experiences.

Easy Moo Shu Pork

Moo shu pork originated in northern China in Shandong Province, where it was traditionally made with thinly sliced pork, scrambled eggs, and wood ear mushrooms. Tim and the children love to make these "Chinese burritos"!

One of the fun things about living in the Appalachians is that we can forage for daylily buds, which I use in this dish. The beauty of daylilies is that they are edible year-round. In the spring, you can eat the young shoots, the flowers, the flower buds, and the tubers. They are plentiful, delicious, and easy to identify.

Yield: 4 to 6 servings

½ cup (10 g) wood ear mushrooms
30 daylily buds or bamboo shoots, sliced (optional)
¼ cup (60 mL) tamari
1 tablespoon grated fresh ginger
2 teaspoons apple cider vinegar
2 teaspoons maple syrup
¼ teaspoon ground black pepper
2 tablespoons (30 mL) coconut oil
1 pound (450 g) pork tenderloin, sliced into very thin strips
½ red or green cabbage, shredded
1 large cucumber, sliced
1 large carrot, julienned
2 garlic cloves, minced
2 large pasture-raised eggs, whisked
6 scallions, cut on the diagonal into 1-inch (2.5 cm) pieces (optional)
Sesame seeds, for garnish (optional)
4 to 6 (6-inch [15 cm]) flour tortillas

Note: You can substitute an equal amount of thinly sliced chicken, turkey, or beef for the pork. Adjust the cooking time accordingly depending on the protein source used.

Put the dried mushrooms in a bowl, cover with warm water, and let soak for 1 hour. Put the daylily buds in a separate bowl, cover with warm water, and let soak for 1 hour. Drain both bowls. Cut the mushrooms into small pieces and cut the daylily buds in half crosswise.

In a small bowl, whisk together the tamari, ginger, vinegar, maple syrup, and pepper until well combined. Set aside.

Heat the coconut oil in a large wok or skillet over medium-high heat until it is melted and hot. Add the pork and cook for 3 to 4 minutes, stirring occasionally, until the pork is browned on all sides and cooked through. Add the mushrooms, daylily buds, cabbage, cucumber, carrot, and garlic and cook, stirring occasionally, for 8 to 10 minutes, until the vegetables are wilted and softened.

Push the pork and vegetable mixture to one side of the skillet and add the eggs to the other side. Use a spatula to scramble the eggs until cooked through, 2 to 3 minutes, then mix them in with the pork and vegetables.

Pour in the sauce and stir gently to coat everything evenly. Cook for 1 to 2 minutes, until the sauce has thickened slightly.

If desired, garnish with scallions and sesame seeds before assembling.

Warm the tortillas in a skillet, on a griddle, or in the oven. (I like to warm a cast-iron skillet or griddle over medium-high heat and heat each tortilla for 20 to 30 seconds on each side.)

To assemble, spoon a generous amount of the pork mixture onto the center of a tortilla. Fold the bottom of the tortilla up over the filling, like a taco, or fold the sides in to make a roll, similar to a burrito. Serve immediately.

Vietnamese Steamed Egg Meatloaf
(CHẢ TRỨNG HẤP)

At restaurants, we often find ourselves ordering an extra serving or two of this delicious and savory side dish because it's never enough to share! However, when I make it at home, there's plenty for everyone. This recipe is a go-to option for when we have an abundance of eggs on our homestead. The steamed egg meatloaf perfectly complements the flavors and textures of Lemongrass Bone-in Pork Chops (page 174). To prepare this recipe, you'll need a heatproof glass or ceramic baking dish and a steamer that can accommodate the dish. With these simple tools, you'll be able to create a satisfying and crowd-pleasing meal that will leave everyone asking for seconds!

Yield: 4 to 6 servings

½ cup (10 g) dried wood ear mushrooms
1 cup (120 g) mung bean noodles
5 large pasture-raised eggs, divided
1 pound (450 g) ground pasture-raised pork
1 or 2 shallots, minced
1 medium carrot, shredded
2 to 3 garlic cloves, minced
2 tablespoons (30 mL) fish sauce or
  Fermented Anchovy Sauce (page 70)
1 tablespoon maple syrup
1 teaspoon fine sea salt
1 teaspoon ground black pepper
1 teaspoon avocado oil (optional)
Thinly sliced scallions, for garnish
Steamed rice (pages 62–63), for serving
Vietnamese Dipping Sauce (page 68),
  for serving

Note: *You can use ground chicken or turkey in place of the pork in this recipe.*

Put the wood ear mushrooms in a bowl, cover with warm water, and let soak for 1 hour. Drain and mince or slice thinly.

Rinse the mung bean noodles with hot water and set aside to cool, then cut into 2-inch (5 cm) pieces.

Separate 2 of the eggs, putting the whites in one small bowl and the yolks in another.

In a large bowl, combine the mushrooms, noodles, ground pork, shallots, carrot, garlic, 3 whole eggs, reserved 2 egg whites, fish sauce, maple syrup, salt, and pepper and mix well.

Line a baking dish with parchment paper or grease with the avocado oil. Transfer the meat mixture to the dish and smooth the surface.

Whisk the reserved egg yolks with a pinch of salt and pour them over the surface of the meatloaf. Tip the dish if necessary to get the egg yolk to the edges.

Place the dish in a steamer and cover with a lid. Steam over medium heat for 20 to 30 minutes. Carefully remove the lid, taking care to not let condensation drip onto the meatloaf. Insert a toothpick into the center of the meatloaf; if it comes out clean, it's done. You may need to adjust the cooking time if your baking dish is on the small side, as the meatloaf will be thicker.

Let the meatloaf sit in the steamer for a few minutes, then remove the baking dish from the steamer

and run a knife around the edge to loosen the meatloaf. Place a serving plate upside-down on top of the dish and invert to release the meatloaf onto the plate.

Garnish with scallions and serve hot, with steamed rice and dipping sauce.

Vietnamese Grilled Pork Meatballs
(NEM NƯỚNG)

Nem nướng is a type of Vietnamese meatball that is commonly used as a filling for spring rolls or served as a main dish. Savory and easy to make, they are perfect for a family dinner or a gathering with friends. Our whole family loves nem nướng, but when you buy them in stores or restaurants, they often have added sodium nitrate to the pork, which acts as a preservative and gives a pink color to the meatballs. When you make them at home, you can control what goes inside! To make the dish more nourishing and increase the fiber and micronutrient content, serve nem nướng with a variety of fresh vegetables, such as lettuce, herbs, cucumber, and carrot. Serve with a dipping sauce made with high-quality, nutrient-dense ingredients, such as fish sauce, lime juice, garlic, chili peppers, and coconut sugar or honey, to add more flavor and nutritional value to the dish.

Yield: 4 to 6 servings

1 pound (450 g) ground pasture-raised pork
2 garlic cloves, minced
2 tablespoons (35 g) minced shallots
2 tablespoons (30 mL) fish sauce or
    Fermented Anchovy Sauce (page 70)
1 tablespoon coconut sugar or maple syrup
1 tablespoon tapioca starch or
    arrowroot starch
½ teaspoon fine sea salt
½ teaspoon ground black pepper

FOR SERVING
Cooked noodles
Fresh herbs, such as mint or cilantro
Lettuce leaves
Cucumber slices
Julienned carrots
Vietnamese Dipping Sauce (page 68)

Note: You can substitute ground chicken or turkey for the pork in these meatballs.

If using bamboo skewers, soak them in water for 30 minutes.

In a large bowl, combine the ground pork, garlic, shallots, fish sauce, coconut sugar, tapioca starch, salt, and pepper. Mix the ingredients together until everything is evenly distributed.

Shape the mixture into 1-inch (2.5 cm) meatballs. You can adjust the size according to your preference; 4 to 6 meatballs per skewer works well for grilling. Carefully thread the meatballs onto the skewers, ensuring that they are evenly spaced.

Preheat a grill or stovetop grill pan to medium-high heat. Grill the meatballs for 5 to 7 minutes per side, until they are browned and cooked through.

Serve hot over noodles, with fresh herbs, lettuce, cucumbers, carrots, and dipping sauce.

Holy Basil Pork Stir-Fry

(PAD KRA PAO)

The variety of basil known as holy basil or tulsi is commonly used in traditional medicine in Southeast Asia, particularly in Ayurvedic and Thai medicine. It is believed to have a range of medicinal properties, including as an antioxidant, anti-inflammatory, and antimicrobial. It is used to treat a variety of conditions, such as coughs, colds, flu, headaches, digestive issues, and even anxiety and stress. We have an abundance of holy basil growing in our backyard medicinal garden. Every year we dry some to use in our teas and our cooking. Holy basil has a distinct flavor that pairs well with the other ingredients in this dish, so be sure to use it if you can find it. If you can't find holy basil, regular basil or Thai basil can be used as a substitute. This stir-fry is a super-quick, nourishing dish to put together in less than 10 minutes. It is traditionally served with steamed jasmine rice, but if you prefer a lower-carb option, cauliflower rice is a great substitute.

Yield: 4 to 6 servings

3 tablespoons (45 g) ghee or
  unsalted grass-fed butter, divided

2 shallots, thinly sliced

7 garlic cloves, thinly sliced

3 bird's eye or Holland chilies,
  seeded if desired and thinly sliced

1 pound (450 g) ground pasture-raised pork

⅓ cup (80 mL) Gelatinous Chicken Bone
  Broth (page 48) or spring water

1 tablespoon fish sauce or Fermented
  Anchovy Sauce (page 70)

1 tablespoon tamari

2 teaspoons oyster sauce

1 teaspoon coconut sugar or raw honey

1½ cups (60 g) packed fresh holy basil leaves

Steamed Jasmine Rice (page 62) or
  cauliflower rice, for serving

> **Note:** You can substitute ground
> chicken, turkey, or beef for the
> pork in this dish.

Heat 1 tablespoon of the ghee in a large wok or skillet over medium-high heat until melted and shimmering. Add the shallots, garlic, and chilies and stir-fry for 1 to 2 minutes, until fragrant and slightly softened. Add the ground pork and stir-fry until it's cooked through and lightly browned, 5 to 7 minutes. Use a spatula or wooden spoon to break up any large clumps of meat and ensure it cooks evenly.

Meanwhile, in a small bowl, combine the chicken broth, fish sauce, tamari, oyster sauce, and coconut sugar to make the sauce. Whisk until the sugar is fully dissolved and the ingredients are well combined. When the pork is cooked, pour the sauce over the pork mixture in the skillet and stir to coat evenly, scraping up any browned bits from the bottom of the pan.

Add the holy basil leaves and stir-fry for another 1 to 2 minutes, until the leaves are wilted and fragrant. Serve hot, over rice.

Caramelized Pork Spare Ribs
with Quail Eggs
(THIT SUON KHO)

This is a beloved and comforting dish that reflects the rich and complex flavors of Vietnamese cuisine. The use of caramelized sugar in Vietnamese cuisine is thought to have originated during the French colonial period, when the French introduced sugarcane to Vietnam and encouraged its cultivation. I grew up loving this dish, and when I went away to college across the country, my mother used to send these ribs packed in zip-top bags to store in the freezer. Today, I make this dish for my family, and it still takes me back to my days in college!

Yield: 4 to 6 servings

2 pounds (900 g) pasture-raised pork spare ribs, cut into 1-inch (2.5 cm) pieces

1 shallot, minced

4 garlic cloves, minced

3 tablespoons (45 mL) fish sauce or Fermented Anchovy Sauce (page 70)

4 tablespoons (60 g) panela, divided

¼ teaspoon ground black pepper

1 tablespoon sesame oil

1 cup (240 mL) Gelatinous Chicken Bone Broth (page 48) or Beef Bone and Marrow Broth (page 50)

¼ teaspoon fine sea salt

FOR SERVING

Crispy Fried Shallots (page 86)

1 scallion, thinly sliced

1 Fresno chili, seeded and thinly sliced lengthwise

Steamed rice (pages 62–63)

12 to 16 Soft-Boiled Quail Eggs (recipe follows)

Fill a large pot with enough water to cover the spare ribs. Bring the water to a rolling boil, then carefully add the ribs. Blanch the ribs for 8 to 10 minutes, until you notice scum rising to the surface. Transfer the blanched ribs to a colander and rinse thoroughly under cold running water to remove any remaining impurities.

In a large bowl, whisk together the shallot, garlic, fish sauce, 1 tablespoon of the panela, and the pepper. Add the pork, toss to coat, and set aside to marinate for 15 minutes.

To make the caramel sauce, combine the remaining 3 tablespoons (45 g) panela and the sesame oil in a large saucepan over medium-high heat. Cook, stirring constantly with a wooden spoon to prevent the sugar from burning. As you stir, the sugar will gradually darken in color. Be attentive, as the sugar can quickly go from amber to burnt. Once the sugar reaches a dark amber color, swiftly and carefully add the pork and marinade and stir to coat the pork with the caramel. The caramelized sugar may start to clump, but the heat will eventually dissolve these clumps.

Pour in the broth and bring to a boil, then cover and reduce the heat to medium-low. Allow the pork to braise for 40 to 45 minutes, stirring occasionally.

continued on page 169

Uncover, reduce the heat to low, and continue simmering the pork for 30 to 45 minutes, until the liquid evaporates, resulting in a glaze that coats the ribs. Season with the salt.

Garnish with the fried shallots, scallion, and chili, and serve over rice, with the soft-boiled quail eggs.

▶ HOW TO MAKE SOFT-BOILED QUAIL EGGS

Soft-boiled quail eggs are a delicious and nutritious addition to a variety of dishes. They can be eaten on their own as a snack, used as a topping for salads, or served with ramen or other noodle dishes. They can also be used as a garnish for other dishes, such as avocado toast.

Fill a pot with enough water to cover the eggs. Bring the water to a boil. Fill a bowl with cold water and ice.

Using a spoon, carefully lower the quail eggs into the boiling water. Boil the eggs for 2 to 3 minutes for a soft-boiled egg with a slightly runny yolk. If you prefer a firmer yolk, boil for an additional minute or two.

Using a slotted spoon, transfer the eggs to the ice bath. Allow the eggs to cool in the ice water for at least 1 minute before peeling.

Note: Cooking time may vary depending on the size of the quail eggs and personal preference, so it may take some experimentation to get the perfect soft-boiled quail egg for your taste.

Five-Spice Pork Belly Bánh Mì

This braised five-spice pork belly bánh mì is an explosion of flavor that will have your taste buds dancing with joy! The complex combination of sweet, sour, savory, and spicy notes creates a perfectly balanced dish that is simply irresistible. The pork is first caramelized for a nice crispy exterior, then slow-cooked in sauce, which allows it to become tender and absorb all the flavors. The baguette complements the pork belly, creating a perfect harmony. This sandwich is the perfect choice for when you're looking for something hearty and satisfying that won't disappoint.

Yield: 4 to 6 servings

FOR THE PORK BELLY

1½ to 2 pounds (675–900 g) pasture-raised pork belly
3 tablespoons (18 g) Chinese five-spice powder
1 tablespoon garlic powder
½ teaspoon fine sea salt, plus more for seasoning
1 tablespoon avocado oil
2 tablespoons (30 g) panela
3 tablespoons (45 mL) tamari
2 star anise pods
1 cup (240 mL) spring water
Ground black pepper

Note: You can substitute boneless, skinless chicken thighs for the pork in this recipe.

To make the pork belly, rinse the pork under cold running water and pat it dry with paper towels. Cut the pork into 1-inch (5 cm) long strips.

Fill a pot with enough water to cover the pork. Bring the water to a boil, add the pork, skin-side down, and boil for 10 minutes, skimming off any scum. Remove the pork and rinse under cool running water. Set aside to cool.

In a large bowl, combine the five-spice powder, garlic powder, and salt. Add the pork and toss to combine. Make sure the pork is evenly coated with the seasoning.

In a large cast-iron skillet, heat the oil and panela over medium-high heat. When the sugar melts into the oil, add the pork and sear for 5 to 8 minutes on each side.

Add the tamari, star anise, and water to the skillet and stir. Turn the heat up to high and cook until the mixture comes to a boil. Reduce the heat to low, cover, and simmer for 1 hour, or until the pork is tender.

Remove the lid and cook over high heat to reduce the sauce. Stir occasionally to prevent it from burning. Season with salt and pepper to taste. Transfer the pork to a plate. You can make this pork ahead of time and store it in an airtight container in the refrigerator for up to 2 days.

To assemble the bánh mì, preheat the oven to 350°F (175°C).

Slice the baguette lengthwise and place the two halves on a rimmed baking sheet, cut side up. Warm the bread in the oven for about 5 minutes, until the outside is crispy and the inside still soft.

FOR THE BÁNH MÌ

1 French baguette

Vietnamese Mayonnaise (page 77)

Tamari or soy sauce

Vietnamese Chicken Liver Pâté (page 231)

Vietnamese Pickled Carrots and Daikon
   (page 97)

1 cucumber, thinly sliced

Fresh cilantro leaves

1 jalapeño, thinly sliced (optional)

Fried eggs (optional)

Spread a generous amount of mayonnaise on the cut sides of the baguette. Drizzle a bit of tamari on top of the mayonnaise for added umami. To the bottom half of the baguette, add the following in layers: pâté, braised pork belly, pickled carrots and daikon, cucumber, cilantro, jalapeño, and fried eggs (if using).

Close the sandwich with the top half of the baguette and press it lightly to compress the ingredients. Cut the bánh mì sandwich into sections and serve immediately, or wrap it tightly in parchment paper with a rubber band to seal and refrigerate for up to 2 days.

Pork || 171

Vietnamese Grilled Pork Noodle Salad
(BÚN THỊT NƯỚNG)

This dish is one of my favorites when I'm in the mood for a refreshing and light salad but Tim wants something a little heartier. It's the perfect compromise because I can easily leave out the noodles and add more fresh vegetables, while Tim can load up on the juicy pork belly. The combination of flavors and textures in this dish is just so satisfying, and it's easy to customize however you like. Start by choosing a high-quality pork belly, preferably pasture raised, which is higher in nutrients compared to conventionally raised pork. Serve the pork and noodles with a variety of fresh vegetables to increase fiber, probiotics, and micronutrient content.

Yield: 4 to 6 servings

2 lemongrass stalks
2 shallots, roughly chopped
4 garlic cloves, roughly chopped
3 tablespoons (45 mL) tamari
2 tablespoons (30 mL) Hoisin Sauce
   (page 80)
1 tablespoon raw honey
1 tablespoon ground black pepper
2 pounds (900 g) pasture-raised
   pork belly, or your preferred cut
4 cups (250 g) vermicelli rice noodles

FOR SERVING
1 head romaine lettuce, chopped
1 cup (40 g) chopped fresh mint
2 cucumbers, julienned
Vietnamese Pickled Carrots and Daikon
   (page 97)
Vietnamese Dipping Sauce (page 68)
2 tablespoons (36 g) white sesame seeds,
   lightly toasted

Reserve 1 or 2 lemongrass ends and cut an X through the tip to use as a basting brush later on. Remove the tough outer layer and cut the remaining lemongrass into manageable pieces. Add the lemongrass, shallots, and garlic to a food processor and blend until finely chopped; alternatively, you can use a knife to finely chop them by hand. In a large bowl, whisk together the tamari, hoisin sauce, honey, and pepper. Add the chopped aromatics to the hoisin mixture and stir to combine.

Remove the skin from the pork belly by running a sharp knife through the fat just next to the skin. (Save the skin for making pork rinds or discard it.) Cut the pork into ¼-inch by 2 inch (6 mm × 5 cm) slices. Add the pork to the marinade and mix well to coat. Cover and marinate in the refrigerator for at least 2 hours, or preferably overnight.

Heat a grill over medium-high heat. Put the pork on the grill (in a grill basket if you prefer) and baste the meat with the marinade, using a lemongrass end as a brush. Grill the pork for 5 to 8 minutes per side, until it's cooked through and has a nice char but is not burnt.

Meanwhile, bring a large pot of water to a boil and cook the rice noodles according to the package instructions until al dente. Drain.

Cut the pork into bite-size pieces and serve on a bed of rice noodles with lettuce, mint, cucumbers, and pickled carrots and daikon. Drizzle with dipping sauce and sprinkle with the sesame seeds.

Teppanyaki with Egg and Vegetables

This Japanese dish is often served with rice and miso soup and is popular for its delicious flavor and sizzling presentation. It's perfect for a nourishing meal, providing a balance of protein, fiber, and healthy fats.

Yield: 4 servings

2 tablespoons (30 mL) lard or coconut oil, divided

1 pound (450 g) pork tenderloin, cut into ¼-inch (6 mm) slices

1 large onion, sliced

2 bell peppers, any color, seeded and sliced

2 cups (140 g) sliced shiitake mushrooms

2 cups (180 g) broccoli florets

2 garlic cloves, minced

2 teaspoons grated fresh ginger

2 tablespoons (30 mL) tamari

1 tablespoon raw honey

1 tablespoon rice vinegar

1 tablespoon toasted sesame oil

4 large pasture-raised eggs, lightly beaten

2 scallions, sliced

Note: *You can substitute boneless chicken thighs or breasts, or beef sirloin or rib eye, for the pork.*

Heat a large skillet or teppanyaki griddle over medium-high heat. Add 1 tablespoon of the lard and allow it to melt. Add the pork to the skillet and cook for 3 to 4 minutes, stirring occasionally, until it's browned on all sides. Transfer the pork to a plate.

Add the remaining 1 tablespoon lard to the skillet, along with the onion, bell peppers, and mushrooms. Cook for 5 to 7 minutes, stirring occasionally, until the vegetables are tender. Add the broccoli, garlic, and ginger and cook for 3 to 5 minutes, until the broccoli is tender but still has a bit of crispiness to it.

Meanwhile, in a small bowl, whisk together the tamari, honey, rice vinegar, and sesame oil and set aside.

Push the vegetables to the side of the skillet and add the eggs to the other side. Use a spatula to scramble the eggs until cooked through, 2 to 3 minutes, then mix them in with the vegetables.

Return the pork to the skillet, then pour in the tamari mixture. Stir well to ensure that everything is coated in the sauce. Cook for 2 to 3 minutes, stirring occasionally, until the sauce has thickened slightly. Serve hot, garnished with the scallions.

Note for Vietnamese Grilled Pork Noodle Salad (opposite): *Chicken thighs can be substituted for the pork in this dish. Grill them at 375 to 425°F (190–220°C) for 25 to 35 minutes if using bone-in thighs or 20 to 25 minutes if using boneless thighs. It's always recommended to use a meat thermometer to ensure the chicken reaches an internal temperature of 165°F (75°C) for safe consumption.*

Lemongrass Bone-in Pork Chops

This dish is a classic that my children have come to know and love because it's always served alongside their favorite Steamed Egg Meatloaf. The star of the show is a juicy, flavorful lemongrass-scented bone-in pork chop that's been marinated and grilled to a smoky, charred perfection. This is a dish to please the whole family, with its combination of bold flavors and comforting familiarity. For best results, marinate the chops overnight.

Yield: 4 servings

FOR THE PORK CHOPS

2 tablespoons (30 mL) fish sauce or
　　Fermented Anchovy Sauce (page 70)
1 tablespoon maple syrup
1 tablespoon spring water
1 tablespoon avocado oil
6 garlic cloves, minced
2 shallots, minced
4 lemongrass stalks, tough outer layer
　　removed, minced
¼ teaspoon ground black pepper
4 (1-inch-thick [2.5 cm]) bone-in
　　pasture-raised pork chops
1 tablespoon grass-fed beef tallow or
　　additional avocado oil
4 large pasture-raised eggs

FOR SERVING

Steamed rice (pages 62–63), for serving
1 head lettuce, chopped
2 cucumbers, chopped
2 tomatoes, sliced
Vietnamese Steamed Egg Meatloaf
　　(page 162)
¼ cup (15 g) sliced scallions
¼ cup (10 g) chopped fresh cilantro
Fine sea salt
Vietnamese Dipping Sauce (page 68)
Vietnamese Pickled Carrots and Daikon
　　(page 97)

In a large bowl, whisk together the fish sauce, maple syrup, water, and avocado oil. Add the garlic, shallots, lemongrass, and pepper and mix well.

Using a meat mallet, tenderize the pork chops. Add the pork chops to the bowl with the lemongrass mixture and toss to ensure they are well coated. Cover and refrigerate for at least 4 hours, or preferably overnight.

When ready to grill, take the pork chops out of the refrigerator and rest at room temperature for 30 minutes. Set up your grill for two-zone grilling, or grill with indirect heat.

Remove the pork chops from the bowl and reserve the marinade. Place the pork chops on the grill, baste with the marinade, and grill, turning frequently, for 10 to 12 minutes, or until they are cooked through (145°F [60°C]).

Transfer the chops to a plate and tent with aluminum foil to keep warm.

Heat the tallow in a large skillet over medium-high heat. Crack the eggs into the pan and fry sunny-side up. Allow the undersides of the eggs to get slightly crispy and cook until the whites are set but the yolks are still runny, 2 to 3 minutes. Transfer the eggs to a plate.

To assemble the dish, divide the rice among serving plates. Arrange the lettuce, cucumbers, and tomatoes around the edge of the plates. Top each plate of rice with a pork chop, a serving of meatloaf, scallions, cilantro, and a fried egg. Sprinkle with salt to season. Serve with dipping sauce and pickled carrots and daikon on the side.

CHAPTER 8

Beef

During the early years of our marriage, Tim struggled with eczema. We tried every cream available, but he would still wake up in the middle of the night scratching. One evening, we had dinner at a restaurant and tried grass-fed beef for the first time. The next morning, I realized that Tim hadn't woken me up in the middle of the night. This was the defining moment! It made us realize the connection between our diet and its effect on our bodies and immune system.

Nearly twenty years later, we now raise our own 100 percent grass-fed and grass-finished dairy cows and beef cattle on our regenerative homestead. From the moment we tried grass-fed beef, we wanted to know our local farmers and understand their practices. We believe it's important to support farmers who are transparent about their practices and prioritize animal welfare and environmental sustainability.

Aligning with our belief in the value of transparency and conscious consumer choices, Joel Salatin, a prominent advocate of transparent farming practices, emphasizes the importance of knowing our local farmers and supporting those who prioritize animal welfare and environmental sustainability. Salatin advises against purchasing products from farms that are not open about their practices.

When you know your local farmer, it comes with several benefits that go beyond just getting fresh produce. For one, you'll have a better understanding of the quality and safety of the food you're eating. Supporting local farmers helps boost the local economy and creates a sense of community. And most importantly, it provides an opportunity to learn about where your food comes from and how it's produced.

Here on our homestead, we take pride in caring for our dairy and meat cows by milking and rotating them to new pasture daily. This way, we have a better understanding of their diet and living conditions. We also make sure to use every part of the animal—meat, bones, fat, and organ meats—which are packed with essential nutrients. By doing so, we reduce waste and add extra flavor and nutrition to our meals.

Grass-Fed, Grass-Finished Beef Is Better

Here are a few reasons to eat 100 percent grass-fed and grass-finished beef:

- Better for the environment and animal welfare: Grass-fed and -finished beef typically comes from cows that have been raised on pasture and have not been fed any grains or other supplements. This means that the production of this beef has a smaller environmental impact than conventionally raised beef, which is often fed large quantities of corn and soy that require significant amounts of water, fertilizer, and fossil fuels to produce. Cows raised on pasture are able to engage in natural behaviors like grazing and socializing with other cows, which leads to a better quality of life for the animals.

- Higher in nutrients: Grass-fed and -finished beef is generally higher in nutrients like omega-3 fatty acids, conjugated linoleic acid (CLA), and antioxidants than is conventionally raised beef. This is because the grass and other plants that the cows eat contain more of these nutrients than corn and soy do.

- Better for human health: Some studies suggest that eating grass-fed and -finished beef may be better for human health than conventionally raised beef. For example, grass-fed beef has been linked to lower levels of inflammation and a lower risk of heart disease in some studies.

Thai Beef Larb with Zucchini

This is my go-to recipe whenever I'm craving something easy and comforting but a little out of the ordinary. The complex flavors and aromas of Thai spices, succulent beef, and zucchini make each mouthful a tantalizing experience. This is a super simple recipe that makes me feel like I'm walking through the bustling streets of Thailand with every single bite, right in my own kitchen.

Yield: 4 servings

2 tablespoons (30 mL) lime juice
2 tablespoons (30 mL) fish sauce or Fermented Anchovy Sauce (page 70), divided
1 tablespoon coconut sugar
2 tablespoons (30 g) ghee or coconut oil, divided
1 pound (450 g) grass-fed ground beef
2 cups (230 g) chopped zucchini
2 garlic cloves, minced
½ teaspoon red pepper flakes
¼ cup (10 g) chopped fresh cilantro
¼ cup (10 g) chopped fresh mint
2 tablespoons (5 g) chopped fresh basil
2 scallions, thinly sliced
Fine sea salt and ground black pepper

In a small bowl, whisk together the lime juice, fish sauce, and coconut sugar. Set aside.

Melt the ghee in a large skillet over medium-high heat. Add the ground beef and cook for 8 to 10 minutes, stirring occasionally, until the beef is browned and fully cooked.

Add the zucchini, garlic, and red pepper flakes and cook for 2 to 3 minutes, until the zucchini is tender. Add the cilantro, mint, basil, and scallions. Pour the lime juice mixture over everything and stir well to combine. Cook for 1 to 2 minutes, until everything is heated through and the flavors are well combined. Season with salt and pepper to taste and serve immediately.

Vietnamese Beef Carpaccio
(BÒ TÁI CHANH)

I grew up watching my parents eating this popular dish together. However, I didn't start to enjoy it with them until after I came home from college in Washington, DC, where I was beginning to enjoy more international food. I had become a more adventurous eater! As with ceviche, the acidic lime juice "cooks" the beef in the sense that it changes the structure of the beef but doesn't cook it in the traditional sense of applying heat.

The lime juice, fish sauce, and maple syrup provide a balance of sour, salty, and sweet flavors to the dish, and the sharp, pungent flavor of the shallots and garlic adds depth and complexity to the marinade. The toppings add color, texture, and richness to the dish.

Yield: 4 servings

8 to 10 ounces (225–280 g) grass-fed beef tenderloin or eye filet (see Note)

¼ cup (60 mL) lime juice

2 tablespoons (30 mL) fish sauce or Fermented Anchovy Sauce (page 70)

1½ teaspoons maple syrup

2 tablespoons (30 g) thinly sliced shallots

1 tablespoon minced garlic

1 scallion, thinly sliced

¼ cup (15 g) Crispy Fried Shallots (page 86)

¼ cup (60 g) salmon roe (see Note)

4 quail eggs

Fine sea salt and ground black pepper

Freeze the beef for about 1 hour to harden it slightly so it will be easier to cut into thin slices.

Remove the beef from the freezer and slice against the grain as thinly as possible (ideally ⅛ inch [3 mm] thick). If the pieces are coming out thicker, place the slices between sheets of parchment paper or plastic wrap and gently pound with the flat end of a meat mallet or a heavy rolling pin until the slices are paper-thin. Arrange the sliced beef on a plate.

In a small bowl, whisk together the lime juice, fish sauce, and maple syrup. Add the sliced shallots and the garlic and stir to combine. Pour the lime juice mixture over the beef, making sure to evenly coat all of the slices. Allow the beef to marinate at room temperature for 10 to 15 minutes.

Divide the beef onto individual plates. Top it with sliced scallions and fried shallots. Add a dollop of salmon roe and crack a raw quail egg on each plate. Season with salt and pepper to taste. Serve immediately.

Note: It is important to use high-quality, fresh beef when making this dish since it is eaten raw. If you're unsure about the quality of the beef or have any concerns about eating raw meat, you may want to cook the beef slightly before serving. When sourcing salmon roe, wild-caught salmon roe is preferred over roe from farmed salmon. Either way, seek out reputable and sustainable sources.

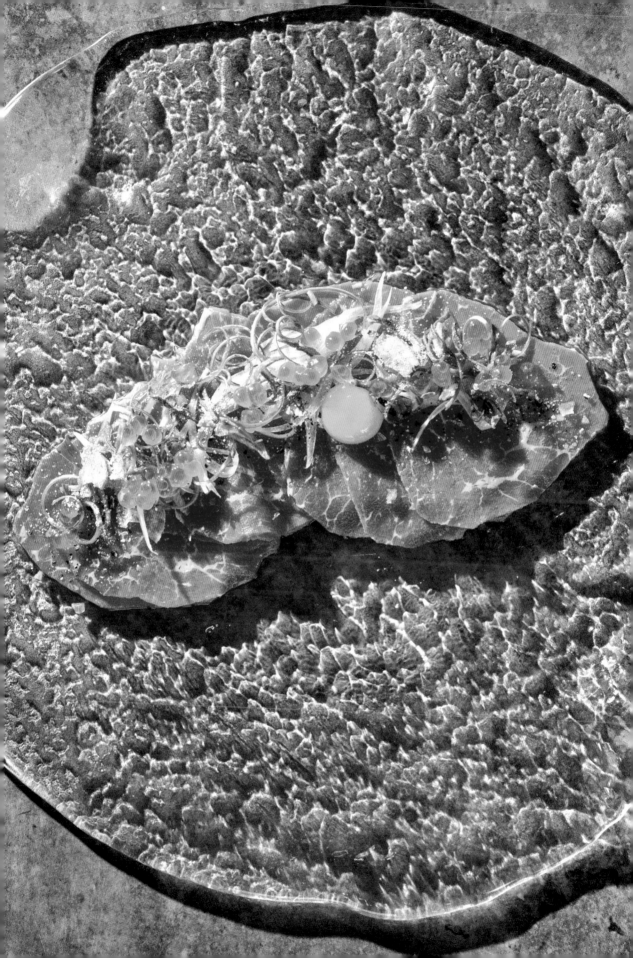

Vietnamese Beef and Onion Rolls
(BÒ NƯỚNG HÀNH)

This dish was served at a local Vietnamese restaurant near West Point, New York, that Tim would frequent on the weekends after his military training. It had understandably become his comfort food away from home, and this was the first dish that he asked me to make. I had never heard of bò nướng hành before, but I re-created it simply by his description of what it looked and tasted like. This dish is perfect for a nourishing and flavorful meal that is sure to satisfy your taste buds.

Yield: 4 servings

3 scallions
1 tablespoon tamari
1 tablespoon maple syrup (optional)
1½ teaspoons Chinese five-spice powder
1 garlic clove, minced
1 pound (450 g) grass-fed beef eye of round, thinly sliced
1 large onion, cut into thick matchsticks
2 tablespoons (30 g) ghee or grass-fed beef tallow
1 teaspoon toasted sesame oil

Fill a small saucepan with water and bring to a boil over high heat. Fill a medium bowl with cold water and ice.

While the water is heating up, cut the scallion greens into thin 4-inch (10 cm) strips. Thinly slice the scallion whites and set aside. Blanch the scallion greens in the boiling water for 10 seconds, then use a slotted spoon to transfer them to the ice bath to stop the cooking process. Let them chill for 1 minute, then remove them from the ice water and pat them dry with a paper towel.

In a large bowl, whisk together the tamari, maple syrup (if using), five-spice powder, and garlic. Add the beef and toss to coat each piece thoroughly in the marinade, then cover and refrigerate for 30 minutes.

Remove the beef from the refrigerator and lay it out on a cutting board. Place two pieces of onion in the center of a beef slice and roll the meat into a tight cylinder. Use a scallion green to tie the roll together. Repeat with the remaining beef, onion, and scallions.

In a cast-iron skillet, heat the ghee over medium-high heat. Add the beef rolls and sear for 2 to 3 minutes on each side, until they are browned and cooked to your liking. Transfer the rolls to a platter and drizzle with the sesame oil. Garnish with the reserved scallion whites, if desired, and serve hot.

Vietnamese Shaking Beef
with Watercress Salad
(BÒ LÚC LẮC)

Bò lúc lắc, also known as "shaking beef," is a tasty Vietnamese dish that has its roots in southern Vietnam. The dish has a bit of French influence and traditionally features filet mignon. In our family, we serve it with sourdough bread, and everyone loves to dip the bread into the savory steak juice (or sauce). To make this dish even better, we lay it on top of a bed of fresh watercress salad. Watercress is a wonderful, nutrient-rich green that is both delicious and healthy. Depending on where you live, you might be able to forage for watercress or grow it yourself for an even fresher taste.

Yield: 4 servings

FOR THE BEEF

1 tablespoon tamari

1 tablespoon fish sauce or Fermented
  Anchovy Sauce (page 70)

1 tablespoon raw honey

1 garlic clove, minced

¼ teaspoon ground black pepper

1 pound (450 g) grass-fed beef filet,
  tenderloin, or sirloin, cut into 1-inch
  (2.5 cm) cubes

2 tablespoons (30 g) unsalted
  grass-fed butter, divided

½ yellow onion, roughly chopped

½ red bell pepper, roughly chopped

½ yellow bell pepper, roughly chopped

FOR THE WATERCRESS SALAD

4 cups (130 g) watercress leaves

1 cucumber, sliced

1 tomato, cut into wedges

¼ cup (30 g) chopped red onion

¼ cup (10 g) chopped fresh cilantro

¼ cup (10 g) chopped fresh mint

Juice of ½ lime

2 tablespoons (30 mL) apple cider vinegar

To make the beef, in a large bowl, whisk together the tamari, fish sauce, honey, garlic, and pepper. Add the beef and toss until evenly coated. Cover and let the beef marinate at room temperature for 30 minutes, or refrigerate overnight.

In a large cast-iron skillet or wok, heat 1 tablespoon of the butter over high heat until melted and sizzling. Add the onion and bell peppers and stir-fry for 2 to 3 minutes, until they start to soften and brown. Transfer the vegetables to a plate.

Add the remaining 1 tablespoon butter to the skillet. Remove the beef from the marinade and add it to the hot skillet, in batches if necessary (do not crowd the pan). Stir-fry for 2 to 3 minutes per side, until browned and crispy. Transfer the beef to the plate with the vegetables.

To make the salad, in a large bowl, toss together the watercress, cucumber, tomato, red onion, cilantro, and mint.

In a small bowl, whisk together the lime juice, vinegar, olive oil, tamari, and maple syrup. Season with salt and pepper to taste.

Add some of the dressing to the watercress salad and toss to coat the greens evenly. Add more if needed, being careful not to overdress the salad, as this can make it soggy.

1 tablespoon extra-virgin olive oil

1 tablespoon tamari

1 tablespoon maple syrup

Fine sea salt and ground black pepper

To serve, transfer the watercress salad to a platter. Top the salad with the stir-fried beef and vegetables, arranging them in an attractive pattern. Drizzle any remaining dressing over the beef and vegetables, if desired.

Szechuan Peppercorn Beef
with Garlic Mustard Greens

In the springtime, we forage delicious wild garlic mustard greens around our property when they're still young. They make a perfect side dish to pair with spicy meats like this Szechuan peppercorn beef. Szechuan peppercorns are known for their unique flavor and their ability to numb the mouth slightly. They are used in traditional Chinese medicine to treat a variety of ailments, including stomach pain, toothache, and coughs. Szechuan peppercorns contain essential oils and antioxidants, which may have anti-inflammatory and antimicrobial properties. For a kid-friendly version, you can omit them.

Yield: 4 servings

1 tablespoon Szechuan peppercorns, lightly toasted and ground

1 tablespoon coconut sugar

1 tablespoon tamari

2 teaspoons rice vinegar

2 teaspoons sesame oil

1 pound (450 g) boneless grass-fed beef sirloin steak, thinly sliced against the grain

1 tablespoon arrowroot starch

2 tablespoons (30 g) ghee or grass-fed beef tallow, divided

2 garlic cloves, minced

1 teaspoon grated fresh ginger

8 ounces (225 g) garlic mustard greens, chopped

¼ cup (60 mL) Beef Bone and Marrow Broth (page 50) or spring water

Fine sea salt and ground black pepper

Steamed rice (pages 62–63) or cooked vermicelli noodles, for serving

Sliced scallions, for garnish (optional)

Toasted sesame seeds, for garnish (optional)

In a large bowl, whisk together the Szechuan pepper, coconut sugar, tamari, rice vinegar, and sesame oil. Add the beef and toss to coat. Cover and let the beef marinate at room temperature for 30 minutes, or refrigerate overnight.

Put the arrowroot in a shallow dish. Heat 1 tablespoon of the ghee in a large skillet or wok and swirl to coat the pan. Remove the beef from the marinade and coat each piece in the arrowroot. Add the beef to the skillet and stir-fry for 2 to 3 minutes, until browned and crispy on the outside. Transfer the beef to a plate.

Add the remaining 1 tablespoon ghee to the skillet, along with the garlic and ginger. Stir-fry for 30 seconds to 1 minute, or until fragrant. Add the broth, then add the garlic mustard greens and stir-fry for 2 to 3 minutes, until wilted and tender. Season with a pinch of salt and pepper.

Return the beef to the pan and stir-fry with the garlic mustard greens for a minute or two, until everything is well combined and heated through. Serve the beef and garlic mustard greens hot, over a bed of rice or noodles, garnished with scallions and sesame seeds, if desired.

Foraging Wild Greens

Wild garlic mustard greens are often foraged in the springtime, when they're young and tender. They are rich in vitamins A, C, and K, as well as minerals such as calcium, iron, and magnesium. Additionally, garlic mustard greens contain compounds called glucosinolates, which have been shown to have anti-inflammatory and anticancer properties.

Foraging for wild edible plants can be a fun and rewarding experience, but it's important to exercise caution and proper identification skills to avoid accidentally consuming a poisonous plant. Always do thorough research and seek guidance from a trusted expert or field guide before consuming any wild plants, and never eat anything that you can't positively identify. It is also important to be aware of potential allergens and to consume wild plants in small quantities until you are certain how your body will react. If you experience any adverse symptoms after consuming a wild plant, seek medical attention immediately.

► **HOW TO TOAST SZECHUAN PEPPERCORNS**

Toasting Szechuan peppercorns is optional, but it enhances their flavor and aroma, adding depth and complexity to your dishes. If you prefer a milder flavor, use them untoasted. Here is a simple method for toasting Szechuan peppercorns:

Heat a dry nonstick or cast-iron skillet over medium heat. Add a small amount of Szechuan peppercorns to the pan and gently shake or stir the peppercorns in the pan to ensure they toast on all sides. Toast the peppercorns until they become fragrant and turn slightly darker in color, 1 to 2 minutes. Keep a close eye on them to prevent overtoasting. Immediately transfer the toasted peppercorns to a plate to cool.

Grilled Vietnamese Beef
Wrapped in Wild Grape Leaves
(BÒ LÁ NHO)

This delicious and flavorful dish is perfect for barbecues and other outdoor gatherings. Traditional Vietnamese grilled beef is wrapped in betel leaves, but they can be difficult to find. Some Asian grocery stores carry them frozen, or you can use foraged wild grape leaves as an alternative to betel leaves. We have wild grapes growing on our land, and they can be invasive, so I am happy to use these leaves as we take down the vines. You will need 10-inch-long skewers to make this dish.

Yield: 4 servings

½ cup (50 g) minced lemongrass

3 tablespoons (27 g) minced garlic

¼ cup (35 g) minced shallots

2 tablespoons (30 mL) fish sauce or Fermented Anchovy Sauce (page 70)

2 tablespoons (30 mL) tamari

1½ teaspoons maple syrup (optional)

1 teaspoon ground black pepper

1 pound (450 g) grass-fed ground beef

20 wild grape leaves (see Note), rinsed and dried

Chopped peanuts, for garnish (optional)

Note: *Not all plants and their parts are safe to eat. Consult a reliable guidebook or a knowledgeable person before consuming wild plants. Alternatively, you can use store-bought grape leaves.*

If using bamboo skewers, soak them in water for 30 minutes.

In a large bowl, whisk together the lemongrass, garlic, shallots, fish sauce, tamari, maple syrup (if using), and pepper. Add the beef and mix well to ensure that the beef is evenly coated. Cover and refrigerate for at least 30 minutes, or up to 24 hours.

Preheat a grill to medium-high heat.

Bring a large pot of water to a boil. Fill a bowl with cold water and ice. Blanch the grape leaves in the boiling water for 30 seconds, then immediately use tongs or a slotted spoon to transfer them to the ice bath to stop the cooking process. Let them chill for 1 minute, then remove them from the ice water and pat them dry with a paper towel. Remove the hard stems with a sharp knife or scissors.

Take a grape leaf and lay it flat on a cutting board. Spoon about 2 tablespoons (30 g) of the ground beef mixture on top of the grape leaf and roll it up tightly, tucking in the sides as you go. Thread the roll onto a skewer. Repeat with the remaining grape leaves and beef mixture, threading 4 or 5 rolls on each skewer.

Grill the skewers for 2 to 3 minutes per side, until the beef is cooked through and the grape leaves are lightly charred. Serve the beef wraps hot off the grill, topped with some chopped peanuts, if you like.

Korean-Style Grilled Short Ribs

This is my favorite meal to make if I'm hosting an outdoor party, bringing food on a camping trip, or simply craving an extraordinary meal—and it is arguably our family's favorite Korean dish. Beef short ribs are marinated in a signature Korean blend and served with kimchi and rice. Sautéed mushrooms, bell peppers, and onions make great accompaniments to this dish. You may need to request these thinly sliced short rib cuts from your local butcher.

Yield: 4 servings

¼ cup (60 mL) tamari

3 tablespoons (45 mL) raw honey

3 tablespoons (45 mL) rice vinegar

1 tablespoon sesame oil

1 tablespoon minced garlic

1 tablespoon grated fresh ginger

1 teaspoon ground black pepper

2 tablespoons (4 g) chopped scallion (optional)

2 pounds (900 g) flanken-style grass-fed beef short ribs

1 tablespoon unsalted grass-fed butter (optional)

In a large bowl, whisk together the tamari, honey, vinegar, sesame oil, garlic, ginger, pepper, and scallion, if using. Add the beef and toss to coat. Cover and let the beef marinate in the refrigerator for at least 2 hours, or overnight.

Preheat a grill or stovetop grill pan to medium-high heat. If using a grill pan, add the butter to prevent sticking.

Remove the beef from the marinade and shake off any excess. Grill the beef for 2 to 3 minutes per side, until cooked to your desired doneness. Be careful not to overcook the beef, as it can become tough and chewy. Transfer the beef to a platter and let it rest for a few minutes before serving.

Chinese Five-Spice Beef with Sautéed Bok Choy

Get ready to elevate your taste buds with the tantalizing flavors of Chinese cuisine. The combination of ingredients in this dish come together to provide a burst of flavor with simple ingredients. Chinese five-spice powder is a traditional blend of spices that typically includes cinnamon, cloves, fennel seed, star anise, and Szechuan peppercorns. The richness of the beef pairs perfectly with the freshness of sautéed bok choy, adding a delightful crunch and a hint of natural sweetness to each bite.

Yield: 4 servings

FOR THE BEEF

1 tablespoon Chinese five-spice powder

2 tablespoons (30 mL) tamari

2 tablespoons (30 mL) raw honey

2 tablespoons (30 mL) rice vinegar

1 garlic clove, minced

1 teaspoon grated fresh ginger

1 pound (450 g) grass-fed beef flank or skirt steak, sliced ½ inch (13 mm) thick

2 tablespoons (30 g) ghee or coconut oil, plus more if needed

FOR THE BOK CHOY

4 cups (300 g) chopped bok choy

1 garlic clove, minced

Fine sea salt and ground black pepper

Toasted sesame seeds, for garnish

Prepare the beef: In a large bowl, whisk together the five-spice powder, tamari, honey, vinegar, garlic, and ginger. Add the beef and toss to coat. Cover and marinate at room temperature for 30 minutes, or refrigerate overnight.

In a large skillet or wok, melt the ghee over medium-high heat. Remove the beef from the marinade and add it to the skillet. Stir-fry for 2 to 3 minutes, until the beef is browned and cooked through. Transfer the beef to a plate.

Make the bok choy: If needed, add a little more ghee to the skillet and add the bok choy and garlic. Sauté for 3 to 4 minutes, until the bok choy is tender but still retains some of its crunch. Season with salt and pepper to taste.

Transfer the bok choy to a platter and top it with the stir-fried beef. Garnish with sesame seeds, and serve hot.

Japanese Miso Beef Stew

This dish takes the traditional concept of a hearty stew and infuses it with the unique flavors of Japan. Umami-rich miso is the secret ingredient that makes this nutritious beef stew full of flavor. I prefer to use organic red miso, which is made from fermenting rice and soybeans for a long time to create a distinctly rich taste.

Yield: 6 servings

2 tablespoons (30 g) ghee or coconut oil

2 pounds (900g) boneless grass-fed beef chuck roast, cut into 1-inch (2.5 cm) cubes

1 large onion, diced

4 garlic cloves, minced

1 (1-inch [2.5 cm]) piece fresh ginger, peeled and grated

1 quart (1 L) Beef Bone and Marrow Broth (page 50)

¼ cup (60 mL) tamari

2 tablespoons (30 mL) raw honey

2 tablespoons (30 mL) rice vinegar

2 tablespoons (30 mL) tomato paste

2 tablespoons (30 mL) organic red miso paste

½ teaspoon ground black pepper

2 carrots, peeled and cut into 1-inch (2.5 cm) pieces

2 potatoes, peeled and cut into 1-inch (2.5 cm) pieces

2 cups (130 g) chopped kale or other leafy greens

2 tablespoons (16 g) arrowroot starch (optional)

2 tablespoons (30 mL) cold spring water (optional)

Sliced scallions and/or chopped fresh herbs, for garnish (optional)

Melt the ghee in a large pot or Dutch oven over medium-high heat. Working in batches as necessary so as not to crowd the pot, add the beef and brown on all sides, 5 to 7 minutes. Transfer the beef to a plate.

Add the onion, garlic, and ginger to the pot and sauté until the onion is soft and translucent, about 5 minutes.

In a medium bowl, whisk together the beef broth, tamari, honey, vinegar, tomato paste, miso, and pepper. Add the broth mixture to the pot and stir to combine with the onion mixture. Return the beef to the pot and bring the mixture to a boil. Reduce the heat to low, partially cover, and simmer for 1 to 2 hours, stirring occasionally, until the beef is nearly tender.

Add the carrots and potatoes and continue to simmer until the vegetables are tender and the flavors have melded together, 30 to 45 minutes. Add the kale and stir until wilted, about 5 minutes.

If you prefer a thicker stew, in a small bowl, whisk together the arrowroot and spring water and add this slurry to the pot. Simmer the stew for 5 more minutes, or until it thickens. Serve hot, garnished with scallions and/or fresh herbs, if desired.

CHAPTER 9

Lamb

For centuries, sheep and lamb have been an important part of many traditional Asian cuisines, partly because their meat is so highly nutritious. Sheep, like cows, are ruminants, which means they have a four-chambered stomach that allows them to efficiently break down tough plant materials such as grass and hay. This unique digestive system also enables them to extract important nutrients and vitamins from their food, making them an excellent source of nutrient-dense meat.

Sheep and lamb meat is high in protein, vitamins B12 and B6, iron, zinc, and niacin, which are essential for maintaining good health. Lamb meat is also a great source of conjugated linoleic acid (CLA), a type of healthy fat that has been linked to a reduced risk of heart disease, cancer, and inflammation. In some parts of Asia, sheep and lamb are also used in traditional medicine. For example, in Chinese medicine, lamb is believed to have warming properties and is often used to treat colds and other respiratory illnesses. The meat is also thought to nourish the blood and boost energy levels.

As it turns out, our family loves lamb! In fact, it may be our favorite protein. As a family, we especially enjoy a Mongolian hot pot, also known as shabu-shabu, which involves cooking thin slices of lamb or mutton in a hot pot filled with a flavorful broth, along with an array of vegetables, mushrooms, and other ingredients.

On our regenerative homestead, our sheep play an important role by contributing to soil health, providing a source of nutrient-dense food, and promoting biodiversity. After moving from our urban homestead with chickens, we explored other poultry options like turkeys and ducks. When we felt confident enough to venture into larger animals, we decided to bring sheep onto our six acres and graze them rotationally. Sheep are known for their ability to graze on grass and other plants, which helps keep fields and pastures healthy and well maintained. Additionally, their manure naturally fertilizes the soil, promoting healthy soil biology and nutrient cycling.

Lamb Bulgogi

With its diverse population and a strong interest in different cuisines, Los Angeles is home to a vibrant international restaurant scene, including some of the best Korean American food I've ever had. Bulgogi is a Korean dish made with slices of beef (or sometimes pork or chicken) that are marinated and then grilled or stir-fried. The term *bulgogi* literally means "fire meat" in Korean, which refers to the cooking method of grilling over an open flame. Lamb bulgogi is delicious served over rice for a complete and satisfying meal that is sure to impress. I also love it wrapped in a spring roll with fresh vegetables (see page 195). The marinade gives the lamb a wonderful blend of sweet and savory flavors with a touch of tanginess. The nuttiness of the sesame seeds and the freshness of the scallions add a beautiful contrast to the rich and savory flavors of the lamb.

Yield: 4 servings

FOR THE MARINADE

1 Asian pear or Fuji apple, cored and grated
4 garlic cloves, minced
¼ cup (60 mL) tamari
2 tablespoons (30 mL) raw honey
1 tablespoon toasted sesame oil
1 tablespoon sake (rice wine) or mirin
2 teaspoons grated fresh ginger
¼ teaspoon ground black pepper

FOR THE LAMB

1 pound (450 g) boneless pasture-raised
   lamb, thinly sliced
1 tablespoon sesame oil
1 onion, sliced

FOR SERVING

2 scallions, sliced
1 tablespoon sesame seeds
Steamed rice (pages 62–63)

Make the marinade: In a large bowl, combine the pear, garlic, tamari, honey, toasted sesame oil, sake, ginger, and pepper and whisk together.

Add the lamb to the marinade and toss to coat evenly. Cover and marinate in the refrigerator for at least 1 hour, or preferably overnight.

Heat the sesame oil in a large skillet or wok over high heat and swirl to coat the pan. Add the onion and cook for 1 to 2 minutes, until slightly softened. Remove the lamb from the marinade with a slotted spoon and add it to the pan. (Discard any remaining marinade.) Stir-fry for 5 to 7 minutes, until the lamb is browned and cooked through.

Sprinkle the scallions and sesame seeds over the lamb and toss to combine. Serve hot, over a bed of rice.

How to Assemble Spring Rolls

Rolling a spring roll takes a little bit of practice to perfect. Follow these steps to create beautiful and delicious spring rolls. You can add other ingredients like sliced avocado, various greens, cooked chicken, sliced pork belly, and fun herbs. Use your favorite ingredients to make the spring rolls your own!

YOU WILL NEED

Rice paper wrappers

Lettuce leaves

Vermicelli noodles, cooked and cooled (optional)

Wild-caught shrimp, peeled, deveined, and cooked (optional)

Lamb Bulgogi (page 193)

Bean sprouts

Julienned carrots or Vietnamese Pickled Carrots and Daikon (page 97)

Julienned cucumbers

Sliced radishes

Fresh herb leaves, such as cilantro, mint, and Thai basil

Dipping sauce, such as Hoisin Sauce (page 80), Vietnamese Peanut Dipping Sauce (page 81), or Vietnamese Dipping Sauce (page 68)

Dip a rice paper wrapper in a bowl of warm water for a few seconds. You want the wrapper to become soft and pliable, but not so soft that it tears.

Remove the wrapper from the water and lay it flat on a clean work surface, such as a plate or cutting board. Place a lettuce leaf on the bottom third of the rice paper, leaving a border of about 1 inch (2.5 cm) at the bottom. This will act as a barrier to prevent the filling from falling out. Layer a small amount of vermicelli noodles on top of the lettuce leaf, followed by a few shrimp (if using), a few pieces of lamb, bean sprouts, carrots, cucumbers, radishes, and fresh herbs. Arrange the ingredients in neat rows, leaving some space at the top of the wrapper for rolling.

Fold the bottom edge of the rice paper up over the filling, tucking it under the filling at the top to secure it. This creates a tight seal at the bottom of the roll. Fold the sides of the rice paper in toward the center. Roll the spring roll up tightly, starting from the bottom and rolling upward, until the entire wrapper is rolled up around the filling. Use your fingers to tuck in any loose bits of filling as you go.

Repeat with the remaining ingredients to make as many spring rolls as desired. Serve the spring rolls with dipping sauce on the side.

Vietnamese-Style Lamb Burgers

These burgers are a family tradition. With just a few simple ingredients, we can have a delicious and healthy way to enjoy a classic burger with a flavorful twist! Since we grind most of our lamb, this is our go-to for what to do with ground lamb. When I want to stretch out our lamb meat, I will combine it in a 50:50 blend with ground beef. This allows our family to enjoy more of our lamb meat when we have it, and the family loves this blend as well!

Yield: 4 servings

1 pound (450 g) ground pasture-raised lamb

1 lemongrass stalk, tough outer layer
    removed, minced

2 garlic cloves, minced

1 tablespoon (15 mL) raw honey (optional)

1 tablespoon grated fresh ginger

1 tablespoon tamari

1 tablespoon fish sauce or Fermented
    Anchovy Sauce (page 70)

1 tablespoon toasted sesame oil

¼ teaspoon ground black pepper

1 tablespoon ghee or grass-fed beef tallow

4 burger buns, toasted, or lettuce leaves

Toppings: sliced avocado, sliced red onion,
    sliced cucumber, fresh cilantro or
    mint leaves

Lime wedges, for serving (optional)

In a large bowl, combine the lamb, lemongrass, garlic, honey, ginger, tamari, fish sauce, sesame oil, and pepper. Mix the ingredients well so that they are evenly distributed throughout the lamb.

Divide the lamb mixture into four equal portions and shape them into patties. Press down gently on the patties to ensure that they are uniform in thickness so they will cook evenly.

Heat the ghee in a grill pan or large skillet over medium-high heat. Add the lamb patties and cook for 4 to 5 minutes per side, until they are browned and fully cooked through.

To assemble the burgers, place a cooked lamb patty on the bottom half of each bun or lettuce leaf. Add your desired toppings, and finish with a squeeze of fresh lime juice if desired. Cover with the top half of the bun or another lettuce leaf and serve.

Ground Lamb Stir-Fry

In less time than it takes to order takeout, you'll have this delicious, home-made meal on your table. This dish is perfect for those busy weeknights when time is of the essence. Serve with a bowl of rice for a complete, nourishing meal the whole family will love.

Yield: 4 servings

2 tablespoons (30 mL) tamari
1 tablespoon raw honey
1 tablespoon fish sauce or Fermented Anchovy Sauce (page 70)
1 tablespoon toasted sesame oil
1 tablespoon apple cider vinegar
2 tablespoons (30 mL) coconut oil
1 tablespoon grated fresh ginger
3 garlic cloves, minced
1 pound (450 g) ground pasture-raised lamb
1 red bell pepper, sliced
1 yellow onion, sliced
2 cups (180 g) broccoli florets
1 tablespoon arrowroot starch
2 tablespoons (30 mL) cold spring water
Fine sea salt and ground black pepper
Sliced scallions, for garnish (optional)
Toasted sesame seeds, for garnish (optional)
Steamed rice (pages 62–63), for serving

In a small bowl, whisk together the tamari, honey, fish sauce, sesame oil, and vinegar until well combined; set aside.

Heat the coconut oil in a large skillet or wok over medium-high heat. Add the ginger and garlic and cook for 1 to 2 minutes, stirring frequently to prevent burning. Add the lamb and cook, breaking up the meat into smaller pieces with a wooden spoon, until browned, about 5 minutes. Add the bell pepper and onion and cook for 3 to 4 minutes, until they're slightly softened. Add the broccoli and stir-fry everything together for an additional 2 to 3 minutes.

Pour the tamari mixture over the lamb and vegetables in the skillet, stirring to coat evenly. Continue to stir-fry for an additional minute or two until the sauce is heated through.

In a small bowl, whisk together the arrowroot and spring water to make a slurry. Add the slurry to the skillet and stir everything together. Cook until the sauce thickens slightly.

Season with salt and pepper to taste, garnish with scallions and sesame seeds, if desired, and serve immediately, with rice.

Thai Basil–Lemongrass Lamb Chops with Pea Shoots

My children have so much fun eating these delicious and flavorful Thai-inspired lamb "lollipops"! As a mom who is focused on feeding my kids a balanced diet, I appreciate that lamb chops are a good source of protein and other nutrients, such as iron, zinc, and vitamin B12, which are important for growing children. Lemongrass is a fragrant and citrusy herb commonly used in Southeast Asian cuisine, and it pairs well with lamb, which has a slightly gamy flavor. When cooked properly, the lamb chops are crispy on the outside and juicy on the inside, with a complex and flavorful marinade that permeates the meat. The salad provides a light, refreshing complement to the rich flavors of the lamb chops, and lime wedges add a zesty citrus flavor to the dish.

Yield: 4 to 6 servings

2 lemongrass stalks, tough outer layer removed, thinly sliced

4 garlic cloves, minced

1 (1-inch [2.5 cm]) piece fresh ginger, peeled and grated

2 Thai chilies, thinly sliced

¼ cup (60 mL) tamari

¼ cup (60 mL) fish sauce or Fermented Anchovy Sauce (page 70)

2 tablespoons (30 mL) raw honey

1 tablespoon toasted sesame oil

1 tablespoon avocado oil

8 pasture-raised lamb rib chops

FOR THE SALAD

1 cup (30 g) pea shoots, cut into 2- to 3-inch (5–7.5 cm) pieces

½ cup (25 g) chopped fresh Thai basil

½ cup (25 g) fresh mint leaves

Lime wedges, for serving

In a large bowl, combine the lemongrass, garlic, ginger, chilies, tamari, fish sauce, honey, sesame oil, and avocado oil and mix well. Add the lamb chops and toss them well to coat each piece evenly. Cover and refrigerate for at least 2 hours, or preferably overnight.

Make the salad: In a large bowl, toss together the pea shoots, Thai basil, and mint; set aside.

Preheat a grill or stovetop grill pan to medium-high heat. Remove the lamb chops from the marinade and grill them for 3 to 4 minutes per side, depending on your desired level of doneness. Remove the lamb chops from the grill and let them rest for a few minutes to allow the juices to redistribute throughout the meat.

Serve the lamb chops hot, with the salad and lime wedges on the side.

Roast Lamb with Shallots and Lemongrass

Leg of lamb is a traditional dish to serve for special celebrations with friends and family, and this Chinese-inspired recipe provides a unique twist on the classic preparation. The marinade not only adds flavor but also helps tenderize the meat, resulting in a juicy and succulent roast. It is our new family favorite for Passover dinner! If you have any leftovers, these would be great to put into spring rolls or bánh mì.

Yield: 8 servings

4 garlic cloves, minced

1 shallot, sliced

3 lemongrass stalks, tough outer layer removed, chopped

1 (1-inch [2.5 cm]) piece fresh ginger, peeled and roughly chopped

2 tablespoons (21 g) Chinese five-spice powder

2 tablespoons (30 g) grass-fed beef tallow

1 tablespoon tamari

2 teaspoons fine sea salt

1 teaspoon ground black pepper

1 (5-pound [2.25 kg]) bone-in pasture-raised lamb leg

Preheat the oven to 350°F (180°C).

Combine the garlic, shallot, lemongrass, ginger, five-spice powder, tallow, tamari, salt, and pepper in a blender or food processor. Blend until the spice rub mixture becomes a smooth paste. If the mixture is too thick, add a little spring water to thin it out and create a more spreadable consistency.

Place the lamb in a large roasting pan. Use a sharp knife to make small slits all over the lamb so that the flavors of the rub can penetrate the meat. Apply the spice rub generously to the lamb, making sure to coat it evenly on all sides.

Roast for 3 to 4 hours, until it reaches the desired temperature (145°F [60°C] for medium-rare). Remove the lamb from the oven and let it rest for 10 to 15 minutes to allow the juices to redistribute throughout the meat. Carve the meat off the bone to serve.

Szechuan Lamb Stir-Fry

For those special occasion dinners when I want to serve a spicy, flavorful dish for adults, this is my go-to! The secret to this lamb recipe is the marbling of the fat in the lamb. Boneless lamb shoulder is the best cut to use, although any boneless lamb will work. Cooking over high heat will sear the meat but keep it tender as well. Szechuan red pepper flakes have a unique flavor that is both spicy and tingly, in a good way! You can buy Szechuan red pepper flakes at most Asian grocery stores or online retailers. Serve this dish with plenty of white rice.

Yield: 4 servings

1 tablespoon toasted sesame oil
1 tablespoon tamari
2 garlic cloves, minced
1 tablespoon ground cumin
1 teaspoon arrowroot starch
1 pound (450 g) boneless pasture-raised lamb, patted dry and cut into ½-inch by 2-inch (13 mm × 5 cm) pieces
1 tablespoon cumin seeds
2 tablespoons (30 g) grass-fed beef tallow or coconut oil
2 dried red chilies, chopped
½ teaspoon Szechuan red pepper flakes or chili powder
2 scallions, sliced
2 tablespoons (5 g) chopped fresh cilantro
Fine sea salt
Steamed rice (pages 62–63), for serving

In a large bowl, whisk together the sesame oil, tamari, garlic, ground cumin, and arrowroot. Add the lamb and stir until the lamb is evenly coated. Set aside and let it marinate for 30 minutes or preferably overnight.

Heat a wok or large skillet over medium heat. Add the cumin seeds and toast them until fragrant, 1 to 2 minutes; keep an eye on them and stir frequently to prevent burning. Transfer the cumin seeds to a plate and set aside.

Heat the wok over high heat until it starts to smoke. Add the tallow and tilt the wok to coat, then immediately add the lamb. Spread the meat out in a single layer to ensure even cooking. Sear the meat until it turns brown and starts to crisp slightly, about 5 minutes.

Add the cumin seeds, dried chilies, red pepper flakes, scallions, cilantro, and season with salt. Toss everything together quickly so that the scallions and cilantro are just slightly cooked. Transfer to a serving dish and serve hot, with rice.

Lamb Makhani

For our family, there is one Indian dish that's worth making at home, and it's this ridiculously easy-to-make butter curry. The aromatic spices are commonly found in any grocery store. With our own dairy cow, we often have lots of butter and cream, which help make this dish shine with the richness of the lamb. Serve with basmati rice and sourdough naan on the side.

Yield: 4 servings

2 tablespoons (30 g) ghee or unsalted grass-fed butter
1 pound (450 g) boneless pasture-raised lamb, cut into bite-size pieces
1 onion, finely chopped
1 tablespoon grated fresh ginger
1 tablespoon minced garlic
2 teaspoons ground cumin
2 teaspoons ground coriander
1 teaspoon ground turmeric
1 teaspoon garam masala
1 teaspoon paprika
1 teaspoon dried fenugreek leaves (kasuri methi)
1 cup (225 g) tomato puree
2 potatoes, peeled and cut into bite-size pieces
2 carrots, peeled and cut into bite-size pieces
½ cup (120 mL) heavy cream, preferably raw
Fine sea salt
Chopped fresh cilantro, for garnish
Lime wedges, for serving

Melt the ghee in a large cast-iron skillet or Dutch oven over medium-high heat. When it starts to shimmer and sizzle slightly, add the lamb and cook until it is browned on all sides, about 2 to 3 minutes on each side. Transfer the lamb to a plate and set aside.

Add the onion to the drippings left in the pan and cook over medium heat, stirring occasionally to prevent it from burning, until soft and translucent, 3 to 4 minutes. Add the ginger and garlic and cook for another minute, stirring occasionally. Add the cumin, coriander, turmeric, garam masala, paprika, and fenugreek to the pan and cook, stirring, for 1 to 2 minutes, until fragrant.

Add the tomato puree and stir everything together. If the mixture looks too dry, you can add a splash of water or chicken broth to thin it out slightly. Reduce the heat to medium-low and bring the mixture to a simmer. Cook for 15 to 20 minutes, stirring occasionally.

Return the lamb to the pan, along with the potatoes and carrots. Stir everything together and let it simmer until the lamb is tender and the vegetables are cooked through, about 30 minutes.

Stir in the cream and let the mixture simmer for another 5 to 10 minutes.

Taste the curry and season it with salt as needed. Garnish with chopped cilantro and serve hot, with lime wedges.

Chinese Mutton Stew with Daikon Radish

A popular dish in Chinese cuisine, mutton stew with daikon radish is a comforting and hearty meal. For this dish, tender chunks of mutton or lamb are slow-cooked in a flavorful broth infused with garlic and ginger. The long, slow cooking time allows the flavors to fully develop and the meat to become tender and juicy. The inclusion of daikon radish provides a hint of sweetness and adds a delightful crunch to the stew. The fresh herbs add a pop of color and brightness to the dish, as well as some extra flavor. This warm and satisfying meal is perfect for cold weather or any time you desire a bowl of hearty goodness.

Yield: 4 servings

1 pound (450 g) boneless
    pasture-raised mutton or lamb,
    cut into 1-inch (2.5 cm) pieces
2 tablespoons (30 g) ghee or coconut oil
1 onion, chopped
2 or 3 garlic cloves, minced
1 (4-inch [10 cm]) piece fresh ginger,
    tenderized (see page 44)
4 cups (1 L) spring water
2 tablespoons (30 mL) tamari
1 teaspoon fine sea salt
½ teaspoon ground black pepper
1 daikon, peeled and chopped
2 tablespoons (16 g) arrowroot starch
    (optional)
2 tablespoons (30 mL) cold spring water
    (optional)
2 scallions, sliced (optional)
Chopped fresh cilantro, for garnish (optional)

Heat a large pot or Dutch oven over medium-high heat. Add the mutton and pour in enough water to cover the meat. Bring to a boil and cook for 1 to 2 minutes, skimming off any scum. Drain and rinse the lamb chunks under cool running water. Set aside. Rinse out the pot.

Add the ghee to the pot and melt it over medium heat. Add the onion and garlic and cook until the onion is soft, about 5 minutes. Increase the heat to high and return the mutton to the pot. Cook for 10 minutes, or until the pieces of lamb are lightly browned around the edges.

Add the ginger, spring water, and tamari and season with the salt and pepper. Bring the mixture to a boil, then reduce the heat and let it simmer for 1 to 2 hours, until the meat is tender and the flavors have melded together.

Gently stir in the daikon and cook for 45 minutes, until the daikon is tender.

If you prefer a thicker sauce, dissolve the arrowroot in the cold water to make a slurry, then pour the slurry into the simmering sauce and stir until the sauce thickens slightly and becomes glossy in appearance. If you find that the sauce is still too thin for your liking, add more arrowroot slurry until it reaches your desired consistency.

Remove the stew from the heat and let it cool for a few minutes. Serve garnished with scallions and cilantro, if desired.

CHAPTER 10

Seafood

As a child, I learned how to shop for the different varieties of fish and shellfish with my mother at many various grocery stores. She would search high and low throughout the San Francisco Bay Area and even venture to Half Moon Bay to get the freshest seafood. I learned to look at the overall appearance of a fish, from the eyes to the gills to the scales, and touch the fish to assess its firmness. I even learned to identify the mild, oceanic smell of fresh fish compared to the "fishy" smell of those past their prime. I loved watching the fish swim through live fish tanks, and she would make sure she let the fishmonger know the exact fish she wanted and how she wanted it cleaned and prepared.

Most Asian countries are known for their love of seafood and have access to a wide variety of fish, shellfish, and seaweed. Wild-caught fish such as salmon, mackerel, and sardines are excellent sources of omega-3 fatty acids and other important nutrients. These also happen to be staple ingredients in Vietnamese, Japanese, and Korean cooking. Vietnam is known for a variety of dishes made with fish, shrimp, squid, and other seafood, such as Vietnamese Sweet-and-Sour Tamarind Soup (page 126) and seafood hot pot (lẩu hải sản, see page 138). With its long coastline and ancient fishing traditions, Japan is renowned for its consumption of seafood, especially sushi, sashimi, and grilled fish. China also has a long coastline, with popular dishes such as steamed fish, hot and sour soup with seafood, and fried shrimp. Thailand's cuisine is known for its bold and spicy flavors, and seafood plays a significant role in many Thai dishes.

To source high-quality, clean seafood, look for wild-caught seafood from sustainable sources. You can start by finding a reputable fishmonger or seafood market that sources their products from sustainable fisheries. Look for labels or certifications such as Marine Stewardship Council (MSC), an independent organization that sets standards for sustainable fishing practices.

Another resource is Seafood Watch from the Monterey Bay Aquarium, which provides recommendations for seafood choices. They offer a free app for your phone or on the web that allows you to search for specific types of seafood and see their recommendations for each one.

When choosing seafood, it's important to consider not only the environmental impact but also the quality and safety of the seafood. Look for seafood that is fresh and firm and has only a mild odor, and avoid seafood that smells overly fishy or has a strong ammonia smell. It's also important to follow safe food handling and cooking practices to prevent foodborne illness.

Ensuring that seafood is properly cooked is not only crucial for safety but also for savoring the exquisite flavors and textures of these ocean treasures. While having a food thermometer may be the best tool to guarantee that seafood reaches the recommended internal temperature of 145°F (63°C), there are other handy indicators you can rely on if you ever find yourself without one.

When it comes to fish, look for telltale signs that it's cooked to perfection: the flesh should transform into a beautiful, opaque hue, and it should readily separate into delicate flakes with just a gentle touch of a fork. This is not only a visual delight but also a sensory confirmation of its readiness.

For seafood such as shrimp, scallops, crab, and lobster, the transition to doneness involves a change in the texture. As they cook, their flesh undergoes a transformation, becoming firm and turning opaque. This change in texture is a clear signal that they are ready to be enjoyed.

Now, when you're dealing with the bivalve wonders of the sea, such as clams, mussels, and oysters, their shells offer a distinctive sign of readiness during cooking. These creatures have a unique way of expressing their doneness by opening up during the cooking process, which signifies that these shellfish are fully cooked and safe to enjoy. You should discard any clams, mussels, or oysters that remain tightly shut after cooking, as this may indicate that they were not alive before cooking and are, therefore, unsafe to consume.

Chinese Fish Balls

While you can buy fish balls ready-made at Asian grocers, it's really easy to make them at home with just a few ingredients. Plus, if you make extra, you can always store them in the freezer for a quick and tasty meal on a busy day. These fish balls can be enjoyed on their own as a snack, added to noodle soups, or served as a side dish with a dipping sauce. You can use cod or any other white fish, but I especially love using salmon for its vibrant natural color, texture, and taste.

Yield: 6 to 8 servings as a side

1 pound (450 g) fresh salmon fillet or any white fish (cod, tilapia, bass, grouper)
1 tablespoon fish sauce or Fermented Anchovy Sauce (page 70)
1 tablespoon grated fresh ginger
1 tablespoon minced garlic
½ teaspoon ground white pepper
1 large pasture-raised egg white
3 tablespoons (24 g) arrowroot starch

Mince the fish using a chopper or food processor. Add the fish sauce, ginger, garlic, white pepper, egg white, and arrowroot and pulse until it has a smooth and pasty texture. (Alternatively, you can finely chop the fish and beat it with the blunt edge of a cleaver to flatten it until the fish is tender and paste-like, then mix in the remaining ingredients.)

Fill a small bowl with cold water to periodically dip your hands into to prevent sticking. Form the fish mixture into 1-inch (2.5 cm) balls by rolling them between your palms. Place the fish balls spaced out on a rimmed baking sheet until you're ready to cook them.

Bring a large pot of water to a boil and cook the fish balls for 3 to 5 minutes, until cooked through. Scoop them out with a skimmer and serve, or set aside for use in soup or hot pot.

Korean Seafood Pancake

This recipe is a tasty, nourishing twist on a traditional Korean favorite. It uses sprouted wheat flour for better digestion, bone broth for added minerals and gelatin, and coconut oil or lard for healthy fat. The scallions and kimchi add a savory kick to the pancake, while the seafood provides a healthy dose of protein and omega-3 fatty acids.

Yield: 2 to 4 servings

FOR THE PANCAKE

1 cup (125 g) sprouted wheat flour
½ cup (60 g) rice flour
1 cup (240 mL) Fish Broth (page 47) or
  Gelatinous Chicken Bone Broth (page 48)
1 large pasture-raised egg, beaten
½ teaspoon toasted sesame oil
½ teaspoon fine sea salt
½ cup (100 g) chopped seafood, such as
  oysters, shrimp, or scallops
½ cup (120 g) chopped kimchi,
  plus more for garnish
½ cup (30 g) sliced scallions,
  plus more for garnish
¼ cup (30 g) chopped onion
¼ cup (15 g) chopped garlic chives
Coconut oil or lard, for frying

FOR THE DIPPING SAUCE

3 tablespoons (45 mL) tamari
1½ teaspoons rice vinegar
1 teaspoon panela
1 teaspoon toasted sesame oil
½ teaspoon toasted sesame seeds

Combine the wheat flour and rice flour in a large bowl. Add the broth, egg, sesame oil, and salt and stir until the mixture is smooth. Let it sit for 30 minutes at room temperature to allow the flour to absorb the liquid.

Meanwhile, make the dipping sauce by whisking together the tamari, rice vinegar, panela, sesame oil, and sesame seeds in a small bowl; set aside.

Once the batter has rested, add the seafood, kimchi, scallions, onion, and garlic chives and mix well to incorporate all the ingredients.

Heat a large skillet or griddle over medium-high heat and add enough coconut oil to coat the bottom. Pour the batter into the skillet and spread it evenly to make a pancake. Cook the pancake for 3 to 4 minutes on each side, until it is golden brown and crispy.

To serve, cut the pancake into wedges, garnish with more scallions and kimchi, and serve with the dipping sauce.

Easy Shrimp and Vegetable Stir-Fry

In just minutes, this colorful and nutritious meal will satisfy both your taste buds and your busy schedule. The succulent shrimp and crisp vegetables come together in a delightful medley of flavors, while stir-frying them seals the freshness and crunch. This is yet another reliable go-to dish for a wholesome, delicious weeknight dinner or a great option for entertaining guests of all ages!

Yield: 4 to 6 servings

2 tablespoons (30 mL) tamari

2 tablespoons (30 mL) fish sauce or Fermented Anchovy Sauce (page 70)

1 tablespoon honey

1 teaspoon arrowroot starch

1 tablespoon unsalted grass-fed butter

1 tablespoon sesame oil

1 red bell pepper, seeded and thinly sliced

1 yellow onion, thinly sliced

2 garlic cloves, minced

1 tablespoon grated fresh ginger

1 cup (60 g) sugar snap peas, trimmed

1 cup (70 g) sliced button mushrooms

1 cup (70 g) shredded green cabbage

1 pound (450 g) wild-caught jumbo shrimp, peeled and deveined

2 scallions, thinly sliced

½ cup (20 g) chopped fresh cilantro

Steamed rice (pages 62–63), for serving

In a small bowl, whisk together the tamari, fish sauce, honey, and arrowroot; set aside.

Melt the butter with the sesame oil in a wok or large skillet over high heat. Add the bell pepper and onion and stir-fry for 1 to 2 minutes, until they start to soften. Add the garlic and ginger and stir-fry for 30 seconds, until fragrant. Add the sugar snap peas, mushrooms, and cabbage and stir-fry for 1 to 2 minutes, until the vegetables are just cooked. Add the shrimp and stir-fry for 2 to 3 minutes, until they turn pink and are cooked through.

Rewhisk the sauce if necessary, pour it over the stir-fry, and toss to coat evenly. Cook for 1 to 2 minutes, until the sauce thickens. Garnish with the scallions and cilantro and serve hot, with rice.

Hanoi Turmeric Halibut with Dill
(CHẢ CÁ LÃ VỌNG)

In our home, the ingredients for this dish are laid out on the dining table, and everything is cooked at the table for the family to enjoy either as a noodle bowl or wrapped in rice paper for a fresh spring roll. The layers of flavor and texture make this delicious, versatile, nourishing dish one of our favorites. The turmeric not only adds a warm, earthy flavor to the fish but also has anti-inflammatory compounds that are good for your health. Coconut oil is the perfect complement, adding depth and complexity, as the dill lends a bright, herbaceous note that balances out the richness of the fish. You can use any white fish for this dish, but I love the flakiness of halibut. Serve with a fermented shrimp paste dipping sauce (page 84) or nước chấm (page 68).

Yield: 4 to 6 servings

2 tablespoons (30 mL) fish sauce or Fermented Anchovy Sauce (page 70)

2 tablespoons (18 g) grated fresh ginger

1 tablespoon minced garlic

1 tablespoon ground turmeric

Fine sea salt and ground black pepper

1 pound (450 g) halibut or other white fish fillet, cut into bite-size pieces

3 tablespoons (45 mL) coconut oil

1 onion, sliced

½ cup (25 g) chopped fresh dill

1 bunch scallions, cut into 2-inch (5 cm) pieces

1 (1-pound [450 g]) package rice vermicelli noodles, cooked according to package instructions, or 1 (8-ounce [226 g]) package rice paper wrappers

1 head lettuce, cored and chopped

Fresh cilantro and/or mint leaves

Chopped peanuts

Vietnamese Dipping Sauce (page 68) or other dipping sauce, for serving (optional)

In a large bowl, mix together the fish sauce, ginger, garlic, and turmeric. Season with salt and pepper. Add the fish and toss with the marinade, making sure all pieces are fully coated. Cover and marinate in the refrigerator for at least 1 hour, or preferably overnight.

Heat the coconut oil in a large cast-iron or other heavy skillet over high heat. Add the fish, onion, dill, and scallions and cook until the fish is cooked through and nicely browned, 3 to 4 minutes per side.

To serve the fish as is, place it on a bed of noodles, with lettuce, cilantro, and chopped peanuts, along with your choice of dipping sauce.

To enjoy the fish wrapped in a spring roll (this is my favorite way!), fill a large, shallow dish with warm water. Dip a rice paper wrapper into the water and let it soak for 5 to 10 seconds, until it is soft and pliable. Place the wrapper on a clean, flat surface. Spoon some of the fish mixture, noodles, lettuce, herbs, and chopped peanuts down the center of the wrapper. Fold the wrapper over the filling, tuck in the sides, then roll it up tightly, like a burrito. Repeat with the remaining wrappers and filling. Serve with your choice of dipping sauce.

Supercharged Sushi with Turmeric-Spiced Salmon and Kimchi

My kids just love sushi! They ask for it all the time, and not just for school lunches—we even pack it for picnics. I like to make it extra nutritious by using forbidden black rice, which provides a beautiful color contrast and makes it super healthy. Sometimes, when the kids aren't in the mood for raw fish, I cook salmon for them, and they love it just as much. If we're feeling really fancy, I'll add some salmon roe on top for an extra burst of flavor. It's amazing how something as simple as sushi can be so versatile and loved by everyone in the family. For this recipe, you will need a bamboo rolling mat.

Yield: *4 to 6 servings*

FOR THE RICE

2 cups (360 g) forbidden black rice or sushi rice (see Note)

3 cups (720 mL) spring water

3 tablespoons (45 mL) rice vinegar

2 tablespoons (30 mL) maple syrup

1 teaspoon fine sea salt

FOR THE SUSHI ROLLS

½ teaspoon ground turmeric

8 ounces (225 g) wild-caught salmon fillet, skinned and cut into thin ½-inch strips (see Note)

1 teaspoon sesame oil (optional)

1 (0.6-ounce [17 g]) package (7¾ inches [20 cm] square) roasted nori sheets

Note: If you prefer to use short-grain Japanese rice (sushi rice), use only 2¼ cups (600 mL) water and cook for only 15 to 20 minutes

If you prefer raw salmon, you can omit the cooking step and use slices of fresh, sushi-grade salmon in your sushi rolls.

Rinse the rice in a fine-mesh strainer under cold running water until the water runs clear. Put the rice in a bowl, cover with water, and soak for at least 30 minutes. Drain.

In a medium saucepan, combine the rice and spring water and bring to a boil over medium-high heat. Cover, reduce the heat to low, and simmer for 30 to 35 minutes, until all the water has been absorbed and the rice is tender.

While the rice is cooking, combine the vinegar, maple syrup, and salt in a small saucepan. Heat the mixture over low heat, stirring, until everything dissolves completely. Set aside to cool.

Transfer the hot rice to a large, shallow, nonmetal bowl and let it rest for 10 minutes. Stir in the vinegar mixture and let it cool to room temperature. The rice grains should be slightly sticky and hold together when formed into a lump. To help with cooling and drying, you can fan the rice with a handheld fan or a table fan. Set aside.

Make the rolls: In a small bowl, create a paste by mixing the turmeric with a splash of water. Rub this paste onto the salmon slices, coating them evenly.

Heat a skillet or grill pan over medium-high heat and lightly coat the pan with sesame oil. Place the salmon slices in the hot pan and cook for 1 to 2 minutes on each side. Once the salmon is cooked to your liking, remove it from the pan and let cool.

Chopped kimchi

Cucumber sticks

Carrot sticks

Radish slices

Avocado slices

Broccoli or sunflower sprouts

FOR SERVING

Salmon roe and tobiko (flying fish eggs)

Tamari

Wasabi paste

Pickled Ginger (recipe follows)

To assemble the sushi rolls, place the bamboo mat flat on a cutting board and lay one sheet of nori on the mat with the shiny side facing down. Take about ½ cup (100 g) of the cooked rice and spoon it onto the seaweed. Moisten your hands with water to prevent the rice from sticking. Gently spread the rice to the edges, leaving a 1-inch (2.5 cm) border at the far end of the seaweed.

Place the fish slices in a row across the rice, slightly below the center of the nori. Add a strip of your desired sushi toppings (kimchi, cucumber, avocado slices, etc.) across the end of the seaweed closest to you. Using the mat to help you, start rolling and pressing the seaweed and rice mixture to form a roll. Roll it to the far end of the seaweed, then stop rolling and dampen the open edge with your fingers dipped in water to seal the roll. Gently press the roll to seal.

Place the finished roll on a plate and continue making the remaining rolls. To serve, slice each roll into 5 or 6 sections and arrange them on a serving plate, topped with salmon roe. Wet the knife with water between each slice to prevent sticking. Serve the rolls with tamari, wasabi paste, and pickled ginger.

Pickled Ginger

Yield: about 1 cup (240 mL)

1 (8-ounce [225 g]) piece fresh ginger, peeled and julienned or cut into thin rounds

1 cup (240 mL) rice vinegar

½ cup (120 mL) maple syrup

½ teaspoon fine sea salt

Note: If you want to add a pop of color to your pickled ginger, you can add a small amount of beet juice to the vinegar mixture before pouring it over the ginger. This will give a pink hue similar to the pickled ginger served at sushi restaurants.

Put the ginger slices in a clean jar.

In a small saucepan, combine the vinegar, maple syrup, and sea salt. Heat the mixture over low heat until the maple syrup dissolves, stirring occasionally. Once the mixture is smooth, pour it over the ginger slices in the jar, making sure they are fully submerged.

Allow the ginger to cool to room temperature, then cover the jar and refrigerate for at least 24 hours before using. During this time, the ginger will absorb the sweet and tangy flavors of the vinegar mixture and become tender and slightly translucent.

The pickled ginger will keep in the fridge for up to 1 month, but it's best to consume it within a few weeks for optimal flavor and texture.

Vietnamese Sweet Potato and Shrimp Fritters
(BÁNH TÔM HÀ NỘI)

This is one of my mother's favorite appetizers, which she would make on special occasions. It reminded her of one of her early memories with her father. When she would go with him to the barber shop in Hanoi, there was a street vendor who would fry these shrimp fritters right outside the barber shop. She would ask him for an order of two fritters while she was waiting for my grandfather and would have the vendor cut them into quarters so that she could stretch them out. I have grown to love this dish, and because of the abundance of sweet potatoes we grow on our land, Mom can enjoy it even more often. The fritters are served with lettuce leaves and pickled carrots and daikon.

Yield: 4 to 6 servings

4 teaspoons (20 mL) apple cider vinegar
6 cups (1.5 L) spring water
2½ teaspoons fine sea salt, divided
2 large pasture-raised eggs
1 pound (450 g) sweet potatoes, peeled and cut into ¼-inch-thick (6 mm) sticks
½ cup (70 g) rice flour
½ cup (70 g) cassava flour
½ cup (64 g) arrowroot starch
½ teaspoon ground turmeric
¼ teaspoon ground black pepper
1 cup (240 mL) whole milk (preferably raw)
Grass-fed beef tallow or avocado oil, for frying
1 pound (450 g) wild-caught jumbo shrimp, deveined, shell left on

FOR SERVING (OPTIONAL)
Lettuce leaves
Chopped fresh herbs such as cilantro or mint
Vietnamese Pickled Carrots and Daikon (page 97)
Vietnamese Dipping Sauce (page 68)

In a large bowl, combine the vinegar, spring water, and 2 teaspoons of the salt and stir until the salt is dissolved. Add the sweet potato sticks and soak for 30 minutes to help crisp them up. Drain, then rinse the potatoes, pat dry, and set aside.

In a large bowl, whisk together the eggs, rice flour, cassava flour, arrowroot starch, turmeric, remaining ½ teaspoon salt, and pepper. Gradually whisk in the milk until you get a thick batter with no clumps; you might not need all the milk. Cover and let the batter rest for 15 minutes.

Line a plate with paper towels. Fill a wok or large, deep skillet about one-third of the way with tallow and heat over high heat. The oil is ready when a chopstick or wooden spoon dipped into the oil forms small bubbles. Dunk 10 to 15 sweet potato sticks in the batter and, using a spoon, carefully scoop the mixture into the oil, forming small fritters. Cook for 2 minutes, then dunk a piece of shrimp in the batter, put it on top of the sweet potatoes, and cook for 4 to 5 minutes, until the shrimp is pink and cooked through. Transfer the fritter to the paper towels and season with salt. Repeat until all the sweet potatoes, batter, and shrimp are used.

To serve, arrange the fritters on a platter with lettuce leaves, fresh herbs, pickled carrots and daikon, and dipping sauce, if desired.

Crispy Sea Bass with
Ginger and Scallion Sauce

This was always my favorite dish that I looked forward to at weddings, and when I started making it at home, it brought back those cherished memories and became a regular part of my culinary repertoire. The aroma of the fragrant spices, the tender fish melting in my mouth, and the rich, flavorful sauce evoke a sense of comfort and joy. It has become a beloved tradition in my household, creating a warm and inviting atmosphere whenever I prepare it. Sharing this dish with loved ones brings us closer together, fostering a connection to our cultural heritage and the joy of gathering around a delicious meal. The gluten-free coating is made from tapioca starch and gives the fish a crispy texture when deep-fried. Serve with steamed rice and vegetables.

Yield: 2 to 4 servings

Avocado oil, for frying

1 (1½- to 2-pound [675–900g]) whole wild-caught sea bass, cleaned and deboned

1 tablespoon tapioca starch

1 tablespoon fine sea salt

1 teaspoon ground black pepper

2 tablespoons (30 mL) tamari

1 tablespoon extra-virgin olive oil

1 (2-inch [5 cm]) piece fresh ginger, peeled and cut into thin strips, plus more for garnish

4 scallions, cut into thin strips

Pour about 2 inches (5 cm) of avocado oil into a wok or deep skillet and heat over high heat until it reaches 350°F (175°C). Line a rimmed baking sheet with paper towels and set a wire rack over it.

While the oil heats, pat the sea bass dry with paper towels and cut into 2-inch chunks. In a large, shallow bowl, whisk together the tapioca starch, salt, and pepper. Add the fish pieces to the tapioca mixture and coat them thoroughly, shaking off any excess.

Working in batches as necessary to avoid crowding, use a pair of long tongs to carefully place the fish pieces in the hot oil. Cook for 6 to 8 minutes on each side, until the skin is crispy and golden brown and the fish is cooked through. Transfer the fish to the wire rack to drain.

Meanwhile, in a small bowl, whisk together the tamari, olive oil, ginger, and scallions.

Transfer the fried fish to a serving platter and pour the sauce over the top. Garnish with additional sliced scallions and serve immediately.

Thai Green Curry Mussels in Creamy Coconut Broth

In this dish, the succulent mussels bathe in a fragrant green curry sauce. With the rich creaminess of coconut milk, this dish delivers an explosion of Thai flavors. Experience the perfect blend of tender mussels, vibrant vegetables, and aromatic spices in every delightful spoonful.

Yield: 4 to 6 servings

2 tablespoons (30 mL) coconut oil

1 large onion, diced

4 garlic cloves, minced

1 (1-inch [2.5 cm]) piece fresh ginger, peeled and minced

2 tablespoons (30 mL) Thai green curry paste

1¾ cups (420 mL) Coconut Milk (page 273)

1 cup (240 mL) Fish Broth (page 47) or Gelatinous Chicken Bone Broth (page 48)

1 red bell pepper, seeded and sliced

1 yellow bell pepper, seeded and sliced

1 large zucchini, sliced

8 ounces (225 g) green beans, trimmed

2 pounds (900 g) mussels, scrubbed and debearded

1 tablespoon fish sauce or Fermented Anchovy Sauce (page 70)

1 tablespoon coconut sugar

Juice of 1 lime

½ cup (20 g) fresh Thai basil leaves

Steamed rice (pages 62–63), for serving

Heat the coconut oil in a large pot or Dutch oven over medium-high heat. Add the onion, garlic, and ginger and cook for 2 to 3 minutes, until fragrant and softened. Add the green curry paste and cook for 1 minute, stirring, until fragrant.

Pour in the coconut milk and broth and stir well to combine. Bring to a simmer, then add the bell peppers, zucchini, and green beans and cook for 5 to 7 minutes, until the vegetables are tender.

Add the mussels and stir gently. Cover and simmer for 5 to 7 minutes, until the mussels open. Discard any mussels that do not open.

Stir in the fish sauce, coconut sugar, and lime juice. Remove from the heat and stir in the Thai basil leaves. Serve hot, over steamed rice.

Vietnamese Caramelized Fish
(CÁ KHO TỘ)

It may come as a surprise, but when we dine out, the dishes we order are often similar to those that we enjoy at home. On a typical night out, we might expect to be served bubbling cá kho tộ in a clay pot, alongside Vietnamese Sweet-and-Sour Tamarind Soup (canh chua cá; page 126), white rice, and a selection of vegetable side dishes. Even with an affordable cut of fish, you'll be amazed at how moist and tender the fish becomes after being braised. Use high-quality, wild-caught fish and make your own caramel sauce using natural sweeteners like unrefined whole cane sugar. The clay pot imparts a unique flavor and texture to the dish, but even with a regular pot, you will still have a satisfying and flavorful dish. This classic dish is best served with steamed rice and some vegetables on the side.

Yield: 4 to 6 servings

¼ cup (60 mL) fish sauce or Fermented Anchovy Sauce (page 70), plus more if needed

2 shallots, minced

1 tablespoon grated fresh ginger (optional)

2 garlic cloves, minced

3 tablespoons (45 g) panela, divided, plus more if needed

2 pounds (900 g) wild-caught fish steaks (such as salmon or cod)

2 tablespoons (30 mL) coconut oil or lard

1½ cups (360 mL) coconut water

1 Thai chili (optional), minced

2 teaspoons fresh cracked pepper

Chopped fresh cilantro, for garnish

In a large bowl, whisk together the fish sauce, shallots, ginger (if using), garlic, and 1 tablespoon of the panela. Add the fish and marinate at room temperature for 20 minutes.

To make the caramel sauce, heat the remaining 2 tablespoons (30 g) panela in a clay pot or Dutch oven over medium-high heat, stirring, until the sugar melts and caramelizes to a dark amber color, 5 to 7 minutes. Immediately add the oil to stop the caramelization process and stir.

Add the fish to the caramel sauce and sear until golden brown, 2 to 3 minutes, then flip the fish and sear the other side for another 2 to 3 minutes.

Pour the coconut water into the pot and reduce the heat to low. Cover and simmer for 20 minutes, until the fish is firm and has a beautiful caramel color. Remove the cover to allow the sauce to reduce to about half in volume, 20 to 30 minutes. Taste the sauce and season with more fish sauce or panela if desired. If you prefer some heat, stir in the optional Thai chili. Sprinkle with the pepper, garnish with cilantro, and serve.

Chinese Garlic-Butter Lobster Noodles

In Chinese culture, noodles are regarded as a symbol of longevity and are often eaten on special occasions such as weddings and birthdays. The long, unbroken strands of noodles are believed to represent long life, prosperity, and good fortune. Garlic is believed to have many health benefits as well, and is often used in traditional Chinese medicine.

Yield: 2 to 4 servings

1 live (2- to 4-pound [900–1,800 g]) lobster

5 tablespoons (75 g) unsalted grass-fed butter, divided

5 garlic cloves, minced

2 tablespoons (18 g) grated fresh ginger

4 scallions, sliced, plus more for garnish

1½ teaspoons minced fresh Thai chilies (optional)

4 teaspoons (20 mL) fish sauce or Fermented Anchovy Sauce (page 70), divided

1½ teaspoons maple syrup (optional)

1 teaspoon ground white pepper

¼ cup (32 g) arrowroot starch

3 tablespoons (45 mL) spring water

1½ teaspoons toasted sesame oil

1 pound (450 g) gluten-free cassava spaghetti noodles, cooked according to package instructions

Lime or lemon wedges, for serving

Note that you may see green stuff inside the lobster, which is called tomalley. It will turn orange when baked and is a delicious delicacy.

Gently rinse the lobster in cool water to remove all dirt.

Fill a large pot with water and bring to a boil. Fill a large bowl with cold water and ice and set aside. Add the lobster to the boiling water and cook for 9 minutes for a 2-pound (900 g) lobster; add an extra minute for every additional 8 ounces (225 g) of lobster. When it is fully cooked, the outer shell will turn bright red. Transfer the lobster to the ice bath.

While the lobster is boiling, in a small saucepan, melt 2 tablespoons (30 g) of the butter over low heat. Add the garlic, ginger, scallions, Thai chili (if using), 1 teaspoon of the fish sauce, and the maple syrup (if using). Let simmer for 10 minutes, until cooked through; set aside.

Preheat the broiler to high.

Once the lobster is cooled, put it on a rimmed baking sheet and cut it in half. Pour the butter sauce over the lobster halves and broil for 3 to 4 minutes. Turn off the broiler, but leave the lobster in the oven to keep warm.

In a small bowl, whisk together the arrowroot and water. In a large skillet, combine the remaining 3 tablespoons (45 g) butter, remaining 1 tablespoon fish sauce, sesame oil, and arrowroot mixture. When the sauce has come to a simmer, add the noodles and cook for 1 to 2 minutes, stirring, to flavor the noodles and warm them through. If the noodles are too dry, add a splash of water to loosen the sauce.

Transfer the noodles to a large serving dish and pour the juice from the baking sheet over the noodles. Top with the lobster and squeeze fresh lime or lemon juice on top. Garnish with scallions and serve.

Korean Pan-Fried Mackerel

Grilled mackerel is a beloved dish in Korean cuisine, often served in restaurants. Our children love this fish! In fact, it's common in our family to order an extra grilled mackerel for the children as an appetizer before the main course arrives. And now we make this dish for dinner at home, and it is done in just a few minutes! Not only is it tasty, but it's also incredibly nutritious. Mackerel is a fatty fish that's rich in omega-3 fatty acids, vitamins D and B12, and minerals such as selenium and magnesium. Soaking the fish in water left over from making rice removes a lot of the odor from the skin. Alternatively, you can soak the fish in milk, as there is a substance in milk called casein that binds to the fish odor. Enjoy the dish with a bowl of hot rice, and be careful of the fish bones.

Yield: 4 servings

4 (8-ounce [250 g]) mackerel, cleaned,
  heads and tails removed
Rice water or milk, enough to submerge fish
¼ cup (32 g) tapioca starch
¼ cup (24 g) curry powder
Avocado oil, for frying
Lemon wedges, for serving (optional)

If you're going to eat this dish with rice, make your rice first and reserve the water from rinsing the rice.

Soak the fish in the rice water or milk for 10 to 15 minutes, then rinse it thoroughly under cold running water. Use paper towels to pat the fish dry.

In a small bowl, whisk together the tapioca starch and curry powder. Sprinkle this mixture over the fish, making sure to coat both sides evenly. Lightly pat the fish with paper towels to remove any excess.

Pour about ½ inch (13 mm) of the oil into a large skillet and heat over medium-high heat. Add the fish, skin-side down, and cook for about a minute, until the skin turns crispy. Flip the fish over to the other side and reduce the heat to low. Cook for 3 to 5 minutes, until the fish is cooked through. Transfer the fish to plates and squeeze fresh lemon juice on top, if desired.

CHAPTER 11

Offal

Growing up, I always looked forward to eating the food that my mom cooked for us at home. Her cooking was a fusion of traditional Vietnamese dishes and a smattering of American cuisine. I loved the way the flavors blended together, the bold and savory spices that she used, and the aromas that filled our home.

However, whenever I brought my lunch to school, it was a different story. I vividly remember the teasing and humiliation that I endured from my classmates for eating certain types of Asian food, like offal, that they considered to be strange or gross. I was constantly reminded that my food was different from their sandwiches or pizza, and that it was weird or smelly. The looks of disgust on my classmates' faces when they saw me eating foods that were unfamiliar to them were hurtful and made me feel like an outsider, even though I was born and raised in the same country as they were.

Now as an adult, I have a deeper appreciation for the food and culture of my upbringing. I've come to understand that my love for these foods is a reflection of my identity and heritage. It's a part of me that I can never separate from, nor would I want to. I am now proud of my heritage and the diverse range of foods that I grew up eating.

I'm beyond excited to see that in recent years, there has been a resurgence of interest in nose-to-tail eating, which involves using all parts of the animal, including offal. Offal, also known as organ meats, refers to the internal organs and other parts of a butchered animal, including heart, liver, tongue, kidney, sweetbreads, lungs, brain, cheeks, and feet. This trend has been driven in part by a growing awareness of the nutrient density of offal, which is rich in vitamins, minerals, and other beneficial compounds that are not found in muscle meat. Additionally, as food costs have risen in many parts of the world, using offal has become a cost-effective way to make nutritious and satisfying meals. Some chefs and food enthusiasts are also interested in offal for its unique and interesting flavor and texture profiles and enjoy the challenge of finding creative and delicious ways to prepare it.

As more people embrace nose-to-tail eating, they are discovering the many delicious and creative ways that offal can be prepared and are coming to appreciate the unique flavors and textures that these cuts offer. By using all parts of the animal, we can reduce waste while also enjoying the many health benefits that come from a varied and nutrient-dense diet.

Chicken Feet Dim Sum Style

Chicken feet are popular in Chinese dim sum cuisine. Chinese dim sum consists of bite-size portions of food traditionally served in small steamer baskets or on small plates. Dim sum is typically enjoyed during breakfast or lunchtime as a communal meal, where a variety of small dishes are ordered and shared among diners. When we go out for dim sum, my parents always order this dish of gelatinous chicken feet, which is rich in collagen and protein. As a little girl, I also remember ordering chicken feet for my grandparents. As an adult now, I make this dish for my parents after cooking a batch of chicken broth with the chicken feet. Because our chickens are raised on pasture on organic feed, we want to get the most out of them by enjoying two delicious and nourishing dishes. If you don't raise your own chickens, you can find high-quality chicken feet at health food stores, or ask your local butcher or farmer.

Yield: 2 to 4 servings

1 tablespoon avocado oil

1 (1-inch [2.5 cm]) piece fresh ginger, peeled and sliced

2 garlic cloves, minced

2 tablespoons (30 mL) Hoisin Sauce (page 80)

1 tablespoon tamari

2 teaspoons maple syrup

8 pasture-raised chicken feet leftover from making broth (see page 48)

1 tablespoon Lemongrass Chili Oil (page 90; optional)

1 tablespoon arrowroot starch (optional)

1 tablespoon spring water (optional)

In a wok or large saucepan, heat the avocado oil over medium heat. Add the ginger and garlic and cook, stirring frequently, until fragrant, about 1 minute. Add the hoisin sauce, tamari, and maple syrup and stir until well combined. Let the sauce simmer for 3 to 5 minutes to allow the flavors to meld.

Add the chicken feet and stir them around to coat them in the sauce. Cover and simmer for 10 minutes.

If you like extra spice, add the chili oil. If your sauce is too thin, whisk together the arrowroot and water in a small bowl. Add the slurry to the wok and stir it in, cooking until the sauce has thickened to your liking. Serve hot.

Note: Chicken feet should not fall apart during the broth cooking process if cooked properly. Chicken feet have a lot of collagen, which gives the broth a gelatinous texture and mouthfeel, but this also helps keep the chicken feet intact during cooking. When cooked for the recommended time, the chicken feet should be tender but still hold their shape. If the chicken feet do fall apart, it could be an indication that they were cooked for too long.

Japanese Beef Tongue Rice Bowl
(GYUTAN-DON)

Gyutan-don is a popular Japanese delicacy that is surprisingly quick, easy, and tasty to make at home. This does require the beef tongue to be cut super thin, so either use a very sharp knife or a slicer, or if you're lucky, you can find it presliced at some Asian grocery stores.

Yield: 4 to 6 servings

2 tablespoons (30 mL) sesame oil, divided
2 tablespoons (30 mL) tamari
2 tablespoons (30 mL) mirin
1 tablespoon maple syrup
1 teaspoon fine sea salt
1 (1-pound [450 g]) grass-fed beef or ox tongue, cleaned and very thinly sliced
2 shallots, thinly sliced
1 scallion, finely chopped
3 bird's eye chilies, finely chopped
Steamed rice (pages 62–63), for serving

In a large bowl, whisk together 1½ teaspoons of the sesame oil, the tamari, mirin, maple syrup, and salt and mix well. Add the beef slices and marinate at room temperature for 15 minutes, or cover and refrigerate overnight.

Heat a large cast-iron skillet over medium heat. Remove the beef from the marinade and let the excess drip off; reserve the marinade. Once the pan is hot, add the beef tongue and cook until brown, 1 to 2 minutes, then flip and cook for another 1 to 2 minutes on the other side, being careful not to overcook it. Set the pieces aside on a plate.

Reduce the heat to low and add the shallots and reserved marinade. Cook for a minute or two, until the shallots are slightly softened. Return the tongue slices to the skillet and cook for 1 to 2 minutes. Top with scallions and chilies and serve over a bed of rice.

Stewed Tripe

If you haven't had tripe before, it's worth trying at least once. This dish is a great way to incorporate nutrient-rich organ meats into your diet. It is cooked low and slow in a flavorful beef broth to make it more nourishing. Enjoy this hearty and satisfying stew as a main dish or serve it as a side with steamed rice or other grains.

Yield: 4 to 6 servings

2 pounds (900 g) grass-fed beef tripe

White vinegar, for soaking

1 quart (1 L) Beef Bone and Marrow Broth (page 50)

¼ cup (60 mL) tamari

¼ cup (60 mL) rice vinegar

2 tablespoons (30 g) coconut sugar

1 (2-inch [5 cm]) piece fresh ginger, peeled and thinly sliced

4 garlic cloves, minced

2 star anise pods

2 cinnamon sticks

1 teaspoon Szechuan peppercorns

¼ teaspoon red pepper flakes (optional)

2 cups (150 g) chopped bok choy

¼ cup (15 g) sliced scallions

Clean the tripe thoroughly under cold running water to remove any impurities or debris. Fill a bowl with enough vinegar to cover the tripe, add the tripe, and soak for 45 to 60 minutes. Rinse the tripe and cut it into bite-size pieces.

In a large pot or Dutch oven, combine the tripe, broth, tamari, vinegar, coconut sugar, ginger, garlic, star anise, cinnamon sticks, Szechuan peppercorns, and red pepper flakes, if using. Stir to combine. Bring the mixture to a boil over high heat, stirring occasionally.

Reduce the heat to low, cover, and simmer for 2 to 3 hours, stirring occasionally to prevent sticking, until the tripe is tender and fully cooked.

Remove the pot from the heat, add the bok choy, and cover the pot to allow the bok choy to steam for a few minutes. Serve hot, garnished with the scallions.

Vietnamese Chicken Liver Pâté

Pâté was introduced to Vietnamese cuisine during the French colonial period and became an integral part of the Vietnamese culinary repertoire. The Vietnamese adapted this French-style pâté, combining French techniques with Vietnamese herbs and spices, resulting in a delightful fusion of flavors. Chicken liver, the star ingredient of this pâté, is a nutritional powerhouse. It is an excellent source of high-quality protein, essential amino acids, and various vitamins and minerals. It is also particularly rich in iron and contains significant amounts of vitamin A, vitamin B12, folate, and other B vitamins that support immune function, brain health, and overall vitality. Enjoy this delicious and rich pâté as a spread on your bánh mì sandwich (see page 170) or as a snack with crackers.

Yield: 6 to 8 servings

1½ pounds (675 g) pasture-raised chicken liver

Whole milk (preferably raw), for soaking

2 cups (220 g) sourdough bread pieces

4 tablespoons (60 g) unsalted grass-fed butter, divided, plus more for greasing

3 shallots, chopped, divided

5 garlic cloves, minced, divided

1½ pounds (675 g) pasture-raised ground turkey

1 onion, chopped

1 tablespoon ground black pepper

2 teaspoons fish sauce or Fermented Anchovy Sauce (page 70)

3 bacon strips

Flaky salt and cracked black pepper

Wash the chicken liver thoroughly under cold running water and remove the white fatty parts with a sharp knife or kitchen shears, making sure to remove as much of the fatty tissue as possible. Put the liver in a bowl and pour in enough milk to fully submerge it. Set aside for 15 minutes.

While the liver is soaking, place the bread in a separate small bowl and pour over enough milk to cover the bread. Set aside to soak for 5 minutes, then drain.

Melt 2 tablespoons of the butter in a cast-iron skillet over medium heat. Add half of the shallots and half of the garlic and cook, stirring, for 1 to 2 minutes, until fragrant.

Remove the liver from the milk and rinse under cold running water. Add the liver to the skillet and stir-fry until done to medium-rare, 2 to 4 minutes. The liver should still be slightly pink in the center. Transfer the liver to a plate. Add the remaining 2 tablespoons butter to the skillet and add the remaining shallots and garlic. Cook, stirring, for 1 to 2 minutes, then add the turkey and onion. Stir-fry, breaking up the meat with a spatula, until the turkey is no longer pink, about 5 minutes.

continued on page 232

Transfer the turkey mixture to a food processor. Add the pepper, fish sauce, soaked bread, and liver and blend until smooth.

Butter the sides and bottom of a glass or ceramic baking dish that can fit in a steamer and line the bottom with the bacon strips. Transfer the pâté mixture to the baking dish and smooth the top. Don't fill the baking dish to the top, as the pâté may overflow during steaming. Season with flaky salt and cracked black pepper. Cover with aluminum foil. Place the dish in a steamer, cover, and steam for 1½ to 2 hours, depending on the size of

your container. The pâté should be firm and set in the center, with a smooth and creamy texture. Gently touch the top or insert a toothpick in the center to see if it comes out clean. Let the pâté cool a bit, then refrigerate for 4 to 6 hours.

When ready to serve, remove the pâté from the fridge and run a knife around the edge of the dish. Place a serving plate upside-down on top of the dish and invert it to release the pâté onto the plate. Store leftovers in an airtight container in the refrigerator for up to 5 days or in the freezer for up to 3 months.

Pan-Fried Chicken Liver and Hearts

Chicken hearts may not be as popular as other cuts, but they can be a nutritious and flavorful addition to your diet. Liver is a nutritional powerhouse and is possibly one of the most nutrient-dense foods available. Both liver and heart are among the most economical cuts of meat and are a great source of protein. Most grocery stores and butchers have them readily available. My favorite way to prepare both chicken heart and liver is this quick and simple recipe, perfect for an appetizer or side dish.

Yield: 4 to 6 servings

8 ounces (225 g) pasture-raised chicken liver
1 pound (450 g) pasture-raised
   chicken hearts
1 tablespoon grass-fed beef tallow
2 tablespoons (30 mL) Hoisin Sauce
   (page 80)
1 tablespoon tamari
1½ teaspoons sriracha or Sambal Oelek
   (page 85; optional)
1 teaspoon fine sea salt
Sliced scallions, for garnish

Wash the chicken liver thoroughly under cold running water and remove the white fatty parts with a sharp knife or kitchen shears, making sure to remove as much of the fatty tissue as possible.

Wash the chicken hearts thoroughly under running water and dry them well with paper towels.

In a wok or large skillet, heat the tallow over medium heat. Add the hoisin sauce, tamari, sriracha (if using), and salt, and stir to combine. Allow the sauce to simmer for a few minutes, stirring occasionally, until it has thickened slightly and the flavors have melded together.

Add the chicken hearts and let them cook in the sauce for about 3 minutes, until fragrant and starting to brown and caramelize in the sauce.

Add the chicken liver and stir well to coat it in the sauce. Cook until the liver is no longer pink, turning the pieces occasionally so that they cook evenly on all sides. The liver should be cooked through but still tender and juicy.

Transfer the liver and hearts to a serving dish. Season with salt, garnish with scallions, and serve hot.

Chicken Gizzard Yakitori

This delightful Japanese dish showcases the unique and delicious flavors of chicken gizzards, the muscular organs found in the digestive system of chickens. They are a good source of protein, collagen, and essential amino acids. Yakitori, meaning "grilled chicken skewers," is a popular street food in Japan, and chicken gizzards are a prized ingredient in this traditional dish. Marinated in a savory and slightly sweet sauce, the gizzards are skewered and grilled to perfection, resulting in a tender and juicy texture with a hint of charred smokiness. This recipe makes a great appetizer or main dish and pairs well with a variety of side dishes, such as rice, pickled vegetables, or a simple salad.

Yield: 4 servings

1 pound (450 g) pasture-raised chicken gizzards
¼ cup (60 mL) tamari
¼ cup (60 mL) mirin
2 tablespoons (25 g) coconut sugar
1 tablespoon toasted sesame oil
2 garlic cloves, minced
1 teaspoon grated fresh ginger
2 scallions, sliced, plus more for garnish

If using bamboo skewers, soak them in water for 30 minutes.

Rinse the chicken gizzards thoroughly under cold running water and use a sharp knife to remove any white membranes or fat. Cut the gizzards into bite-size pieces and set aside.

In a large bowl, whisk together the tamari, mirin, coconut sugar, sesame oil, garlic, and ginger until the sugar is fully dissolved. Add the gizzard pieces and scallions to the marinade and stir to coat each piece. Cover and refrigerate for at least 2 hours, or preferably overnight.

Preheat a grill or stovetop grill pan to medium-high. While the grill is heating up, thread the marinated chicken gizzard pieces onto skewers, leaving a little space between each piece so that they cook evenly.

Grill the yakitori skewers for 2 to 3 minutes on each side, until cooked through and lightly charred. Turn the skewers over only once to ensure that the gizzards cook evenly and don't dry out.

Remove the skewers from the grill and let them rest for a minute or two before serving. Serve hot, garnished with additional sliced scallions.

Asian Haggis Soup

This hearty and nutrient-dense soup can be enjoyed as a meal on its own or served as a starter. It's a great way to incorporate lamb organs into your diet and enjoy the health benefits they offer.

Yield: 4 to 6 servings

1 pound (450 g) pasture-raised lamb organs, such as liver, heart, kidney, and lung, rinsed and chopped
2 tablespoons (30 mL) coconut oil or lard
1 large onion, chopped
2 garlic cloves, minced
2 tablespoons (18 g) grated fresh ginger
1 tablespoon tamari
1 tablespoon rice vinegar
1 tablespoon coconut sugar
1 teaspoon ground cinnamon
1 teaspoon ground cumin
½ teaspoon ground coriander
¼ teaspoon cayenne pepper
1 quart (1 L) Gelatinous Chicken Bone Broth (page 48)
1 cup (75 g) chopped kale or bok choy
Fine sea salt and ground black pepper
Chopped fresh cilantro and/or scallions, for garnish (optional)

Bring a large pot of water to boil.

Rinse the lamb organs thoroughly under cold running water and remove any white membranes or fat. Blanch the organs in the boiling water for 20 minutes, or until the scum floats to the top. Drain. Rinse the pot, return the organs to the pot, and fill with enough fresh water to cover. Bring to a boil and cook over medium-high heat for 30 minutes. Drain and set aside to cool. Cut the organs into thin strips and set aside.

Rinse the pot again, then add the coconut oil and heat over medium-high heat. Add the onion, garlic, and ginger and sauté until the onion is translucent and fragrant, about 5 minutes. Add the organs, tamari, vinegar, coconut sugar, cinnamon, cumin, coriander, and cayenne. Stir to coat the organs in the seasonings.

Pour in the broth and bring to a boil over high heat. Reduce the heat to low, cover, and simmer for about 1 hour, until the organs are tender.

Add the kale and simmer for 10 minutes, until it is wilted and tender. Season the soup with salt and pepper to taste and serve hot, garnished with cilantro and/or scallions, if desired.

Beef Liver Stir-Fry

This stir-fry combines tender slices of beef liver with an array of colorful vegetables, creating a delicious and well-balanced meal. The liver is quickly seared to maintain its tenderness while being infused with the rich flavors of the savory sauce. Packed with essential nutrients such as iron, vitamin B12, and vitamin A, beef liver is known for its nutritional value. This stir-fry not only offers a burst of flavors but also provides a nourishing and wholesome option for a quick and easy weeknight dinner. Serve it over steamed rice or noodles for a complete and satisfying meal that will please your taste buds and provide you with a healthy dose of nutrients.

Yield: 2 to 4 servings

10 ounces (285 g) grass-fed beef liver, membranes and veins removed, cut into 2-inch (5 cm) pieces

1½ cups (360 mL) whole milk (preferably raw)

Fine sea salt

4 tablespoons (60 g) unsalted grass-fed butter, divided

1 large onion, chopped

2 celery ribs, sliced

1 tablespoon tamari

Rinse the beef liver under cold running water and cut off any unwanted parts. Put the liver in a bowl and pour over the milk. Soak the liver for 30 minutes at room temperature, or cover and refrigerate overnight.

Drain the liver, rinse off the milk, and season with salt.

In a large wok or cast-iron skillet, melt 2 tablespoons of the butter over medium heat. Add the onion and celery and cook, stirring, until tender and soft, 5 to 7 minutes. Transfer to a bowl.

Melt the remaining 2 tablespoons butter in the same skillet. Increase the heat to high and add the liver. Stir-fry for 3 to 4 minutes, until browned. Turn the liver as little as possible, and be careful not to overcook the liver as it has a tendency to get tough. Return the onion and celery to the skillet and reduce the heat to medium. Stir in the tamari and cook for a minute or so until everything is evenly coated. Serve hot.

Indonesian Beef and Kidney Curry

This vibrant and aromatic dish celebrates the bold flavors of Indonesian cuisine. Tender pieces of beef and succulent kidney are cooked in a rich and delicious sauce. The combination of the tender meat and the unique texture of the kidney creates a delightful contrast. Serve with steamed rice so you can fully appreciate the robust flavors and rich textures.

Yield: 4 to 6 servings

2 pounds (900 g) grass-fed beef kidneys

1 tablespoon fine sea salt, plus more
    for seasoning

2 tablespoons (30 g) grass-fed beef tallow

1 large onion, chopped

3 garlic cloves, minced

1 teaspoon grated fresh ginger

1 pound (450 g) grass-fed beef stew meat

1 teaspoon ground turmeric

1 teaspoon ground coriander

1 teaspoon ground cumin

1 teaspoon paprika

1¾ cups (420 mL) Coconut Milk (page 273)
    or full-fat canned coconut milk

2 tablespoons (30 mL) tamarind paste

2 tablespoons (20 g) coconut sugar

1 tablespoon fish sauce or Fermented
    Anchovy Sauce (page 70)

2 makrut lime leaves

Ground black pepper

Chopped fresh cilantro and/or scallions,
    for garnish (optional)

Rinse the kidneys under cold running water. Fill a large bowl with water, add the salt, and stir until dissolved. Add the kidneys and soak for 2 hours. Drain, rinse, and cut them into bite-size pieces.

In a large pot or Dutch oven, heat the tallow over medium-high heat. Add the onion, garlic, and ginger and sauté until the onion is translucent and fragrant, about 5 minutes. Add the stew meat, kidneys, turmeric, coriander, cumin, and paprika and stir to coat the meat in the spices. Pour in the coconut milk and add the tamarind paste, coconut sugar, fish sauce, and lime leaves. Stir to combine.

Bring to a boil over high heat, then reduce the heat to low, cover, and simmer for about 2 hours, until the meat and kidneys are tender and cooked through. Season with salt and pepper to taste. Serve hot, garnished with cilantro and/or scallions, if desired.

CHAPTER 12

Beverages and Desserts

Asian cultures have a rich tradition of beverages and desserts that emphasize natural ingredients, such as fruits, grains, nuts, and seeds, and tend to be low in sugar and fat. In many parts of Asia, tea is a central part of daily life and is often imbibed for both social and religious reasons; in China, it has been a part of daily life for more than 5,000 years.

Popular Asian teas include green tea, black tea, oolong tea, and herbal teas made from plants like chrysanthemum, ginseng, and lotus. Tea—especially green tea—is known for its high levels of antioxidants and polyphenols, both of which have been linked to a variety of health benefits, including heart health, brain health, and reduced inflammation. In Japan, green tea is a popular beverage that is often served with meals or enjoyed on its own.

Introduced by Taiwan teahouse owner Liu Han-Chieh in the 1980s, milk tea has evolved into a global phenomenon with numerous variations and flavors available today. Boba tea, sometimes called bubble tea, has become a beloved beverage in many countries, appreciated for its diverse range of flavors and textures. Hong Kong–style milk tea and Thai iced tea are two of our favorite milk tea variations.

Kombucha and kefir are both fermented beverages that have been enjoyed for centuries in various parts of Asia, including China, Japan,

Korea, and Russia. While the exact origins of these drinks are unclear, it's believed that they were first created as a way to preserve milk and tea. While both kombucha and kefir have their roots in traditional Asian cultures, they've since become popular worldwide. Today, you can find a variety of different flavors and types of kombucha and kefir, and they're often enjoyed as an alternative to sugary sodas and other less healthy drinks.

Asian cultures also have a wide variety of sweet treats that range from simple fruit-based dishes to more complex confections made with rice flour, beans, and other ingredients. Some popular Asian desserts include mochi (a sweet rice cake), red bean soup, and shaved ice with fruit and condensed milk. One notable aspect of Asian desserts is their focus on natural sweetness, often through the use of fruit or honey instead of refined sugar. In addition, many Asian desserts incorporate ingredients that are believed to have health benefits, such as matcha (green tea powder), ginger, and goji berries.

In many Asian cultures, meals are seen as a balance between cooling and heating foods. Desserts are often viewed as overly sweet and warming, which can upset this balance. Instead, my mother would often serve a full plate of cut-up fresh fruit, such as oranges, mangoes, pineapple, watermelon, lychee, dragon fruit, jackfruit, and even durian to eat after meals. Fresh fruit is seen as a healthier and more refreshing way to balance the palate and aid in digestion. Additionally, fruit is a natural source of sweetness and a healthier alternative to desserts that are high in sugar and processed ingredients.

Born and raised in California, Tim and I witnessed a resurgence of interest in traditional Asian desserts, as well as the development of new and innovative dessert creations that combine traditional flavors with modern techniques and ingredients. Tapioca pearls (boba) have become a popular addition to many Asian desserts, such as milk tea and shaved ice. Almond jelly and rice pudding remain popular traditional desserts but have also been reinvented in creative ways, such as almond jelly with fresh fruit or matcha-flavored rice pudding.

Before Tim and I had children, our first business together was a self-serve frozen yogurt and boba shop in Albuquerque, New Mexico, where our Asian American–inspired desserts brought the community of all ages and nationalities together.

Additionally, there has been a growing trend toward using healthier and more nourishing ingredients in Asian desserts, such as coconut milk, fresh fruit, and natural sweeteners. Overall, the evolution of modern Asian desserts has brought about a fusion of traditional and contemporary flavors, textures, and presentation styles.

Homemade Sweetened Condensed Milk

Traditional condensed milk is typically made with lots of refined sugar and often includes additives and preservatives. However, you can make a more nourishing version of condensed milk at home using natural sweeteners and whole ingredients.

I use fresh organic milk and panela, which is a type of unrefined whole cane sugar commonly used in Latin American cuisine. By using panela instead of refined sugar, you can avoid the need for high heat and retain more of the natural nutrients and minerals present in the unrefined cane sugar. Using raw whole milk instead of pasteurized milk can also provide additional nutrients and health benefits.

Yield: about 1½ cups (360 mL)

2 cups (480 mL) whole milk (preferably raw)
1 cup (240 g) panela
1 teaspoon vanilla extract
¼ teaspoon fine sea salt (optional)

In a medium saucepan, heat the milk and panela over medium heat, stirring constantly until the panela dissolves and the mixture comes to a gentle boil. Reduce the heat to low and simmer for about 1 hour, stirring occasionally, until the mixture thickens and reduces by half.

Remove from heat and stir in the vanilla extract and salt, if using. Let the mixture cool to room temperature, then transfer to an airtight container and store in the fridge for up to 2 weeks.

Note: *Heat the milk only to a gentle boil at most and maintain on a very low simmer to allow for even heat distribution and to prevent the milk from curdling or separating. You'll also have better control over the rate of evaporation. This allows you to slowly reduce the milk's volume while retaining its smooth and creamy texture, resulting in a rich and thick condensed milk.*

Coconut Condensed Milk

Coconut condensed milk is a nourishing alternative to store-bought condensed milk. It is made with natural sweeteners and does not contain any additives or preservatives. It can be used in a variety of recipes, such as desserts, baked goods, and hot beverages.

Yield: about 2 cups *(480 mL)*

2 (14-ounce) cans full-fat coconut milk
1 cup (240 g) panela or coconut sugar
¼ teaspoon fine sea salt

In a medium saucepan, combine the coconut milk, panela, and salt. Bring the mixture to a boil over medium heat, stirring constantly. Reduce the heat to low and simmer for 30 to 40 minutes, stirring occasionally, until the mixture has thickened and reduced by about half. Remove the saucepan from the heat and let the mixture cool to room temperature. Transfer the coconut condensed milk to an airtight container and store in the refrigerator for up to 2 weeks.

Condensed Milk: A Versatile Ingredient

The popularity of condensed milk in Vietnamese cuisine can be traced back to the colonial period, when the French introduced condensed milk as a way to preserve milk in a hot and humid climate. It soon became a popular ingredient in many Vietnamese desserts and drinks, such as coffee with condensed milk (cà phê sữa đá) and sweetened condensed milk with bread (bánh mì kẹp). Today, condensed milk remains a beloved ingredient in Vietnamese cuisine and is used in both traditional and modern recipes.

One way to bring condensed milk more in line with a traditional diet is to make it at home. This allows you to control the ingredients, using organic, grass-fed dairy and natural sweeteners like coconut sugar or panela (unrefined whole cane sugar). You can avoid adding any artificial flavors, colors, or preservatives that may be found in commercial brands.

The use of condensed milk and other dairy products in Asian drinks and desserts reflects the cultural exchange and globalization that have taken place in the region over the past century. These ingredients have become an integral part of many Asian cuisines and continue to evolve and adapt to new tastes and trends.

Vietnamese Coffee
(CÀ PHÊ SỮA ĐÁ)

Practicing patience is a true art, and when it comes to coffee, it's also an art that can be both beautiful and delicious. I have fond memories of weekends during my childhood, waking up to the enticing aroma of my parents' coffee wafting from the kitchen. As I stood by the counter, I would watch with wonder as droplets of coffee trickled down from the phin (Vietnamese coffee filter). If I stayed long enough, my father would let me stir in the condensed milk. I always loved the marbling effect created as the milk and coffee blended together.

When making Vietnamese coffee, it's important to start with fresh, high-quality coffee grounds. The best Vietnamese coffee is made with robusta beans, though any medium to dark roast coffee will work. The amount of coffee can be adjusted to your taste preferences. Using more coffee will result in a stronger flavor, while using less will create a milder taste. When it comes to adding sweetness, condensed milk is the traditional choice. Start with 1 tablespoon condensed milk in the glass and adjust to your preferred level of sweetness. The condensed milk adds a creamy sweetness to the strong coffee, making it a delicious and indulgent treat. You can also add ice to make iced Vietnamese coffee. If you don't have a phin, you can get great results with a French press.

Yield: 1 serving

1 to 3 tablespoons (5–15 g) coarsely ground coffee

Spring water, brought to a boil

1 to 3 tablespoons (15–45 mL) Homemade Sweetened Condensed Milk (page 241) or Coconut Condensed Milk (page 243)

If using a phin filter:

Place the phin over your cup. Spoon 1 to 2 tablespoons (5–10 g) ground coffee into the phin. Use a spoon to press down lightly on the coffee grounds to ensure that they are evenly distributed and compacted. Pour a small amount of hot water over the grounds and let it sit for about 30 seconds before adding more water. This allows the coffee to release its flavors and aroma. When pouring the hot water, it's important to do so slowly and in a circular motion to ensure even extraction. Leave some space at the top of the phin to allow the coffee to expand and drip through the filter. Once all the water has passed through, remove the lid and place the phin on it. This prevents drips on the table. Add your desired amount of sweetened condensed milk and mix with a spoon.

Note: *When my mother gave up coffee due to her heart palpitations, we found a great substitute for her: Dandy Blend. It's a unique blend of roasted barley, roasted rye, roasted chicory roots, and roasted dandelion roots that comes together to create a delicious and satisfying herbal beverage. Simply mix with hot water right in your cup.*

If using a French press:

Spoon 2 to 3 tablespoons (10–15 g) ground coffee into the French press. Pour hot water over the coffee, filling the French press to the top. Stir the coffee and let it steep for about 4 minutes. This allows the flavors to develop and infuse the coffee. Once the coffee has steeped, slowly and carefully plunge the French press. Pour your desired amount of sweetened condensed milk into your cup. Pour the coffee over the sweetened condensed milk and stir gently to combine.

Vietnamese Egg Coffee
(CÀ PHÊ TRỨNG)

This rich and indulgent beverage is a popular traditional Vietnamese drink, often enjoyed as a midmorning or midafternoon treat rather than at breakfast.

Cà phê trứng is said to have originated in Hanoi, Vietnam, in the 1940s during the French colonial period. Because milk was scarce and expensive in Vietnam, people had to find creative ways to enjoy coffee without it. Adding whipped egg yolks to coffee gives it a creamy texture and richness, as well as being a rich source of nutrients. Whisking the egg yolks until they become light and frothy is an important step in this recipe, as it helps create a smooth and creamy texture. The egg yolks also add a richness to the drink, while the condensed milk provides sweetness and a hint of caramel flavor. Top with a bit of cinnamon, cacao powder, or vanilla for additional flavor and visual appeal.

When brewing the coffee, it is important to use a strong and bold coffee that can stand up to the richness of the egg yolk and condensed milk mixture. A Vietnamese phin filter or French press are great options for brewing a strong and bold coffee (see pages 244–245).

Yield: 1 serving

½ cup (120 mL) strongly brewed Vietnamese Coffee (page 244)
2 large pasture-raised egg yolks
1 tablespoon Homemade Sweetened Condensed Milk (page 241) or Coconut Condensed Milk (page 243)
Optional flavorings: ground cinnamon, cacao powder, vanilla extract

Pour the coffee into a cup.

In a small bowl, whisk together the egg yolks and condensed milk until light and frothy. Carefully pour the egg mixture onto the surface of the coffee. The goal here is to pour the mixture slowly and gently so that it forms a layer on top of the coffee rather than mixing in. Sprinkle with your desired toppings.

Can Coffee Be Nourishing?

Coffee is not considered part of the Nourishing Traditions diet, as it is not a whole, nutrient-dense food. Sally Fallon Morell does not include coffee in her list of recommended foods in *Nourishing Traditions* and, in fact, she recommends reducing or eliminating caffeine from your diet. Additionally, Dr. Weston A. Price does not advocate for drinking coffee or any caffeinated beverages in his studies of traditional diets.

That said, Tim and I drink coffee, and we love indulging in the recipes I've included here. They make us feel closer to our family traditions and roots—and for us, that's all the convincing we need that they're nourishing in their own way.

How to Source Coffee

Choose organic: Coffee plants are often sprayed with pesticides, which can be harmful to both the environment and your health. Look for coffee that is certified organic to ensure it was grown without the use of synthetic pesticides.

Look for shade-grown: Coffee grown in the shade tends to be more flavorful and nutritious than coffee grown in direct sunlight. Shade-grown coffee also helps protect the natural habitat of birds and other wildlife.

Consider the roast: Lighter roasts tend to retain more of the coffee's original nutrients and antioxidants, while darker roasts tend to have a more bitter taste and potentially higher levels of acrylamide, a compound that forms when coffee is roasted at high temperatures.

Buy from a reputable source: Choose fair trade coffee to support sustainable and ethical practices. Look for coffee that is sourced directly from farmers or from companies that prioritize sustainable and ethical practices. This can help ensure that the coffee you're buying is both nourishing for your body and good for the planet.

Finally, like everything, consume in moderation.

Vietnamese Egg Soda

(SODA SỮA HỘT GÀ)

This sweet and creamy drink is made by mixing egg yolks, sweetened condensed milk, sparkling water, and a little bit of lemon juice. This Vietnamese classic is protein-rich with a very light custard texture, almost like a creamy eggnog soda.

Yield: 1 serving

1 large pasture-raised egg yolk

2 tablespoons (30 mL) Homemade Sweetened Condensed Milk (page 241) or Coconut Condensed Milk (page 243)

Crushed ice

¼ cup (60 mL) sparkling water

1 teaspoon lemon juice (optional)

Fresh mint leaves (optional)

In a large glass, use a milk frother or whisk to blend the egg yolk and condensed milk together until smooth.

Fill the glass with crushed ice. Add the sparkling water and lemon juice (if using) and stir vigorously until well combined. Garnish with mint leaves, if desired, and serve immediately.

Preserved Lemon Drink

(SODA CHANH MUỐI)

Growing up, I experienced a plethora of Asian home remedies. There's the practice of cạo gió, where menthol oil and a coin are used to rub the skin and alleviate discomfort. Then there's the wonder that is Vietnamese preserved lemons (chanh muối), which can be enjoyed either hot or cold to treat various ailments such as nausea and the common cold. Tim and the girls love this sweet and salty drink on a hot summer day.

Yield: 1 serving

1 wedge Vietnamese Preserved Lemons (page 89)
Raw honey (optional)
Ice cubes
Sparkling water
Fresh mint leaves (optional)

Put the preserved lemon wedge in a tall glass and use a muddler or wooden spoon to muddle the lemon in the glass to release the juices. Add a spoonful of honey, if using, and stir until the honey is mixed in. Add ice cubes to the glass, then pour in sparkling water and stir to mix everything together. Garnish with fresh mint leaves, if desired.

Note: If you're looking for a different way to ease your cold symptoms, you can steep a wedge of chanh muối in a cup of hot water and add a spoonful of honey. It may sound simple, but trust me, this home remedy really works!

Note: Honey contains enzymes and antioxidants that can be destroyed by heat, especially when exposed to high temperatures for extended periods. Heating honey can also lead to the formation of a compound called hydroxymethylfurfural (HMF), which is known to be harmful when consumed in large quantities. Additionally, heating honey can cause it to lose its unique flavor and aroma. Therefore, it is generally recommended to consume honey in its raw form or use it as a sweetener in cold or warm dishes instead of cooking it.

Kombucha

Discover the tangy and effervescent delight of kombucha! This ancient fermented beverage, made from tea, sugar, and a starter culture, offers a unique flavor and potential health benefits. Sip on the sparkling, homemade elixir with its perfect balance of sweet and tangy notes, while benefiting from probiotics and organic acids.

You will need to obtain a SCOBY (symbiotic culture of bacteria and yeast) from a friend, local brewer, or health food store, or you can purchase a kombucha starter kit online. When sourcing a SCOBY, it's important to ensure its quality and health. Look for SCOBYs that are firm, white or beige in color, and free from mold or other signs of contamination. It is also essential to handle the SCOBY with clean hands and use sanitized equipment during the fermentation process to avoid the introduction of unwanted bacteria. When you acquire a SCOBY, it will be stored in liquid. Save a portion of this liquid to be the starter for your next batch. If you don't have starter liquid, you can substitute ¼ cup (60 mL) distilled white vinegar to acidify the environment and keep the kombucha healthy.

You will need a large glass jar or ceramic crock for brewing, cheesecloth, and flip-top bottles (or other glass bottles with airtight lids) for storage.

Yield: 1 gallon (3.75 L)

1 gallon (3.75 L) spring water, divided
8 black tea bags
1 cup (240 g) panela
1 SCOBY
1 cup (240 mL) starter liquid from a previous batch of kombucha or unflavored store-bought kombucha

Add half of the water to a large pot and bring to a boil. Add the tea bags, remove from the heat, cover, and let steep for about 5 minutes. Remove the tea bags and add the panela, stirring until it is dissolved.

Add the remaining water to cool down the temperature of the sweet tea. Allow the tea mixture to cool to room temperature. Once cooled, pour it into a clean brewing vessel.

Making sure that your hands and tools are clean, add the SCOBY and kombucha liquid. Cover the vessel with a piece of cheesecloth or other breathable cloth (or a coffee filter) and secure it with a rubber band.

Let the kombucha ferment at room temperature, ideally above 70°F (21°C), away from direct sunlight, for 7 to 10 days. Taste the kombucha after 7 days to see if it has reached your desired level of sweetness and tartness. The longer it sits, the tarter it will be.

Once the kombucha has reached your desired flavor, remove the SCOBY and 1 cup of the liquid for your next batch of kombucha. Bottle the rest to drink as is, or use this kombucha as a starter in a secondary fermentation (see variation below). Store the kombucha in the refrigerator for up to a few weeks.

Passion Fruit Kombucha
SECONDARY FERMENTATION

Yield: 1 quart (1 L)

1 quart (1 L) fresh plain kombucha
¼ cup (60 mL) passion fruit juice

Combine the kombucha and passion fruit juice in a large liquid measuring cup or a pitcher. Pour the mixture into flip-top bottles, leaving about 1 inch (2.5 cm) headspace at the top and seal the bottles. Place the bottles in a warm area for 1 to 3 days, depending on the ambient temperature, to allow for a second fermentation to occur. Lightly "burp" the bottles on on day 2 or 3 to release excess gas. Once the desired level of carbonation is achieved, move the bottles to the refrigerator to chill. To prevent spillage, open the bottles cautiously over a sink, as they will be under pressure due to carbonation.

Caution: *It is important to be aware that, especially during secondary fermentation, kombucha can build up carbonation and pressure within the bottles. If not properly handled, there is a risk of the bottles exploding or bursting unexpectedly. To avoid potential accidents and ensure your safety, take precautions when working with kombucha. Use appropriate bottles designed for carbonated beverages and ensure they are properly sealed. Monitor the fermentation process, release excess pressure regularly, and store the bottles in a safe place away from heat or direct sunlight. Always open up the bottles with caution, pointing away from yourself and others.*

Cultured Drinks

Cultured drinks have been consumed in Asia for centuries. Kombucha originated in China over 2,000 years ago and was known as the "tea of immortality." It later spread to Korea, Japan, and Russia. Jun is a traditional Tibetan fermented drink made from green tea and honey. It was originally consumed by Tibetan monks as a health tonic.

Both of these cultured beverages are relatively easy to make at home. Once you have the basic equipment and ingredients, you can easily make them in your own kitchen. To make kombucha, you will need a SCOBY (symbiotic culture of bacteria and yeast), which ferments with sweetened tea in a week or two. Jun is similar to kombucha, but is made with green tea and honey instead of black tea and sugar. The SCOBY used in jun is also different, a mix of bacteria and yeast that is better suited to fermenting honey. Jun has a lighter and more delicate flavor than kombucha, and is often described as having floral or fruity notes.

What Is Kefir?

Kefir is a fermented drink that is made by adding kefir grains to milk. The grains are a mixture of bacteria and yeasts that ferment the lactose in milk, producing a tart and slightly effervescent beverage. Kefir has a thicker consistency than milk and a tangy flavor. It is also rich in probiotics, vitamins, and minerals.

Tim and I like raw milk kefir because it contains a wider variety of beneficial microorganisms than pasteurized milk kefir. These beneficial microorganisms, including various strains of bacteria and yeast, can help support the gut microbiome, improving digestion, boosting immunity, and reducing inflammation. Additionally, raw milk kefir contains higher levels of certain vitamins and minerals that are often destroyed or reduced during pasteurization.

It's worth noting, however, that there are potential risks associated with consuming raw milk due to the possibility of contamination with harmful bacteria. It's important to make sure you're obtaining raw milk from a trusted source that follows proper sanitary procedures.

Milk Kefir

With this simple process, you can enjoy delicious and nutritious homemade kefir anytime. You can buy kefir grains online or from a health food store, or ask someone who already makes kefir if they can spare some grains. You can use dairy milk, nut milk, coconut milk, or water, but the process will vary slightly for each type of liquid.

Yield: 1 quart (1 L)

¼ cup (66 g) kefir grains
1 quart (1 L) whole milk (preferably raw)

Note: The most common way to store kefir grains is in the refrigerator. Place the grains in a glass jar with enough fresh milk or water to cover them. Seal the jar tightly and keep it in the refrigerator. This slows down the fermentation process and allows the grains to enter a dormant state. Change the milk or water every 1 to 2 weeks to provide fresh nutrients for the grains.

Put the kefir grains in a clean jar and pour the milk over them. Cover the jar with a piece of cheesecloth or other breathable cloth (or a coffee filter) and secure it with a rubber band. Leave the jar at room temperature for 12 to 24 hours, depending on how thick and tangy you want your kefir to be. The longer you ferment, the tangier and thicker the kefir will be.

Once the kefir is fermented, use a fine-mesh strainer or cheesecloth to separate the kefir grains from the liquid. The strained kefir can be stored in an airtight container in the fridge for up to 1 week.

Rinse the kefir grains and repeat the process to make another batch of kefir.

Citrus Kefir

Tim and I have fond childhood memories of drinking Yakult, a sweetened probiotic drink. The small, brightly colored bottles and sweet taste made it appealing to kids, and our parents appreciated that it contained beneficial bacteria that could improve digestion and boost the immune system. Now that we're parents, we took our children to visit the Yakult factory in Fountain Valley, California, and it was fascinating to see the pasteurization containers and the effort required to make these little bottles. While we love the flavors of Yakult, kefir has a wider variety of bacteria and yeasts and is more nutrient-dense. This is our Yakult-inspired drink!

The citrus zest contains essential oils and fragrant compounds that will infuse the kefir with flavor and aroma. The citrus juice adds tanginess and acidity, balancing out the sweetness and adding a refreshing flavor. You can use any citrus fruit, such as orange or lemon.

Yield: 4 to 6 servings

1 or 2 oranges, lemons, or other citrus fruits
5 cups (1.5 L) Milk Kefir (page 255)
1 to 2 tablespoons (15–30 mL) raw honey (optional)
Citrus slices or mint sprigs, for garnish

Use a grater or zester to scrape off the outer layer of the fruit peel, being careful to avoid the white pith underneath. You should have at least 2 teaspoons zest. Cut the fruit in half and squeeze out the juice. You will need ½ cup (120 mL) juice.

In a blender, combine the citrus zest and juice, milk kefir, and honey (if using). Blend the ingredients until well combined. The blending process will also help to aerate the milk kefir, creating a light and frothy texture that is easy to drink and digest. Serve in glasses or jars, garnished with a citrus slice or a sprig of mint, if you like. Store in an airtight container in the refrigerator for up to 1 week.

Artichoke and Stinging Nettle Tea

(TRÀ ATISO)

The artichoke plant was brought to Vietnam by French colonists in the late nineteenth century, and it quickly became popular among Vietnamese people. Artichoke tea developed a reputation as a digestive aid and liver protector, which are important aspects of traditional Vietnamese medicine. This artichoke tea is typically consumed after meals to promote good digestion and overall health. In addition to its medicinal benefits, artichoke tea is also enjoyed for its pleasant taste and aroma. Today, artichoke tea can be found in many cafes and restaurants throughout Vietnam, and it is also commonly sold in supermarkets and health food stores. This is a particular favorite of my mother's, and, growing up, I would always find this tea simmering at night on the stove. As a bonus, you can enjoy the artichoke hearts, leaves, and buds with a squeeze of fresh lemon and melted butter as a delicious snack or side dish.

Yield: *4 to 6 servings*

2 artichokes
1 bunch stinging nettles (about 2 cups [180 g])
10 cups (2.25 L) spring water

Note: Stinging nettles have diuretic properties and should be avoided by individuals who have low blood pressure or kidney disease or who are pregnant. If you have any of these conditions, consult with a doctor before consuming stinging nettles.

Wash the artichokes thoroughly and cut off the stems. Use a sharp knife to remove the tough outer leaves until you reach the tender, pale-yellow inner leaves. Cut off the top inch of each artichoke and trim the pointed tips of the remaining leaves with kitchen scissors. Rinse the artichokes under cold running water and set aside.

Wearing gloves, rinse the nettles thoroughly under cold running water. Tie a string around them to keep them together while cooking.

In a large pot, combine the artichokes, nettles, and water. Bring to a boil over high heat, then reduce the heat to low, cover, and simmer for 1 hour, or until the artichokes are tender when pierced with a knife.

Remove the nettles from the pot and discard them. Remove the artichokes from the pot and set them aside to cool. Serve the tea hot or, to serve chilled, transfer the tea to a large pitcher and refrigerate for a few hours or up to 3 days.

Korean Strawberry Milk Tea
with Honey Boba

Making this fun and nourishing drink is a labor of love, but watching the whole family enjoy it makes it all worth it! By making larger batches, we can store the tapioca boba pearls and strawberry compote in the freezer and have it on hand for when we want to assemble the drink. With a little planning, we can put together this treat faster than driving to the boba shop, avoid all the additives and preservatives, and actually feel good about what we are drinking.

Yield: 1 serving

1 pound (450 g) organic strawberries, hulled and quartered

3 tablespoons (45 mL) orange juice or spring water

2 to 3 tablespoons (30–45 mL) maple syrup, or more if needed

3 to 4 tablespoons (45–60 g) Honey Tapioca Boba Pearls (page 263)

3 or 4 pieces Boba Shop Almond Jelly (page 267; optional)

2 cups (480 mL) whole milk (preferably raw)

In a saucepan, combine the strawberries, orange juice, and maple syrup, and bring to a boil over medium-high heat. Reduce the heat to medium and simmer for 5 to 10 minutes, stirring occasionally, until the strawberries are soft and the liquid thickens. Taste, and add more maple syrup if needed. Let cool slightly, then cover and refrigerate until chilled, about 1 hour.

Put the boba pearls in the bottom of a glass, add a few pieces of almond jelly (if using) and a generous spoonful of strawberry compote, and then pour in the milk. Use a long spoon or straw to gently stir. Serve immediately, with a wide straw. Store the remaining strawberry compote in an airtight container in the refrigerator for up to 2 weeks or in the freezer for up to 6 months.

Grandmother and granddaughter make boba together.

Honey Tapioca Boba Pearls

Yield: 1 cup (240 g) boba pearls;
4 to 6 servings

¾ cup (96 g) tapioca starch,
    plus more for dusting
¼ cup (60 mL) boiling spring water
1 cup (240 mL) raw honey

In a medium bowl, combine the tapioca starch and boiling water. Mix well with a silicone spatula until it thickens into a sticky dough.

Transfer the dough to a work surface lightly dusted with tapioca starch. Knead the dough until it becomes soft and elastic. The dough can be very sticky, so extra starch may be needed. To test if the dough is done kneading, pull the dough apart; if it snaps in the middle, it is ready.

Dust a rimmed baking sheet with tapioca starch. Divide the dough in quarters and work with one section at a time. To prevent the unused portions from drying out, cover with a beeswax wrap or clean dish towel. Roll one section of the dough into several long ropes, about ¼ inch (6 mm) in diameter. (The tapioca pearls will expand in size when they are cooked.) Cut the ropes into ½-inch (13 mm) pieces, then roll each piece into a ball between the palms of your hands and place it on the baking sheet. Repeat with the rest of the dough, working quickly so the balls do not dry out. (If making ahead, dust the balls with extra starch and store them in an airtight container in the fridge for up to 1 week.)

Bring a large pot of water to a boil. Add the dough balls, but do not stir. Wait for the boba to float to the top, then lower the heat to medium and simmer for 20 minutes. As the boba pearls cook, they will gradually become translucent. Remove from the heat, cover the pot with a lid, and let rest for 20 minutes.

Drain the boba pearls and rinse them under cold running water to stop the cooking process.

Transfer the boba pearls to a bowl and pour the honey over. Let steep for 20 minutes before using, or store in an airtight container in the refrigerator for up to 2 days.

Okinawa Milk Tea with Boba

Okinawa milk tea takes its name from the renowned Japanese island and features the distinctive kokuto sugar, also known as Okinawa brown sugar. This type of sugar is valued for its rich flavor and health benefits. With its unique caramel and malty taste, kokuto sugar is widely used in Japan, including in milk tea, cakes, and sweet soups. Unlike regular brown sugar, kokuto sugar is made by boiling down sugarcane juice, which allows it to retain more nutrients, resulting in higher levels of calcium, potassium, and iron. This is Tim's favorite milk tea. I like to make it at home so the sweetness is customizable to our preference.

Yield: 1 serving

FOR THE SUGAR SYRUP
¼ to ½ cup (50–100 g) kokuto (Okinawa brown sugar) or panela
¼ cup (60 mL) spring water

FOR THE MILK TEA
2 cups (480 mL) spring water
1 tablespoon Assam, Earl Grey, English Breakfast, or Irish Breakfast tea leaves
½ cup (120 mL) whole milk (preferably raw)
¼ cup (60 g) Honey Tapioca Boba Pearls (page 263)
Ice cubes (optional)

Make the sugar syrup: In a small saucepan, combine the kokuto and the spring water and bring to a boil over medium-high heat, stirring to dissolve the sugar. Reduce the heat to medium and stir until the syrup is sticky and thick, about 5 minutes. (The syrup can be made ahead; store in an airtight container in the fridge for up to 3 weeks.)

Make the milk tea: In another small saucepan, bring the spring water to a boil. Remove from the heat, add the tea leaves, and let them sink to the bottom. Cover and steep for about 5 minutes, depending on how strong you like your tea. Strain the tea and discard the tea leaves.

Pour the tea into a large heatproof glass, three-quarters of the way to the top. Add the milk and stir. Add the boba pearls and as much syrup as you desire. If you prefer a warm drink, serve immediately. It can also be served chilled, with ice cubes and a large straw.

Mango Sticky Rice

Mango sticky rice is a favorite dessert that unites my mother and her beloved grandchildren. This delightful treat combines the sweetness of ripe mangoes and the comforting texture of sticky rice, creating a tropical sensation that captivates the senses. Share in the tradition and create cherished memories as you indulge in this classic Asian dessert.

Yield: 4 servings

1 cup (205 g) glutinous rice
1¾ cups (420 mL) Coconut Milk (page 273)
   or full-fat canned coconut milk
½ cup (100 g) panela or raw honey
½ teaspoon fine sea salt
1 ripe mango, peeled, pitted, and sliced
Toasted sesame seeds and fresh mint
   leaves, for garnish (optional)

Rinse the rice in a fine-mesh strainer under cold running water until the water runs clear. Put the rice in a bowl, cover with water, and soak for at least 2 hours.

Drain the rice and transfer it to a steamer. Steam the rice for 25 to 30 minutes, or until it is cooked through and sticky.

Meanwhile, in a small saucepan, combine the coconut milk, panela, and salt. Heat the mixture over medium heat, stirring constantly, until the sugar has dissolved and the mixture is well combined. Pour the coconut milk mixture over the cooked sticky rice and stir to combine. Let the rice sit for 10 to 15 minutes to absorb the coconut milk.

Serve the sticky rice topped with the mango. Garnish with sesame seeds and mint leaves, if desired.

Boba Shop Almond Jelly

This dessert is a childhood favorite of Tim's and mine because it's light, refreshing, and slightly sweet. My father loves to make this dessert for his grandchildren, and in our boba shop, we offered this as a topping for our boba drinks. Our children love it, and it's a great way to get them to drink more raw milk when we add it to our Strawberry Milk Tea (page 260).

Commercial almond jelly comes out of a bag and is packaged with additives that include thickeners, stabilizers, and emulsifiers. In this homemade version, I use agar-agar, which is a seaweed-derived gelatin substitute that is often used as a thickener. You can find it at health food stores or online. It is a source of dietary fiber and has very few calories.

Yield: 4 to 6 servings

2 cups (480 mL) whole milk (preferably raw)
1½ cups (360 mL) spring water
¼ cup (60 g) panela
1 tablespoon agar-agar powder
1 tablespoon almond extract

Combine all of the ingredients in a medium saucepan. Bring the mixture to a boil, whisking frequently to ensure the agar-agar dissolves. Once it comes to a boil, remove the pan from the stove and pour the mixture into a heatproof glass container.

Let the mixture cool to room temperature, then refrigerate it for at least 1 hour to overnight, to solidify.

Once the jelly is set, cut it into small cubes, and it's ready to serve or add to boba tea or fruit salad.

Note: You can use almond milk or coconut milk instead of dairy milk. You can also add chopped fruit, nuts, or other flavorings for added texture and flavor.

Strawberry-Lychee Panna Cotta

The velvety smoothness of panna cotta, combined with the vibrant sweetness of ripe strawberries and the slightly floral aroma of lychee, creates a dessert that is both nourishing and indulgent.

Yield: 4 servings

1 quart (1 L) heavy cream, preferably raw, chilled, divided
4 teaspoons (10 g) unflavored gelatin
¼ to ½ cup (60–120 mL) maple syrup
4 fresh or canned lychees, peeled and chopped
1 cup (165 g) sliced strawberries

In a saucepan, combine 1 cup (240 mL) of the cream and the gelatin and heat over low heat, stirring, until the gelatin is dissolved. Add the remaining 3 cups (720 mL) cream, the maple syrup, and lychee and mix well. Remove from the heat, cover, and steep for 30 minutes.

Strain and pour the liquid into ramekins or small bowls. Cover and refrigerate until firm, 2 to 3 hours. Top with sliced strawberries and serve.

Variation: For an extra creamy texture, beat 2 large raw egg yolks with the heavy cream before blending with the other ingredients.

Condensed Milk Affogato

Vietnamese affogato is a delicious and unique twist on the classic Italian dessert. Instead of using traditional vanilla ice cream, this recipe features condensed milk ice cream, which adds a rich and creamy sweetness to the dish.

Yield: 1 serving

½ cup (120 g) Condensed Milk Ice Cream (page 275)
½ to ¾ cup (120–180 mL) Vietnamese Coffee (page 244), cooled to room temperature
Chocolate syrup, for topping (optional)
Crushed peanuts, for topping (optional)

Scoop the condensed milk ice cream into a dessert bowl or glass. Pour the cooled coffee over the ice cream, covering it completely. Drizzle with chocolate syrup and sprinkle crushed peanuts over the top, if desired. Serve immediately.

Passion Fruit and Toasted Coconut Rice Pudding

This recipe is our family's all-time favorite rice dessert. It is versatile in flavoring, but the base is solid. To add an extra burst of flavor, I serve it with passion fruit topping and a sprinkle of toasted coconut chips.

Yield: 4 to 6 servings

2 quarts (2 L) whole milk, preferably raw

1 cup (240 g) panela or maple syrup

3 tablespoons (45 g) unsalted
  grass-fed butter

¾ teaspoon fine sea salt

1¼ cups (240 g) Arborio rice

3 large pasture-raised egg yolks,
  at room temperature

¾ cup (180 mL) heavy cream, preferably
  raw, divided

1 tablespoon vanilla or almond extract
  (optional)

Passion Fruit Topping (page 272), for serving

Toasted Coconut Chips (page 272),
  for serving

In a medium saucepan, combine the milk, panela, butter, salt, and rice. Bring the mixture to a boil over medium-high heat, stirring occasionally, then reduce the heat to low and partially cover the pot. Cook for about 45 minutes, stirring frequently to ensure the rice doesn't stick to the bottom of the pot, until the rice is tender and the mixture has thickened. Remove the pan from the heat and let the rice pudding cool for about 5 minutes.

Meanwhile, in a small bowl, whisk the egg yolks and ¼ cup (60 mL) of the cream until well combined. To temper the eggs, gradually add a spoonful of the warm rice pudding mixture to the egg mixture, stirring constantly. This will prevent the eggs from curdling when added to the pot of hot rice pudding. Add the tempered egg mixture to the rice pudding, stirring constantly to ensure that everything is well combined. Cook the mixture over low heat for 5 minutes, stirring constantly to prevent the pudding from sticking to the bottom of the pot. If desired, stir in the vanilla or almond extract. Remove the pan from the heat and let the pudding cool completely.

In a medium bowl, beat the remaining ½ cup (120 mL) cream until soft peaks form. Once the rice pudding is somewhat cooled, fold the whipped cream into the pudding mixture, making sure everything is well combined. Serve with the passion fruit topping and toasted coconut chips.

Passion Fruit Topping

Yield: about 1 cup (240 mL)

4 or 5 ripe passion fruits *or* 1 cup (240 mL) frozen passion fruit puree, thawed

¼ cup (60 mL) plus 1 tablespoon spring water, divided

¼ cup (60 g) panela

1 tablespoon arrowroot starch

Cut the passion fruits in half and scoop the flesh into a small saucepan, or put the passion fruit puree in the saucepan. Add ¼ cup (60 mL) of the water and the panela and stir to combine.

Heat the mixture over medium heat, stirring occasionally, until the panela has dissolved and the mixture comes to a boil. Reduce the heat to low and simmer for 5 to 7 minutes, stirring occasionally, until the passion fruit pulp has broken down and the mixture has thickened slightly.

In a small bowl, whisk together the arrowroot and remaining 1 tablespoon water to create a slurry. Slowly pour the arrowroot slurry into the passion fruit mixture while stirring constantly. Cook for an additional 2 to 3 minutes, stirring constantly, until the mixture has thickened and becomes glossy. Remove from the heat and let the passion fruit topping cool to room temperature before serving.

Toasted Coconut Chips

Yield: 2 cups (200 g)

2 cups (200 g) unsweetened coconut chips or flakes

> *Note:* You can add flavorings to the coconut chips, such as a sprinkle of sea salt or a drizzle of honey, before toasting them in the oven.

Preheat the oven to 325°F (160°C).

Spread the coconut chips evenly on a rimmed baking sheet. Bake for 5 to 10 minutes, stirring every few minutes to ensure even toasting, until the coconut is golden brown and fragrant. Remove the baking sheet from the oven and let the coconut cool on the baking sheet. Serve right way, or store in an airtight container at room temperature for up to 2 weeks.

Coconut Milk or Coconut Cream

Making your own coconut milk at home is easy, affordable, and free from additives or preservatives found in store-bought versions. Use homemade coconut milk in a variety of dishes from smoothies to curries and beyond.

The cream in coconut milk is the thicker, more viscous layer that rises to the top of the coconut milk when it's left to settle. Some coconuts naturally have more cream than others. The cream content of homemade coconut milk can be increased by using more coconut and less water in the recipe, or by blending the coconut milk for a longer period of time.

Yield: 1 quart (**1 L**)

2 cups (200 g) shredded
    unsweetened coconut
1 quart (1 L) hot spring water

Combine the shredded coconut and hot water in a blender. Blend for 2 to 3 minutes, until the coconut is finely ground and the mixture is creamy. Strain the mixture through a cheesecloth or nut milk bag, squeezing out as much liquid as possible. Store in an airtight container in the refrigerator for up to 4 days.

If you want to use coconut milk, shake well before using, as it may have separated. To make thicker coconut cream, let the coconut milk sit in the refrigerator for a few hours or overnight. The cream will rise to the top and can be scooped off.

Matcha's vibrant color, unique flavor, and numerous health benefits are unparalleled. When sourcing clean matcha powder, it's important to look for high-quality options that are pure and free from contaminants. Here are some tips to help you find clean matcha powder:

Choose organic: Opt for matcha powder that is certified organic. This ensures that it is produced without the use of synthetic pesticides, herbicides, or GMOs.

Check for origin: Look for matcha powder that specifies its origin, preferably from regions known for producing high-quality matcha. Matcha from Japan is typically considered to be of superior quality.

Read reviews and certifications: Before making a purchase, read reviews from reputable sources or check for certifications such as USDA organic, JAS (Japan Agricultural Standards), or other recognized quality standards.

Look for ceremonial grade: Ceremonial-grade matcha is generally higher in quality and purity compared to culinary-grade matcha. It is made from the youngest tea leaves and has a smoother taste. Consider choosing ceremonial-grade matcha for the best experience.

Buy from reputable sellers: Purchase matcha powder from trusted and reputable sellers who prioritize quality and transparency in their sourcing and production processes.

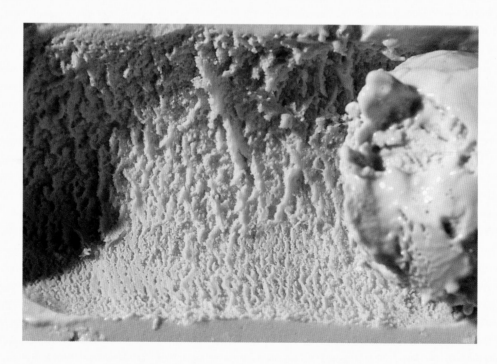

Matcha Green Tea Honey Ice Cream

This light and refreshing ice cream is bursting with antioxidants, making it the perfect frozen treat for summer! Matcha's unique, slightly earthy and umami-rich flavor pairs wonderfully with the sweetness of honey and the creaminess of ice cream. Green tea also offers potential health benefits, such as soothing a sore throat and providing vitamins and minerals.

Yield: about 2 cups (*480 mL*)

2 cups (480 mL) Coconut Cream (page 273)
3 tablespoons (45 mL) raw honey
1 tablespoon organic matcha powder
1 teaspoon vanilla extract

In a large bowl, whisk together the coconut cream, honey, matcha powder, and vanilla until the honey is dissolved and the matcha powder is fully incorporated.

Pour the mixture into an ice cream maker and churn according to the manufacturer's instructions, until the ice cream is thick and creamy. Transfer the ice cream to an airtight container and freeze for several hours, until firm. (Alternatively, line a loaf pan with parchment paper. Pour the ice cream mixture into the pan, cover with beeswax wrap, and freeze.)

Condensed Milk Ice Cream

You will need an ice cream maker for this recipe. Serve with all your favorite toppings, such as fresh berries, mochi (sweet rice cakes), red bean paste, Toasted Coconut Chips (page 272), chocolate chips, cacao nibs, and/or chopped nuts.

Yield: 4 servings

1¾ cups (420 mL) Homemade Sweetened
　　Condensed Milk (page 241) or
　　Coconut Condensed Milk (page 243)
2 cups (480 mL) heavy cream, preferably raw
1 teaspoon vanilla extract
Pinch fine sea salt
4 large pasture-raised egg yolks

In a large bowl, whisk together the condensed milk, cream, vanilla extract, and salt until well combined. In a separate bowl, beat the egg yolks until light and blended completely. Gradually whisk the beaten egg yolks into the condensed milk mixture, mixing well.

Pour the mixture into an ice cream maker and churn according to the manufacturer's instructions, until the ice cream is thick and creamy. Transfer the ice cream to an airtight container and freeze for several hours, until firm.

Adzuki Red Bean Dessert Soup

This cherished Asian treat holds a special place in my mother's heart. It captures the essence of Mom's care and affection as she prepares the velvety, sweet red beans. This sweet soup is nourishing and immune boosting, and you can enjoy it hot or cold.

Yield: 4 servings

1 cup (195 g) adzuki red beans
5 cups (1.25 L) spring water
1 (2-inch [5 cm]) piece orange peel
⅔ cup (160 g) plus 1 tablespoon panela, divided
¾ cup (180 mL) Coconut Milk (page 273)
Pinch fine sea salt

Put the adzuki beans in a bowl, cover with water, and soak overnight. Drain the beans and rinse under cold running water.

In a medium saucepan, bring the spring water and orange peel to a boil. Reduce the heat to low, add the adzuki beans, and simmer for 2 to 3 hours, stirring occasionally, until they are softened. Add ⅔ cup (160 g) of the panela and stir until it is dissolved.

In a small saucepan, bring the coconut milk to a boil, add the remaining 1 tablespoon panela and a pinch of salt, and stir until the sugar is dissolved.

Serve the soup in bowls, with a dollop of coconut milk on top.

You can make the soup ahead and store in the refrigerator (without coconut milk topping) for up to 3 days.

Menu Ideas

As a busy working family, we love to have healthy and nourishing meal plans that incorporate Vietnamese and other Asian cuisines. One of the reasons we are drawn to these types of meals is because they often revolve around umami flavors, which create a unique and satisfying taste that keeps us coming back for more.

Umami is the fifth basic taste, alongside sweet, sour, salty, and bitter, and is often described as a savory, meaty, or brothy flavor. In Asian cooking, umami-rich ingredients such as naturally fermented soy sauce, fish sauce, miso, and mushrooms are often used to enhance the depth and complexity of dishes. In addition to using umami in main dishes, Vietnamese and other Asian cuisines often feature umami-rich side dishes like pickles, kimchi, and sauerkraut, which are fermented foods that are known for their gut-healthy probiotics and unique flavor profiles.

To plan your menu ideas, it's traditional to incorporate complementary umami flavorings. Here are a few tips:

1. Plan your meals around a protein source: Whether it's poultry, pork, beef, lamb, or seafood, choose a protein source that you enjoy.
2. Pick a soup that will complement your protein: Consider how you're cooking the protein. If you're dressing it in a rich sauce, you may want to have a lighter soup. Selecting a soup is about balancing flavors and textures to create a well-rounded meal.
3. Choose side dishes that complement your protein: Pair your protein with a variety of vegetables and fruits that provide different flavors and textures. For example, if you're making a beef stir-fry, add some shiitake mushrooms and bok choy for a lighter balance to the stir-fry.

Meal Option 1
Soup: Vietnamese Sweet-and-Sour Tamarind Soup
(Canh Chua Cá), page 126
Protein: Vietnamese Caramelized Fish (Cá Kho Tộ), page 220
Vegetable: Fermented Bean Sprouts (Dưa Giá), page 100

Meal Option 2
Soup: Chicken Rice Porridge (Cháo Gà), page 136
Protein: Pan-Fried Chicken Liver and Hearts, page 233
Vegetable: Vietnamese Chicken Salad (Gỏi Gà Bắp Cải), page 147

Meal Option 3
Soup: Vietnamese Crab Noodle Soup (Bún Riêu), page 130
Protein: Vietnamese Egg Rolls with Turkey (Chả Giò), page 150
Vegetable: Vietnamese Pickled Carrots and Daikon (Đồ Chua), page 97

Meal Option 4
Soup: Vietnamese Chicken Noodle Soup (Phở Gà), page 123
Protein: Vietnamese Garlic-Butter Chicken Wings, page 155
Vegetable: Daikon Kimchi (Củ Cải Kimchi), page 103

Meal Option 5
Soup: Vietnamese Spicy Beef Noodle Soup (Bún Bò Huế), page 132
Protein: Vietnamese Beef-Onion Rolls (Bò Nướng Hành), page 181
Vegetable: Easy Napa Cabbage Kimchi, page 104

Meal Option 6
Soup: Vietnamese Pork and Shrimp Tapioca Noodle Soup
  (Bánh Canh Giò Heo), page 128
Protein: Caramelized Pork Spare Ribs with Quail Eggs
  (Thịt Sườn Kho), page 167
Vegetable: Fermented Bean Sprouts (Dưa Giá), page 100

Meal Option 7
Soup: Korean Healing Soup (Miyeok-Guk), page 119
Protein: Lamb Bulgogi Spring Rolls, page 193
Vegetable: Vegan Japchae, page 107

Resources

Fermented Food Starters

Cultures for Health
www.culturesforhealth.com
Cultures, equipment, and kits

Kombucha Kamp
www.kombuchakamp.com
Kombucha mothers and water kefir grains

Dairy

Ancient Organics
www.ancientorganics.com
Organic, grass-fed ghee

A Campaign for Real Milk
www.realmilk.com
Listing of raw, grass-fed dairies

Miller's Bio Farm
www.millersbiofarm.com
Sweet and cultured raw butter,
flavored ghee

Pure Indian Foods
www.pureindianfoods.com
Organic, grass-fed ghee

Raw Farm
www.rawfarmusa.com
Raw milk, raw kefir, raw cream,
raw butter

Siggi's
www.siggisdairy.com
Traditional Icelandic skyr, available in
the dairy case at many well-stocked
health foods stores

Fruits and Vegetables

Chaffin Family Orchards
www.chaffinfamilyorchards.com
Fifth-generation biodiverse family farm sell-
ing mandarins, oranges, olives, and olive oil

Local Harvest
www.localharvest.org
Listing of local farms, farmers markets,
and CSAs

Grains and Flours

Anthony's Goods
www.anthonysgoods.com
Organic arrowroot flour

Lundberg Family Farms
www.lundberg.com
Regenerative organic certified white basmati rice, organic wild blend rice, organic
black pearl rice, Arborio rice

Sunrise Flour Mill
www.sunriseflourmill.com
Heritage bread blend and sourdough starter

To Your Health Sprouted Flour
www.healthyflour.com
Organic sprouted brown rice flour, sprouted gluten-free mung bean flour

Lacto-Fermented Vegetables
Fab Ferments
www.fabferments.com
Sauerkraut, kimchi, and other lacto-fermented vegetables

Hex Ferments
www.hexferments.com
Miso, kimchi, fermented vegetables

Condiments
Eden Foods
www.edenfoods.com
Vinegars, mirin, miso, naturally fermented soy sauce, tekka, furikake

Gold Mine Natural Foods
www.goldminenaturalfoods.com
Gluten-free organic, tamari, organic ume vinegar, traditionally fermented organic soy sauce, organic furikake

Great Eastern Sun
www.great-eastern-sun.com
Organic red miso, organic white miso, chickpea miso, wasabi, sesame oil, mirin, tamari

Red Boat Fish Sauce
www.redboatfishsauce.com
Traditionally fermented fish sauce

Grass-Fed and Pasture-Raised Meats
Alderspring Ranch
www.alderspring.com
Organic grass-fed beef bones, organic grass-fed offal, heritage pasture-raised pigs

Polyface Farms
www.polyfaceyum.com
Grass-fed and -finished beef, pasture-raised pork, chicken, lamb, organ meat, beef bones, and chicken feet.

Eat Wild
www.eatwild.com
A listing of grass-fed and pasture-raised meat producers

Force of Nature
www.forceofnature.com
Regenerative beef including an ancestral blend with organ meat, pasture-raised whole chicken

KOL Foods
www.kolfoods.com
Grass-fed beef and lamb, and pasture-raised chicken, turkey, and duck

Schiltz Foods
https://schiltzfoods.com
Goose, duck, pheasant, as well as duck liver, goose liver, and fatty goose liver

US Wellness Meats
www.grasslandbeef.com
Grass-fed beef, certified humane pork and chicken. Many varieties of offal, bones for broth, chicken feet, and beef suet.

Fats and Oils
Fatworks
www.fatworks.com
Organic grass-fed beef tallow, Japanese Wagyu tallow, cage-free duck fat, organic pork lard, organic free-range chicken schmaltz

Green Pasture
www.greenpasture.org
Fermented cod liver oil, fermented skate
liver oil, and high-vitamin butter oil

Jovial Foods
www.jovialfoods.com
Heirloom Italian olive oil

White Oak Pastures
www.whiteoakpastures.com
Grass-fed beef suet, pastured pork fat

Spices and Herbs
Frontier Co-Op
www.frontiercoop.com
Organic spices and herbs

Mountain Rose Herbs
www.mountainroseherbs.com
Organic and wild-crafted dried herbs,
teas, and spices

Simply Organic
www.simplyorganic.com
Organic spices and herbs

Sustainable Seafood
Alaskan Salmon Company
www.aksalmonco.com
Sushi-grade Alaskan seafood, wild-caught
Alaskan salmon and halibut

Caviar Russe
www.caviarrusse.com
Wild salmon roe, and sustainably
farmed trout roe

Japan Gold USA
www.japangoldusa.com
Dried bonito flakes made from fermented
Honkarebushi fish

Vital Choice
www.vitalchoice.com
Wild-caught Alaskan salmon, Oregon pink
shrimp, and other wild seafood and roe

Sweeteners
BLiS
www.blisgourmet.com
Bourbon barrel-aged maple syrup

Healthy Traditions
www.healthytraditions.com
Panela whole cane sugar, raw honey,
maple syrup

Really Raw Honey
www.reallyrawhoney.com
Raw, unfiltered honey and pollen

Real Food Advocacy Groups
Farm-to-Consumer Legal Defense Fund
https://farmtoconsumer.org
A nonprofit organization that works to
defend the rights of small farmers, artisanal
food producers, and consumers to access
locally grown and produced food.

Food Tank
https://foodtank.com
A research and advocacy organization that
works to promote sustainable agriculture,
reduce food waste, and increase access to
healthy food.

Nourishing Our Children
https://nourishingourchildren.org
A nonprofit organization dedicated to edu-
cating the public about the importance of
traditional, nutrient-dense diets for children's health and development.

Organic Consumers Association
https://organicconsumers.org
An organization that advocates for organic farming, fair trade, and consumer access to healthy food.

Price-Pottenger Nutrition Foundation
https://price-pottenger.org
A nonprofit organization that advocates for traditional nutrient-dense diets, natural farming, and holistic healthcare.

Regeneration International
https://regenerationinternational.org
Regeneration International is an organization dedicated to promoting and advancing the regenerative agriculture movement globally.

Rodale Institute
https://rodaleinstitute.org
A nonprofit organization conducting research on regenerative organic agriculture and offering training and resources to farmers, consumers, and policymakers.

Savory Institute
https://savory.global
A nonprofit organization that promotes large-scale restoration of the world's grasslands through holistic management practices.

Seafood Watch
https://seafoodwatch.org
Monterey Bay Aquarium helps consumers and businesses make informed choices about sustainable seafood through Seafood Watch.

Slow Food International
https://slowfood.com
A grassroots organization that advocates for local and sustainable food systems, traditional foodways, and the preservation of biodiversity.

Weston A. Price Foundation
https://westonaprice.org
An organization that promotes the principles of ancestral diets and traditional food preparation techniques for optimal health.

Acknowledgments

After many late nights researching and writing this cookbook, I am humbled by the kindness and support of so many people who have encouraged me along the way these past 12 years.

With humility and reverence, our family acknowledges Yahweh as the author of our stories, reminding us that every recipe, every memory, and every moment is a part of a larger, beautiful mosaic of life.

To my husband, Tim, your unwavering love has been my guiding light. Your encouragement and belief in me, despite my own doubts and busy schedule, have opened a world of possibilities I never imagined. You saw my potential, and you pushed me to explore this dream with all my heart. Thank you for being my partner in every sense—from our shared love for food and travel to the elegant simplicity we've built around our daily home-steading and homeschooling routines. You've shown me the depths of what I can achieve, and I am forever grateful for the warmth and brightness you bring to our family. Our children are blessed to have you as their father, and I am profoundly lucky to have you by my side, sharing and cherishing the life we have built together.

To Mẹ, thank you for teaching me that food is a love language. You are the heartbeat of my culinary identity, and your influence has shaped me since my earliest memories. I witnessed and learned from your grace in the kitchen, creating nourishing meals that celebrate our cherished Vietnamese heritage. Your wisdom, resourcefulness, and willingness to learn new things have been the biggest inspiration on my journey, and I am forever grateful for the tapestry of flavors and traditions you have woven into my life. Your culinary legacy is present in every dish I prepare. I am humbled to follow in your footsteps.

To Bố, thank you for your unwavering support of my unconventional views and choices in life. Your encouragement has empowered me to embrace my individuality and make a positive impact on the world in my own way.

A special thank-you to my wonderful daughters, Emily and Natalie, for inspiring Mama and Dada to be better people and live a healthier lifestyle. Your happiness and well-being are our greatest motivation. Your enthusiasm and support have been the driving force for me to complete our family project with Ông and Bà and create a legacy for you both to cherish for you and future generations to come. I hope this book inspires you to explore the joys of cooking nourishing meals for your own families someday.

I want to express my appreciation to Chelsea Green Publishing. To my editor, Brianne Goodspeed, who shepherded this clueless sheep through the cookbook process from start to finish with unfailing warmth, patience, and kindness. To Melissa Jacobson, Rebecca Springer, Sean Maher, Kirsten Drew, Darrell Koerner, and the entire team at Chelsea Green Publishing, thank you for taking a chance on this book and making it a reality.

I want to thank Sally Fallon Morell, president of the Weston A. Price Foundation, for her influence, especially with her own book, *Nourishing Traditions*. Her championing of whole foods and raw milk has been integral to our family's commitment to traditional pathways of food, farming, and the healing arts. I am deeply grateful for her mentorship and support for this book.

To Joel Salatin, the Lunatic Farmer at Polyface Farm, thank you for being a trailblazer in promoting sustainable and regenerative agricultural practices. Your commitment to ethical, holistic, and beyond organic farming methods has inspired countless people, including myself, to embrace a more conscious approach to food. Thank you, Joel, for your influence and support for my work and for this book.

A heartfelt thank-you to my dear friends and mentors, John and Maggie Culver, for being family to us, encouraging me to write this book, and giving us the confidence to raise dairy cows.

To my wonderful friends for your enthusiasm and honest opinions, especially Maureen Diaz, founder of God's Good Table, for your early support; Dani Hart, my fellow tech sister turned rebel farmer; and Rey Gonzales, my fellow tech foodie, for sharing your favorite recipes as inspiration.

To my photography team, David Peng, Christiane Hur, and Kim Tran, thank you for your hard work in capturing our modern yet traditional family-style home cooking story through your lens.

Lastly, I want to express my heartfelt appreciation to all the readers of Sprinkle With Soil and *The Nourishing Asian Kitchen* and listeners of the Call to Farms podcast. Your interest and support mean the world to our family. I hope this cookbook brings you and your family joy and inspiration to your culinary adventures from our family to yours.

Photography Credits

Neeli Brisky: pages vii, 22, 26, 40, 192, 255

Sophia Nguyen Eng: pages 1, 2, 3, 5, 6, 8, 9, 10, 12, 14, 33, 37, 42, 69, 92, 93, 98, 105, 115, 116, 117, 144, 160, 188, 262

Huy's Photography: page 4

Kelly Jackson: page 298

David K. Peng: pages iv–v, xii, 15, 30, 41, 46, 49, 50, 52, 54, 58–59, 65, 65, 65, 65, 65, 65, 65, 65, 65, 66, 73, 76, 81, 82, 86, 87, 88, 89, 91, 95, 96, 106, 109, 110, 118, 122, 125, 126, 129, 130, 134, 137, 140–41, 143, 146, 151, 154, 157, 159, 163, 164, 168, 171, 175, 179, 180, 183, 187, 191, 194, 195–96, 200, 204, 207, 209, 213, 216, 221, 222, 225, 228, 230, 232, 232, 233, 237, 239, 242, 245, 247, 249, 250, 257, 258, 261, 265, 266, 269, 270

Bang Pham: pages 1, 2

Zofocl Photography: page 17

Index

Note: Page references in *italics* indicate recipe photographs.

About the Author

Kelly Jackson

A first-generation Vietnamese American, Sophia Nguyen Eng left a successful Silicon Valley career in growth marketing to start a 5-acre permaculture mini farm in the Appalachian region of eastern Tennessee. Eng took a greater interest to better understand where her food comes from because it ties directly into health, and she wanted to provide the best for her family and community. While working in tech, Eng led successful growth marketing campaigns for startups and Fortune 500 companies like Workday, InVision, and Smartsheet, which led to opportunities to develop a certificate training program with CXL Institute and being a founder for the tech organization Women in Growth. A sought-after speaker, she has presented at Google HQ, GrowthHackers, and the global SaaStalk tech conferences, and is now using her experiences and knowledge of food, farming, and health to speak at regenerative agriculture conferences, including sharing the stage with Joel Salatin at Polyface Farm. Eng is also a Weston A. Price chapter leader and the founder of the website Sprinkle With Soil and the Call to Farms podcast. With her husband, Tim, she raises grass-fed dairy cows and beef cattle, laying hens, broilers, ducks, sheep, goats, turkeys, and grows a variety of produce for her multigenerational family and local community.